EMERGING ADULTHOOD

EMERGING ADULTHOOD

The Winding Road From the Late Teens
Through the Twenties

JEFFREY JENSEN ARNETT

OXFORD
UNIVERSITY PRESS

OXFORD
UNIVERSITY PRESS

Oxford University Press, Inc., publishes works that further
Oxford University's objective of excellence
in research, scholarship, and education.

Oxford   New York
Auckland   Cape Town   Dar es Salaam   Hong Kong   Karachi
Kuala Lumpur   Madrid   Melbourne   Mexico City   Nairobi
New Delhi   Shanghai   Taipei   Toronto

With offices in
Argentina   Austria   Brazil   Chile   Czech Republic   France   Greece
Guatemala   Hungary   Italy   Japan   Poland   Portugal   Singapore
South Korea   Switzerland   Thailand   Turkey   Ukraine   Vietnam

First published in 2004 by Oxford University Press, Inc.
198 Madison Avenue, New York, New York 10016

www.oup.com

First issued as an Oxford University Press paperback, 2006

Oxford is a registered trademark of Oxford University Press

Library of Congress Cataloging-in-Publication Data
Arnett, Jeffrey Jensen.
Emerging adulthood: the winding road from the late teens through the twenties /
Jeffrey Jensen Arnett.
p. cm.
Includes bibliographical references and index.
ISBN-13 978-0-19-517314-7; 978-0-19-530937-9 (pbk.)

1. Young adults.   I. Title.
HQ799.5 .A72 2004
305.242—dc22   2003023347

7 9 8

Printed in the United States of America
on acid-free paper

PREFACE

THE ORIGIN OF THIS BOOK DATES from about ten years ago, when I was a junior professor at the University of Missouri. As is often the case for those of us who do research in psychology, my interest in the topic was drawn from my own experience. At that point in my life, after many years of education, I finally had a job that I expected to be in for a long time to come. After many years of dating, I had finally met and was living with the person I hoped to marry. After years of moving around from one place to another every year or two or three in pursuit of new opportunities and experiences, I was ready to stay in one place for a while and put down some roots. I felt at last that I had reached adulthood.

I began to wonder, how and when do other people feel they have reached adulthood? It occurred to me that there is no social or communal ritual in American society to mark that passage. Instead, it is left to each of us to determine when the threshold to adulthood has been reached and what signifies it.

I had been doing research on adolescence for several years at the time, so it was easy for me to turn the focus of my research to the question of what it means to move from adolescence to adulthood. I soon learned that there was not much in psychology that had explored the topic, but there was a great deal of research in sociology on what was called the "transition to adulthood." Sociologists defined the transition to adulthood in terms of distinct events, specifically, finishing education, entering full-time work, marriage, and parenthood. This seemed perfectly reasonable to me. My own sense of reaching adulthood had been marked by entering full-time work and, if not marriage, at least feeling ready for marriage.

I was quite surprised, then, when I began to ask college students about what they believed marked the transition to adulthood and found that for them entering full-time work and marriage had nothing to do with it. Nor did the other sociological transitions, finishing education and entering parenthood. In fact, all four of the sociological transitions ended up rock bottom when I surveyed college students about possible criteria for adulthood. Instead of the sociological transitions, the most important criteria for adulthood to these college students were more intangible and psychological: accepting responsibility for one's actions, making independent decisions, and becoming financially independent.

Well, I thought, maybe that's because they're college students, and being in college leads them to think in more abstract and psychological terms. Maybe people in the same age group who are not in college would see the transition to adulthood more in terms of transition events, like the sociologists did. But when I surveyed and interviewed them, I came up with the same results as I had for the college students, and there were very few differences by educational level or socioeconomic background.

By now I was thoroughly intrigued and wanted to know more about what was going on in the lives of people experiencing the transition to adulthood. I started a study in Missouri of young people in their twenties, including both college and noncollege participants, and asked them a broad range of questions—on their family lives, on love and sex and marriage, on their college and work experiences, on what they value most and what they believe about religious questions, and more. I spent a year in San Francisco and continued my research, focusing on Asian Americans and African Americans. I had graduate students conduct interviews with Latinos in Los Angeles and with African Americans in New Orleans.

The more research I did, the more I talked to people in their twenties, the less satisfied I became with describing their development in terms of the transition to adulthood. Yes, the transition to adulthood takes place during this period, but that term does not begin to cover all that is going on in their lives from the time they leave high school to the time they reach full adulthood. Calling it the "transition to adulthood" seemed to diminish it, as if it were merely a brief passage connecting the two more important periods of adolescence and young adulthood. And it lasts so long, at least from age 18 to 25 for most people and usually beyond, as long or longer than any stage of childhood or adolescence. Why shouldn't it be regarded as a distinct period of life in its own right?

I looked for existing theories that would provide a framework for understanding the transition to adulthood as a separate developmental period, but could not find anything satisfying. The most commonly discussed idea was Kenneth Keniston's idea of "youth," but *youth* seemed to me a dubious choice of terms for this age period, because it was already used in so many other ways, to describe people as young as middle childhood and as old as their thirties. Besides, Keniston's ideas on "youth" were based mainly on the college student protesters of the 1960s, an atypical group at an unusual time in American history, and seemed to me to have little application to the present.

So, I decided to create my own theory of development from the late teens through the twenties, and this book is the result of those efforts. Already I have published numerous articles in scholarly journals outlining the theory, but this is my first attempt to present a comprehensive account of it, based on my research over the past decade. I hope scholars will find it compelling and persuasive, but I regard this book as the beginning of forming an understanding of emerging adulthood, not the last word. Many other scholars are now conducting research using the theory of emerging adulthood, and it is a field of study that is growing rapidly. The first scholarly conference was held at Harvard University in November 2003, and there will certainly be more. A group of scholars has been formed to share information and support in studying emerging adulthood (see www.s-r-a.org/easig.html). Now that we are beginning to develop a shared language for talking about this age period, there are surely many exciting discoveries to come.

This is a book not just for scholars but for anyone interested in this topic and this age period. I hope many emerging adults will find it provocative and informative, and I hope their parents will as well. It was my goal to write a book that would make an important contribution to scholarship on emerging adulthood but that most people could read and find engaging whether they are scholars or not. There are no complex statistical analyses, and most of the information comparing my results to other studies on the age period can be found in the notes rather than in the main text. What I have focused on instead are the voices of emerging adults, that is, what they say about their lives on a wide range of topics.

I present some questionnaire results, but mainly I present the results from the interviews, because that is where I learned the most about emerging adults. Questionnaires have a useful place in research, but in my experience there is simply no substitute for sitting face to face with people and talking to them about what they have experienced and what it means to them. I believe that in all psychological research it is important to listen to how people describe and interpret their lives—except infants, of course— but it may be especially important in emerging adulthood, because it is a highly self-reflective time of life, a period when they think a lot about who they are and what they want out of life. And it's fun to listen to them, as you'll see in the course of this book. No matter what their educational background, they are remarkably articulate, often funny, sometimes moving.

I have many people to thank for their support in making this book possible. Although I did most of the interviews myself, I had assistance from numerous students along the way, including Katie Ramos and Diane Rutledge in Missouri and Los Angeles, Terrolyn Carter in New Orleans, and Gretchen Cooke, Colleen O'Connell, and Megan O'Donnell in San Francisco. Several of my colleagues read part or all of the book before publication and provided comments and suggestions, including Jack Brunner, Jim Côté, Bill Damon, Wyndol Furman, Steve Hamilton, Hugh McIntosh, Shmuel Shulman, Jennifer Tanner, and Niobe Way. Special thanks go to my wife, Lene Jensen, who read many a draft without complaint and always offered insightful and helpful comments. Thanks also to Catharine Carlin, psychology editor at Oxford University Press, for understanding what I was aiming for in this book and enthusiastically supporting it. Finally, I wish to thank the hundreds of emerging adults who opened up their lives to me in the interviews that are the foundation of this book. You taught me an immense amount, and I am grateful for it.

CONTENTS

EMERGING ADULTHOOD

1

A Longer Road to Adulthood

IN THE PAST FEW DECADES A QUIET revolution has taken place for young people in American society, so quiet that it has been noticed only gradually and incompletely. As recently as 1970 the typical 21-year-old was married or about to be married, caring for a newborn child or expecting one soon, done with education or about to be done, and settled into a long-term job or the role of full-time mother. Young people of that time grew up quickly and made serious enduring choices about their lives at a relatively early age. Today, the life of a typical 21-year-old could hardly be more different. Marriage is at least five years off, often more. Ditto parenthood. Education may last several more years, through an extended undergraduate program—the "four-year degree" in five, six, or more—and perhaps graduate or professional school. Job changes are frequent, as young people look for work that will not only pay well but will also be personally fulfilling.

For today's young people, the road to adulthood is a long one. They leave home at age 18 or 19, but most do not marry, become parents, and find a long-term job until at least their late twenties. From their late teens to their late twenties they explore the possibilities available to them in love and work, and move gradually toward making enduring choices. Such freedom to explore different options is exciting, and this period is a time of high hopes and big dreams. However, it is also a time of anxiety and uncertainty, because the lives of young people are so unsettled, and many of them have no idea where their explorations will lead. They struggle with uncertainty even as they revel in being freer than they ever were in childhood or ever will be once they take on the full weight of adult responsibilities. To be a young American today is to experience both excitement and uncertainty, wide-open possibility and confusion, new freedoms and new fears.

The rise in the ages of entering marriage and parenthood, the lengthening of higher education, and prolonged job instability during the twenties reflect the development of a new period of life for young people in the United States and other industrialized societies, lasting from the late teens through the mid- to late twenties. This period is not simply an "extended adolescence," because it is much different from adolescence, much freer from parental control, much more a period of independent exploration. Nor is it really "young adulthood," since this term implies that an early stage of adulthood has been reached, whereas most young people in their twenties have not made the transitions historically associated with adult status— especially marriage and parenthood—and many of them feel they have not yet reached adulthood. It is a new and historically unprecedented period of the life course, so it requires a new term and a new way of thinking; I call it *emerging adulthood*.

Many Americans have noticed the change in how young people experience their late teens and their twenties. In the 1990s "Generation X" became a widely used term for people in this age period, inspired by Douglas Coupland's 1991 novel of that title. However, the characteristics of today's young people are not merely generational. The changes that have created emerging adulthood are here to stay—Generations X, Y, Z, and beyond will experience an extended period of exploration and instability in their late teens and twenties. For this reason I believe emerging adulthood should be recognized as a distinct new period of life that will be around for many generations to come.

In this book I describe the characteristics of emerging adults, based mainly on my research over the past decade, plus a synthesis of other research and theories on the age period. In this opening chapter I provide some historical background on the rise of emerging adulthood and describe the period's distinctive features. I also explain why the term *emerging adulthood* is preferable to other possible terms.

The Rise of Emerging Adulthood

Emerging adulthood has been created in part by the steep rise in the typical ages of marriage and parenthood that has taken place in the past half century.[1] As you can see in Figure 1.1, in 1950 the median age of marriage in the United States was just 20 for women and 22 for men. Even as recently as 1970, these ages had risen only slightly, to about 21 for women and 23 for men. However, since 1970 there has been a dramatic shift in the ages when Americans typically get married. By the year 2000 the typical age of marriage was 25 for women and 27 for men, a four-year rise for both sexes in the space of just three decades. Age at entering parenthood has followed a similar pattern. Then as now, couples tend to have their first child about one year after marriage, on average.[2] So, from 1950 to 1970 most couples had their first child in their very early twenties, whereas today most wait until at least their late twenties before becoming parents.

Why this dramatic rise in the typical ages of entering marriage and parenthood? One reason is that the invention of the birth control pill, in combination with less stringent standards of sexual morality after the sexual revolution of the 1960s and early 1970s, meant that young people no longer had to enter marriage in order to have a regular sexual relationship. Now most young people have a series of sexual relationships before entering marriage,[3] and most Americans do not object to this, as long as sex does not begin at an age that is "too early" (whatever that is) and as long as the number of partners does not become "too many" (whatever that is). Although Americans may not be clear, in their own minds, about what the precise rules ought to be for young people's sexual relationships, there is widespread tolerance now for sexual relations between young people in their late teens and twenties in the context of a committed, loving relationship.

Another important reason for the rise in the typical ages of entering marriage and parenthood is the increase in the years devoted to pursuing higher education. An exceptionally high proportion of young people, about

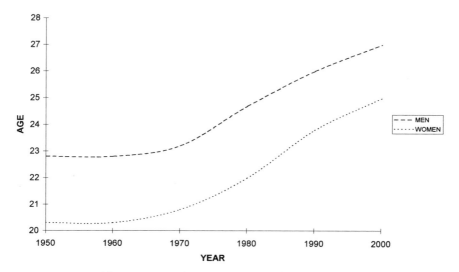

Figure 1.1. Median U.S. Marriage Age, 1950–2000

two thirds, now enter college after graduating from high school.[4] This is a higher proportion than ever before in American history. Among those who graduate from college, about one third go on to graduate school the following year.[5] Most young people wait until they have finished school before they start thinking seriously about marriage and parenthood, and for many of them this means postponing these commitments until at least their mid-twenties.

But it may be that the most important reason of all for the rise in the typical ages of entering marriage and parenthood is less tangible than changes in sexual behavior or more years spent in college and graduate school. There has been a profound change in how young people view the meaning and value of becoming an adult and entering the adult roles of spouse and parent. Young people of the 1950s were eager to enter adulthood and "settle down."[6] Perhaps because they grew up during the upheavals of the Great Depression and World War II, achieving the stability of marriage, home, and children seemed like a great accomplishment to them. Also, because many of them planned to have three, four, or even five or more children, they had good reason to get started early in order to have all the children they wanted and space them out at reasonable intervals.

The young people of today, in contrast, see adulthood and its obligations in quite a different light. In their late teens and early twenties, marriage, home, and children are seen by most of them not as achievements to be pursued but as perils to be avoided. It is not that they do not want marriage, a home, and (one or two) children—eventually. Most of them do want to take on all of these adult obligations, and most of them will have done so by the time they reach age 30. It is just that, in their late teens and early twenties, they ponder these obligations and think, "Yes, but *not yet*." Adulthood and its obligations offer security and stability, but they also represent a closing of doors—the end of independence, the end of spontaneity, the end of a sense of wide-open possibilities.

Women's roles have also changed in ways that make an early entry into adult obligations less desirable for them now compared to 50 years ago. The young women of 1950 were under a great deal of social pressure to catch a man.[7] Being a single woman was simply not a viable social status for a woman after her early twenties. Relatively few women attended college, and those who did were often there for the purpose of obtaining their "m-r-s" degree (in the joke of the day)—that is, for the purpose of finding a husband. The range of occupations open to young women was severely restricted, as it had been traditionally—secretary, waitress, teacher, nurse, perhaps a few others. Even these occupations were supposed to be temporary for young women. What they were really supposed to be focusing on was finding a husband and having children. Having no other real options, and facing social limbo if they remained unmarried for long, their yearning for marriage and children—the sooner the better—was sharpened.

For the young women of the 21st century, all this has changed. At every level of education from grade school through graduate school girls now excel over boys.[8] Fifty-six percent of the undergraduates in America's colleges and universities are women, according to the most recent figures.[9] Young women's occupational possibilities are now virtually unlimited, and although men still dominate in engineering and some sciences, women are equal to men in obtaining law and business degrees and nearly equal in obtaining medical degrees.[10] With so many options open to them, and with so little pressure on them to marry by their early twenties, the lives of young American women today have changed almost beyond recognition from what they were 50 years ago. And most of them take on their new freedoms with alacrity, making the most of their emerging adult years before they enter marriage and parenthood.

Although the rise of emerging adulthood is partly a consequence of the rising ages of marriage and parenthood, marriage ages were also relatively high early in the 20th century and throughout the 19th century.[11] What is different now is that young people are freer than they were in the past to use the intervening years, between the end of secondary school and entry into marriage and parenthood, to explore a wide range of different possible future paths. Young people of the past were constricted in a variety of ways, from gender roles to economics, which prevented them from using their late teens and twenties for exploration. In contrast, today's emerging adults have unprecedented freedom.

Not all of them have an equal portion of it, to be certain. Some live in conditions of deprivation that make any chance of exploring life options severely limited, at best. However, as a group, they have more freedom for exploration than young people in times past. Their society grants them a long moratorium in their late teens and twenties without expecting them to take on adult responsibilities as soon as they are able to do so. Instead, they are allowed to move into adult responsibilities gradually, at their own pace.

What Is Emerging Adulthood?

What are the distinguishing features of emerging adulthood? What makes it distinct from the adolescence that precedes it and the young adulthood that follows it? We will be considering that question throughout this book, but in this initial chapter I want to present an outline of what emerging adulthood is, in its essential qualities. There are five main features:[12]

1. It is the age of *identity explorations*, of trying out various possibilities, especially in love and work.
2. It is the age of *instability*.
3. It is the most *self-focused* age of life.
4. It is the age of *feeling in-between*, in transition, neither adolescent nor adult.
5. It is the age of *possibilities*, when hopes flourish, when people have an unparalleled opportunity to transform their lives.

Let's look at each of these features in turn.

The Age of Identity Explorations

Perhaps the most central feature of emerging adulthood is that it is the time when young people explore possibilities for their lives in a variety of areas, especially love and work. In the course of exploring possibilities in love and work, emerging adults clarify their identities, that is, they learn more about who they are and what they want out of life. Emerging adulthood offers the best opportunity for such self-exploration. Emerging adults have become more independent of their parents than they were as adolescents and most of them have left home, but they have not yet entered the stable, enduring commitments typical of adult life, such as a long-term job, marriage, and parenthood. During this interval of years, when they are neither beholden to their parents nor committed to a web of adult roles, they have an exceptional opportunity to try out different ways of living and different options for love and work.

Of course, it is adolescence rather than emerging adulthood that has typically been associated with identity formation. A half century ago Erik Erikson[13] designated identity versus role confusion as the central crisis of the adolescent stage of life, and in the decades since he articulated this idea, the focus of research on identity has been on adolescence. However, Erikson also commented on the "prolonged adolescence" typical of industrialized societies and the *psychosocial moratorium* granted to young people in such societies, "during which the young adult through free role experimentation may find a niche in some section of his society."[14] Decades later, this applies to many more young people than when he wrote it.[15] If adolescence is the period from age 10 to 18 and emerging adulthood is the period from (roughly) age 18 to the mid-twenties, most identity exploration takes place in emerging adulthood rather than adolescence. Although research on identity formation has focused mainly on adolescence, this research has shown that identity achievement has rarely been reached by the end of high school and that identity development continues through the late teens and the twenties.[16]

In both love and work, the process of identity formation begins in adolescence but intensifies in emerging adulthood. With regard to love, adolescent love tends to be tentative and transient.[17] The implicit question is "Who would I enjoy being with, here and now?" In contrast, explorations in love in emerging adulthood tend to involve a deeper level of intimacy, and the implicit question is more identity-focused: "What kind of person am I, and what kind of person would suit me best as a partner through life?" By becoming involved with different people, emerging adults learn about the qualities that are most important to them in another person, both the qualities that attract them and the qualities they find distasteful and annoying. They also see how they are evaluated by others who come to know them well. They learn what others find attractive in them—and perhaps what others find distasteful and annoying!

In work, too, there is a similar contrast between the transient and tentative explorations of adolescence and the more serious and identity-focused explorations of emerging adulthood. Most American adolescents have a part-time job at some point during high school,[18] but most of their jobs last for only a few months at most. They tend to work in service jobs—restaurants, retail stores, and so on—unrelated to the work they expect to be doing in adulthood, and they tend to view their jobs not as occupational preparation but as a way to obtain the money that will support an active leisure life—CDs, concert tickets, restaurant meals, clothes, cars, travel, and so on.[19]

In emerging adulthood, work experiences become more focused on laying the groundwork for an adult occupation. In exploring various work possibilities and in exploring the educational possibilities that will prepare them for work, emerging adults explore identity issues as well: "What kind of work am I good at? What kind of work would I find satisfying for the long term? What are my chances of getting a job in the field that seems to suit me best?" As they try out different jobs or college majors, emerging adults learn more about themselves. They learn more about their abilities and interests. Just as important, they learn what kinds of work they are *not* good at or *do not* want to do. In work as in love, explorations in emerging adulthood commonly include the experience of failure or disappointment. But as in love, the failures and disappointments in work can be illuminating for self-understanding.

Although emerging adults become more focused and serious about their directions in love and work than they were as adolescents, this change takes place gradually. Many of the identity explorations of the emerging adult years are simply for fun, a kind of play, part of gaining a broad range of life experiences before "settling down" and taking on the responsibilities of adult life. Emerging adults realize they are free in ways they will not be during their thirties and beyond. For people who wish to have a variety of romantic and sexual experiences, emerging adulthood is the time for it, when parental surveillance has diminished and there is as yet little normative pressure to enter marriage. Similarly, emerging adulthood is the time for trying out unusual educational and work possibilities. Programs such as AmeriCorps and the Peace Corps find most of their volunteers among emerging adults,[20] because emerging adults have both the freedom to pull up stakes quickly in order to go somewhere new and the inclination to do something unusual. Other emerging adults travel on their own to a different part of the country or the world to work or study for a while. This, too, can be part of their identity explorations, part of expanding the range of their personal experiences prior to making the more enduring choices of adulthood.

We will examine identity explorations in relation to love in chapters 4 and 5, college in chapter 6, and work in chapter 7. Ideology, the other aspect of identity in Erikson's theory, is the subject of chapter 8, on religious beliefs and values.

The Age of Instability

The explorations of emerging adults and their shifting choices in love and work make emerging adulthood an exceptionally full and intense period of life but also an exceptionally unstable one. Emerging adults know they are supposed to have a Plan with a capital *P*, that is, some kind of idea about the route they will be taking from adolescence to adulthood,[21] and most of them come up with one. However, for almost all of them, their Plan is subject to numerous revisions during the emerging adult years. These revisions are a natural consequence of their explorations. They enter college and choose a major, then discover the major is not as interesting as it seemed—time to revise the Plan. Or they enter college and find themselves unable to focus on their studies, and their grades sink accordingly—time to revise the Plan. Or they go to work after college but discover after a year or two that they need more education if they ever expect to make decent money—time to revise the Plan. Or they move in with a boyfriend or girlfriend and start to think of the Plan as founded on their future together, only to discover that they have no future together—time to revise the Plan.

With each revision in the Plan, they learn something about themselves and hopefully take a step toward clarifying the kind of future they want. But even if they succeed in doing so, that does not mean the instability of emerging adulthood is easy. Sometimes emerging adults look back wistfully on their high school years. Most of them remember those years as filled with anguish in many ways, but in retrospect at least they knew what they were going to be doing from one day, one week, one month to the next. In emerging adulthood the anxieties of adolescence diminish, but instability replaces them as a new source of disruption. We will examine this issue in detail in chapter 10.

The best illustration of the instability of emerging adulthood is in how often they move from one residence to another. As Figure 1.2 indicates, rates of moving spike upward beginning at age 18, reach their peak in the mid-twenties, then sharply decline.[22] This shows that emerging adults rarely know where they will be living from one year to the next. It is easy to imagine the sources of their many moves. Their first move is to leave home, often to go to college but sometimes just to be independent of their parents.[23] Other moves soon follow. If they drop out of college either temporarily or permanently, they may move again. They often live with roommates during emerging adulthood, some of whom they get along with, some of whom they do not—and when they do not, they move again. They may move in with a boyfriend or girlfriend. Sometimes cohabitation leads to marriage, sometimes it does not—and when it does not, they move again. If they graduate from college they move again, perhaps to start a new job or to enter graduate school. For nearly half of emerging adults, at least one of their moves during the years from age 18 to 25 will be back home to live with their parents.[24] Moving home will be one of the topics of chapter 3.

All of this moving around makes emerging adulthood an unstable time, but it also reflects the explorations that take place during the emerging adult years. Many of the moves emerging adults make are for the purpose of some new period of exploration, in love, work, or education. Exploration and instability go hand in hand.

The Self-Focused Age

There is no time of life that is more self-focused than emerging adulthood. Children and adolescents are self-focused in their own way, yes, but they always have parents and teachers to answer to, and usually siblings as well. Nearly all of them live at home with at least one parent. There are household rules and standards to follow, and if they break them they risk the wrath of other family members. Parents keep track, at least to some extent, of where they are and what they are doing. Although adolescents typically grow more independent than they were as children, they remain part of a family system that requires responses from them on a daily basis. In addition, nearly all of them attend school, where teachers set the standards and monitor their behavior and performance.

By age 30, a new web of commitments and obligations is well established, for most people. At that age, 75% of Americans have married and have had at least one child.[25] A new household, then, with new rules and

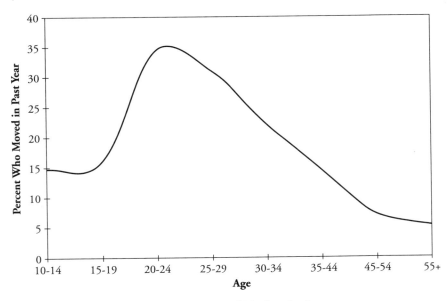

Figure 1.2. Rates of Moving, by Age

Most emerging adults are not quite this self-focused! (CATHY © 1996 Cathy Guisewite. Reprinted with permission of Universal Press Syndicate. All rights reserved.)

standards. A spouse, instead of parents and siblings, with whom they must coordinate activities and negotiate household duties and requirements. A child, to be loved and provided for, who needs time and attention. An employer, in a job and a field they are committed to and want to succeed in, who holds them to standards of progress and achievement.

It is only in between, during emerging adulthood, that there are few ties that entail daily obligations and commitments to others. Most young Americans leave home at age 18 or 19, and moving out means that daily life is much more self-focused. What to have for dinner? You decide. When to do the laundry? You decide. When (or whether) to come home at night? You decide.

So many decisions! And those are the easy ones. They have to decide the hard ones mostly on their own as well. Go to college? Work full time? Try to combine work and college? Stay in college or drop out? Switch majors? Switch colleges? Switch jobs? Switch apartments? Switch roommates? Break up with girlfriend/boyfriend? Move in with girlfriend/boyfriend? Date someone new? Even for emerging adults who remain at home, many of these decisions apply. Counsel may be offered or sought from parents and friends, but many of these decisions mean clarifying in their own minds what they want, and nobody can really tell them what they want but themselves.

To say that emerging adulthood is a self-focused time is not meant pejoratively. There is nothing wrong about being self-focused during emerging adulthood; it is normal, healthy, and temporary. By focusing on themselves, emerging adults develop skills for daily living, gain a better understanding of who they are and what they want from life, and begin to build a foundation for their adult lives. The goal of their self-focusing is self-sufficiency, learning to stand alone as a self-sufficient person, but they do not see self-sufficiency as a permanent state. Rather, they view it as a necessary step before committing themselves to enduring relationships with others, in love and work.

The Age of Feeling In-Between

The exploration and instability of emerging adulthood give it the quality of an in-between period—between adolescence, when most people live in their parents' home and are required to attend secondary school, and young adulthood, when most people have entered marriage and parenthood and have settled into a stable occupational path. In between the restrictions of adolescence and the responsibilities of adulthood lie the explorations and instability of emerging adulthood.

It feels this way to emerging adults, too—like an age in-between, neither adolescent nor adult, on the way to adulthood but not there yet. When asked whether they feel they have reached adulthood, their responses are often ambiguous, with one foot in *yes* and the other in *no*. For example, Lillian, 25, answered the question this way:

> Sometimes I think I've reached adulthood and then I sit down and eat ice cream directly from the box, and I keep thinking, "I'll know I'm an adult when I don't eat ice cream right out of the box any more!" That seems like such a childish thing to do. But I guess in some ways I feel like I'm an adult. I'm a pretty responsible person. I mean, if I say I'm going to do something, I do it. I'm very responsible with my job. Financially, I'm fairly responsible with my money. But sometimes in social circumstances I feel uncomfortable like I don't know what I'm supposed to do, and I still feel like a little kid. So a lot of times I don't really feel like an adult.

As Figure 1.3 demonstrates, about 60% of emerging adults aged 18–25 report this "yes and no" feeling in response to the question "Do you feel that you have reached adulthood?"[26] Once they reach their late twenties and early thirties most Americans feel they have definitely reached adulthood, but even then a substantial proportion, about 30%, still feels in-between. It is only in their later thirties, their forties, and their fifties that this sense of ambiguity has faded for nearly everyone and the feeling of being adult is well established.

The reason that so many emerging adults feel in-between is evident from the criteria they consider to be most important for becoming an adult. The

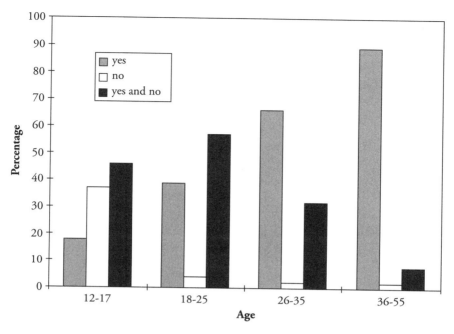

Figure 1.3. "Do you feel that you have reached adulthood?"

criteria most important to them are gradual, so their feeling of becoming an adult is gradual, too. In a variety of regions of the United States, in a variety of ethnic groups, in studies using both questionnaires and interviews, people consistently state the following as the top three criteria for adulthood:[27]

1. Accept responsibility for yourself.
2. Make independent decisions.
3. Become financially independent.

All three criteria are gradual, incremental, rather than all at once. Consequently, although emerging adults begin to feel adult by the time they reach age 18 or 19, they do not feel completely adult until years later, some time in their mid- to late twenties. By then they have become confident that they have reached a point where they accept responsibility, make their own decisions, and are financially independent. While they are in the process of developing those qualities, they feel in between adolescence and full adulthood. We will explore this issue more in chapter 10.

The Age of Possibilities

Emerging adulthood is the age of possibilities, when many different futures remain open, when little about a person's direction in life has been decided for certain. It tends to be an age of high hopes and great expectations, in part because few of their dreams have been tested in the fires of real life. Emerging adults look to the future and envision a well-paying, satisfying job, a loving, lifelong marriage, and happy children who are above average. In one national survey of 18–24-year-olds, nearly all—96%—agreed with the statement "I am very sure that someday I will get to where I want to be in life."[28] The dreary, dead-end jobs, the bitter divorces, the disappointing and disrespectful children that some of them will find themselves experiencing in the years to come—none of them imagine that this is what the future holds for them.

One feature of emerging adulthood that makes it the age of possibilities is that, typically, emerging adults have left their family of origin but are not yet committed to a new network of relationships and obligations. This is especially important for young people who have grown up in difficult conditions. A chaotic or unhappy family is difficult to rise above for children and adolescents, because they return to that family environment every day and the family's problems are often reflected in problems of their own. If the parents fight a lot, they have to listen to them. If the parents live in poverty, the children live in poverty, too, most likely in dangerous neighborhoods with inferior schools. If a parent is alcoholic, the disruptions from the parent's problems rip through the rest of the family as well. However, with emerging adulthood and departure from the family home, an unparalleled opportunity begins for young people to transform their lives. For those who have come from troubled families, this is their chance to try to straighten the parts of themselves that have become twisted. We will see some examples of dramatic transformations in chapter 9.

Even for those who have come from families they regard as relatively happy and healthy, emerging adulthood is an opportunity to transform themselves so that they are not merely made in their parents' images but have made independent decisions about what kind of person they wish to be and how they wish to live. During emerging adulthood they have an exceptionally wide scope for making their own decisions. Eventually, virtually all emerging adults will enter new, long-term obligations in love and work, and once they do their new obligations will set them on paths that resist change and that may continue for the rest of their lives. But for now, while emerging adulthood lasts, they have a chance to change their lives in profound ways.[29]

Regardless of their family background, all emerging adults carry their family influences with them when they leave home, and the extent to which they can change what they have become by the end of adolescence is not unlimited. Still, more than any other period of life, emerging adulthood presents the possibility of change. For this limited window of time—7, perhaps 10, years—the fulfillment of all their hopes seems possible, because for most people the range of their choices for how to live is greater than it has ever been before and greater than it will ever be again.

Who Needs Emerging Adulthood?

Who needs emerging adulthood? Why not just call the period from the late teens through the mid-twenties "late adolescence," if it is true that people in this age group have not yet reached adulthood? Why not call it "young adulthood," if we concede that they have reached adulthood but wish to distinguish between them and adults of older ages? Maybe we should call it the "transition to adulthood," if we want to emphasize that it is a transitional period between adolescence and young adulthood. Or maybe we should call it "youth," like some earlier scholars of this age period did.

I considered each of these alternatives in the course of forming the concept of emerging adulthood. Here is why I concluded each of them was inadequate and why I believe the term *emerging adulthood* is preferable.

Why Emerging Adulthood Is Not "Late Adolescence"

The first time I taught a college course on human development across the lifespan, when I reached the part of the course concerning adolescence I told my students that, by social science terms, nearly all of them were "late adolescents." Social scientists defined adulthood in terms of discrete transitions such as finishing education, marriage, and parenthood. They were students, so clearly they had not finished their education, and few of them were married, and fewer still had become parents. So, they were late adolescents.

They were outraged! OK, they conceded, they had not really reached adulthood yet, not entirely, but they were *not* adolescents, whatever the social scientists might say.

At the time, I was surprised and bewildered at their objections. Now, I realize they were right. Adolescence, even "late adolescence," is an entirely inadequate term for college students or anyone else who is in the age period from the late teens through the mid-twenties that I am calling emerging adulthood. True, adolescents and most emerging adults have in common that they have not yet entered marriage and parenthood. Other than this similarity, however, their lives are much different. Virtually all adolescents (ages 10–18) live at home with one or both parents. In contrast, most emerging adults have moved out of their parents' homes, and their living situations are extremely diverse. Virtually all adolescents are experiencing the dramatic physical changes of puberty. In contrast, emerging adults have reached full reproductive maturity. Virtually all adolescents attend secondary school. In contrast, many emerging adults are enrolled in college, but nowhere near all of them. Unlike adolescents, their educational paths are diverse, from those who go straight through college and then on to graduate or professional school to those who receive no more education after high school, and every combination in between. Adolescents also have in common that they have the legal status of minors, not adults. They cannot vote, they cannot sign legal documents, and they are legally under the authority and responsibility of their parents in a variety of ways. In contrast, from age 18 onward American emerging adults have all the legal rights of adults except for the right to buy alcohol, which comes at age 21.

In all of these ways, emerging adults are different from adolescents. As a result, "late adolescence" is an inadequate term for describing them. The term emerging adulthood is preferable because it distinguishes them from adolescents while recognizing that they are not yet fully adult.

Why Emerging Adulthood Is Not "Young Adulthood"

If not "late adolescence," how about "young adulthood"? There are a number of reasons why the term "young adulthood" does not work. One is that it implies that adulthood has been reached. However, as we have seen, most people in their late teens through their mid-twenties would disagree that they have reached adulthood. Instead, they tend to see themselves as in between adolescence and adulthood, so emerging adulthood captures better their sense of where they are—on the way to adulthood, but not there yet. *Emerging* is also a better descriptive term for the exploratory, unstable, fluid quality of the period.

An additional problem with "young adulthood" is that it is already used in diverse ways. The "young adult" section of the bookstore contains books aimed at teens and preteens, the "young adult" group at a church might include people up to age 40, and "young adult" is sometimes applied to college students aged 18–22. Such diverse uses make "young adulthood" confusing and incoherent as a term for describing a specific period of life. Using *emerging adulthood* allows us to ascribe a clear definition to a new term.

To call people from their late teens through their mid-twenties "young adults" would also raise the problem of what to call people who are in their thirties. They are certainly not middle-aged yet. Should we call them "young adults," too? It makes little sense to lump the late teens, the twenties, and the thirties together and call the entire 22-year period "young adulthood." The period I am calling emerging adulthood could hardly be more distinct from the thirties. Most emerging adults do not feel they have reached adulthood, but most people in their thirties feel they have. Most emerging adults are still in the process of seeking out the education, training, and job experiences that will prepare them for a long-term occupation, but most people in their thirties have settled into a more stable occupational path. Most emerging adults have not yet married, but most people in their thirties are married. Most emerging adults have not yet had a child, but most people in their thirties have at least one child.

The list could go on. The point should be clear. Emerging adulthood and young adulthood should be distinguished as two separate periods. "Young adulthood" is better applied to those in their thirties, who are still young but are definitely adult in ways those in the late teens through the mid-twenties are not.

Why Emerging Adulthood Is Not the "Transition to Adulthood"

Another possibility would be to call the years from the late teens through the twenties the "transition to adulthood." It is true that most young people make the transition to adulthood during this period, in terms of their perceptions of their status and in terms of their movement toward stable adult roles in love and work. However, the "transition to adulthood" also proves to be inadequate as a term for this age period. One problem is that thinking of the years from the late teens through the twenties as merely the transition to adulthood leads to a focus on what young people in that age period are *becoming*, at the cost of neglecting what they *are*. This is what has happened in sociological research on this period. There are mountains of research in sociology on the "transition to adulthood," but virtually all of it focuses on the transitions that sociologists assume are the defining criteria of adulthood—leaving home, finishing education, entering marriage, and entering parenthood.[30] Sociologists examine the factors that influence when young people make these transitions and explain historical trends in the timing of the transitions.

Much of this research is interesting and informative, but it tells us little about what is actually going on in young people's lives from the late teens through the twenties. They leave home at age 18 or 19, and they marry and become parents some time in their late twenties or beyond. But what happens in between? They finish their education? Is that it? No, of course not. There is so much more that takes place during this age period, as we have seen in this chapter and as we will see in the chapters to come. Calling it the "transition to adulthood" narrows our perception and our understanding of it, because that term distracts us from examining all of the changes happening during those years that are unrelated to the timing of transitions such as marriage and parenthood. Research on the transition to adulthood is welcome and is potentially interesting, but it is not the same as research on emerging adulthood.

Another problem with the term "transition to adulthood" is that it implies that the period between adolescence and young adulthood is brief, linking two longer and more notable periods of life, hence better referred to as a "transition" than as a period of life in its own right. This may have been the case 30 or 40 years ago, when most people in industrialized societies finished school, married, and had their first child by their very early twenties. However, today, with school extending longer and longer for more and more people and with the median ages of marriage and parenthood now in the late twenties, referring to the years between adolescence and full adulthood as simply the "transition to adulthood" no longer makes sense. Even if we state conservatively that emerging adulthood lasts from about age 18 to about age 25, that would be a period of seven years—longer than infancy, longer than early or middle childhood, and as long as adolescence. Emerging adulthood *is* a transitional period, yes—and so is every other period of life—but it is not merely a transition, and it should be studied as a separate period of life.

Why Emerging Adulthood Is Not "Youth"

One other possible term that must be mentioned is Kenneth Keniston's "youth," which has been perhaps the most widely used term in the social sciences for the period from the late teens through the twenties.[31] There are a number of reasons why "youth" does not work. First, Keniston wrote at a time when American society and some Western European societies were convulsed with highly visible "youth movements" protesting U.S. involvement in the Vietnam War (among other things). His description of youth as a time of "tension between self and society" and "refusal of socialization" reflects that historical moment rather than any enduring characteristics of the period.[32]

The term "youth" is problematic in other ways as well. "Youth" has a long history in the English language as a term for childhood generally and for what later came to be called adolescence, and it continues to be used popularly and by many social scientists for these purposes (as reflected in terms such as "youth organizations"). Keniston's choice of the ambiguous and confusing term "youth" may explain in part why the idea of the late teens and twenties as a separate period of life never became widely accepted by scholars after his articulation of it.

None of the terms used in the past are adequate to describe what is occurring today among young people from their late teens through their twenties. There is a need for a new term and a new conception of this age period, and I suggest *emerging adulthood* in the hope that it will lead both to greater understanding and to more intensive study of the years from the late teens through the twenties.

The Cultural Context of Emerging Adulthood

Emerging adulthood is not a universal period of human development but a period that exists under certain conditions that have occurred only quite recently and only in some cultures. As we have seen, what is mainly required for emerging adulthood to exist is a relatively high median age of entering marriage and parenthood, in the late twenties or beyond. Postponing marriage and parenthood until the late twenties allows the late teens and most of the twenties to be a time of exploration and instability, a self-focused age, and an age of possibilities.

So, emerging adulthood exists today mainly in the industrialized or "postindustrial" countries of the West, along with Asian countries such as Japan and South Korea. Table 1.1 shows the median marriage age for females in a variety of industrialized countries, contrasted with developing countries.[33] (The marriage age for males is typically about two years older than for females.) In most countries, the entry to parenthood comes about a year after marriage, on average.

Table 1.1.   Median Marriage Age of Females in Selected Countries

Industrialized Countries	Age	Developing Countries	Age
United States	25	Nigeria	17
Australia	26	Egypt	19
Canada	26	Ghana	19
France	26	Indonesia	19
Germany	26	India	20
Italy	26	Morocco	20
Japan	27	Brazil	21

Ages of marriage and parenthood are typically calculated on a countrywide basis, but emerging adulthood is a characteristic of cultures rather than countries. Within any given country, there may be some cultures that have a period of emerging adulthood and some that do not, or the length of emerging adulthood may vary among the cultures within a country. For example, in the United States, members of the Mormon church tend to have a shortened and highly structured emerging adulthood.[34] Because of cultural beliefs prohibiting premarital sex and emphasizing the desirability of large families, there is considerable social pressure on young Mormons to marry early and begin having children. Consequently, the median ages of entering marriage and parenthood are much lower among Mormons than in the American population as a whole, so they have a briefer period of emerging adulthood before taking on adult roles.[35]

Variations in socioeconomic status and life circumstances also determine the extent to which a given young person may experience emerging adulthood, even within a country that is affluent overall.[36] The young woman who has a child outside of marriage at age 16 and spends her late teens and early twenties alternating between government dependence and low-paying jobs has little chance for the self-focused identity explorations of emerging adulthood, nor does the young man who drops out of school and spends most of his late teens and early twenties unemployed and looking unsuccessfully for a job. Because opportunities tend to be less widely available in minority cultures than in the majority culture in most industrialized countries, members of minority groups may be less likely to experience their late teens and early twenties as a period of emerging adulthood. However, social class may be more important than ethnicity, with young people in the middle class or above having more opportunities for the explorations of emerging adulthood than young people who are working class or below. And yet, as we will see in chapter 9, for some young people who have grown up in poor or chaotic families, emerging adulthood represents a chance to transform their lives in dramatic ways, because reaching emerging adulthood allows them to leave the family circumstances that may have been the source of their problems.

Currently in economically developing countries, there tends to be a distinct cultural split between urban and rural areas. Young people in urban areas of countries such as China and India are more likely to experience emerging adulthood, because they marry later, have children later, obtain more education, and have a greater range of occupational and recreational opportunities than young people in rural areas.[37] In contrast, young people in rural areas of developing countries often receive minimal schooling, marry early, and have little choice of occupations except agricultural work. Thus, in developing countries, emerging adulthood may often be experienced in urban areas but rarely in rural areas.

However, emerging adulthood is likely to become more pervasive worldwide in the decades to come, with the increasing globalization of the world economy.[38] Table 1.2 shows an example of how globalization is affecting the lives of young people, by making secondary school a normative experience worldwide.[39] Between 1980 and 2000, the proportion of young people in developing countries who attended secondary school rose sharply. The median ages of entering marriage and parenthood rose in these countries as well.

Table 1.2. Changes in Secondary-School Enrollment in Selected Developing Countries, 1980–2000

	% enrolled 1980		% enrolled 2000	
	Males	Females	Males	Females
Argentina	53	62	73	81
China	54	37	74	67
Egypt	66	41	83	73
India	39	20	59	39
Mexico	51	46	64	64
Nigeria	25	13	36	30
Poland	75	80	98	97
Turkey	44	24	68	48

These changes open up the possibility for the spread of emerging adulthood in developing countries. Rising education reflects economic development. Economic development makes possible the period of independent identity exploration that is at the heart of emerging adulthood. As societies become more affluent, they are more likely to grant young people the opportunity for the extended moratorium of emerging adulthood, because their need for young people's labor is less urgent. Thus it seems possible that by the end of the 21st century emerging adulthood will be a normative period for young people worldwide, although it is likely to vary in length and content both within and between countries.

The Plan of This Book

The challenges, uncertainties, and possibilities of emerging adulthood make it a fascinating and eventful time of life. In the chapters to come, my intention is to provide a broad portrait of what it is like to be an emerging adult in American society. We start out in chapter 2 by looking in detail at the lives of four emerging adults, in order to see how the themes described in this first chapter are reflected in individual lives. This is followed in chapter 3 by a look at how relationships with parents change in emerging adulthood. Then there are two chapters on emerging adults' experiences with love: chapter 4 on dating and sexual issues and chapter 5 on finding a marriage partner. Next comes chapter 6 on the diverse paths that emerging adults take through college and chapter 7 on their search for meaningful work. In chapter 8 we examine emerging adults' religious beliefs and values. Then chapter 9 highlights emerging adulthood as the age of possibilities by profiling four young people who have overcome difficult experiences to transform their lives. Finally, in chapter 10 we consider the passage from emerging adulthood to young adulthood, focusing on the question of what it means to become an adult.

The material in the chapters is based mainly on more than 300 in-depth structured interviews that I and my research assistants conducted in Columbia (Missouri), San Francisco, Los Angeles, and New Orleans. We interviewed young people from age 20 to 29 from diverse backgrounds, about half of them White and the other half African American, Latino, and Asian American.[40] I included people in their late twenties as well as their early to mid-twenties because for many people emerging adulthood lasts through the late twenties. In the lives of those who do leave emerging adulthood by their late twenties we can see what happens in the transition from emerging adulthood to young adulthood. I also draw upon my college students (mostly ages 18–23) at the University of Missouri, where I taught from 1992 to 1998, and the University of Maryland, where I teach now. In addition, I use statistics and information from national surveys and other studies that include 18–29-year-olds.

I present some statistics on the people we interviewed, but for the most part I present excerpts from the interviews to illustrate my points. The interview approach seemed appropriate to me for exploring a period of life that had not been studied much and about which not much was known. Also, emerging adults are a diverse group in terms of their life situations, and the interview approach allows me to describe their different situations and perspectives rather than simply stating that they are "like this," based on an overall statistical pattern. Finally, the interview approach is valuable in studying emerging adults because they are often remarkably insightful in describing their experiences. Perhaps because emerging adulthood is a self-focused period of life, the young people we interviewed often possessed a striking capacity for self-reflection, not only the ones who had graduated from college but also—perhaps especially—the ones who had struggled to make it through high school. Presenting excerpts from the interviews allows for a full display of their everyday eloquence. What they have to say about their lives and experiences is illuminating, moving, and often humorous, as you will see in the chapters to come.

2

What Is It Like to Be an Emerging Adult?

Four Profiles

Douglas Coupland's 1991 novel, *Generation X*, can be credited with first drawing widespread attention to the fact that something new was happening in the lives of young people in their twenties. The novel follows the lives and musings of Andy, Claire, and Dag as they wander through their late twenties together. None of them has been able yet to find enjoyable work, and they refuse to settle into jobs that may pay well but involve "endless stress" and meaningless work "done grudgingly to little applause." As for love, none of them is close to getting married, but as Andy says, "I *do* at least recognize the fact that I don't want to go through life alone."[1] Their feelings about entering adulthood are summed up in the title of one chapter, "Dead at 30 Buried at 70." As good novels often do, *Generation X* not only describes the lives of individual characters but, in doing so, also provides vivid insights into what it is like to live in a certain place at a certain time.

Most emerging adults I talk to about *Generation X* dislike the book, even if—especially if—they have not read it. Who can blame them, given that *Generation X* is responsible for the construction of a rather unflattering stereotype of young people in their twenties as "slackers"—aimless, apathetic, and cynical. Nevertheless, although Coupland's depiction of young people in their twenties was extreme in some ways, in the lives of Andy, Claire, and Dag can be seen many of the features that I described in chapter 1 as defining emerging adulthood. They are exploring (if rather aimlessly); their lives are unstable; they have a sense of being in between adolescence and adulthood (and they are assiduously avoiding adult responsibilities);

and they are self-focused (to an extreme). *Generation X* is also original and funny, and I recommend it to anyone interested in emerging adulthood.

My aim in this book is different than Coupland's, of course, and not just because it is nonfiction rather than fiction. I want to describe common patterns in the lives of emerging adults, not just individual characters, and to illustrate these patterns I will take quotes from various interviews and weave them together. However, there is also much to be gained from describing individuals, so that we can see what a complete life looks like in emerging adulthood. If we only combined isolated parts from the interviews, we would never see how all of the parts fit together. By describing several people in detail, we can get a full sense of what it is like to be an emerging adult, in all of its complexity.

In this chapter we will look at the lives of four emerging adults. I chose the persons for these profiles so that they would represent a broad range of backgrounds and experiences in emerging adulthood. Two are male and two are female; two are White and two are members of ethnic minorities; two are college graduates and two are not; and the four of them grew up in several different parts of the United States. They range in age from 21 to 27. Together they provide a taste of the diversity that exists among emerging adults, as well as some of the qualities that are common to many of them.

Although the persons in the profiles are diverse, they were not chosen to be representative of all persons in my study, much less all persons in their twenties. None of them are married, and none of them have children. None of them are firmly settled into a career path. Rather, the persons in the profiles were chosen because they exemplify the characteristics that define emerging adulthood as a distinct period of life: the age of explorations, the age of instability, the self-focused age, the age of feeling in-between, and the age of possibilities. The profiles presented in this chapter will serve to illustrate the essential characteristics of emerging adulthood described in chapter 1, by connecting them to the real lives of emerging adults. The profiles also preview many of the themes of the chapters to come.

Rosa: "Choking Life for All It's Got"

I arranged to meet Rosa, 24, at a coffee shop near the University of San Francisco, and I had no trouble spotting her when she walked in. She had told me over the phone that her mother was Chinese and her father was Mexican, and in her face I could see clearly the unusual, striking blend of features from both sides of her family. She had just come from her job at an

Internet software start-up company, and she was dressed in casual profes-sional clothes, white slacks and a sweater that matched the jet black of her shoulder-length hair.

We started by talking about her work. Her current job for the Internet start-up requires a variety of skills, including editing, accounting, and human resources management, because it is a small company, only 17 em-ployees. She likes the variety, because it gives her a chance to increase her knowledge and explore possibilities for where she might want to focus her efforts. "I want to be able just to bounce around and learn as much as I can from each of the departments, so I just started doing editing. I want to kind of touch the marketing side, too. Just to see what I want to do."

Working for an Internet company was not what she had in mind when she graduated from the University of California at Berkeley two years ago. An English major in college, she planned to become a teacher in the Oak-land school system she had attended as a child. "I really thought I wanted to go into education," she said. "I graduated from college and I started run-ning an after-school program at a very low-income school because I thought if I was going to teach, I was going to teach where I was needed the most. I didn't want to teach in any district but Oakland, because I grew up in Oakland and I wanted to give back to the city."

However, she soon became disillusioned and depressed with what she witnessed in the schools. "Some of the kids didn't eat all day. A lot of their parents were on crack. A lot of them just lived with their grandmother one week, their aunt the next week; they really just floated. They were cruel to themselves and cruel to each other, just because they needed the attention." Her grim experiences at work seeped into the rest of her life. "I really got attached to my kids, and I couldn't snap out of it when I left the school. Like, I would still be in that zone when I got home, and I'd take it out on my boyfriend."

So she sent out resumes and soon left the school for her current job. But she doesn't see this job as permanent. "I still don't think I'm a businessperson. Eventually I think I'm just going to open my own bakery. That's what I really want to do." She is also considering other possibilities. "I will prob-ably end up taking a career more in editing. I can see myself in front of a computer, writing whatever, because I love to write. But I can also see myself in hard-core marketing for a big corporation, because I do like to work with people and I do like fast-paced stressful work." For now, she is happy to do some temporary exploring during her emerging adult years. "I mean, this is cool for now. I'm just going to hop around for a while."

She is more settled in love than she is in work. She has been seeing her current boyfriend, Mark, for three years, and she expects they will marry, although she is not sure when. "I know that if he proposed to me today, I would say yes. Oh, I love him to death. We've been through so much. I know we can get through anything that came in our way. We communicate really well."

Before Mark, she had another boyfriend for four years. Like many emerging adults with immigrant parents from Asia or Latin America, she never embraced the American way of dating casually in adolescence and emerging adulthood before settling down. Still, now that she is in a relationship that may lead to marriage, she finds herself wondering if she shouldn't explore her options a bit more. As much as she loves her boyfriend, there are also what she calls her "distractions," other men she feels attracted to. "Sometimes there's these little things that happen on the side, or people you meet, and you just kind of wonder, 'God, would this be cool for now?' Because I haven't had very much experience with other people. And sometimes I question if I really want to be in a relationship right now."

She also feels a need to develop her own identity more clearly before she enters marriage, by having a period of being self-focused. "I think I want to get more in touch with myself. I want to be a little selfish for a while, and selfishness and marriage don't seem to go hand in hand. I'd like to be able to experience as much as I can before I get married, just so I can be well-rounded."

This sense of not being ready to commit to marriage, being "wishy-washy," as she puts it, makes her feel that she has not yet fully reached adulthood. But in other ways, she does feel like an adult. "I think the way that I care about people is very adult. The way I express myself is very adult. For the most part I think I'm adult. It's just the wishy-washy part that I don't know about." Overall, then, like so many emerging adults she feels in-between, on the way to adulthood but not there yet. "Maybe I am an adult. I don't know. I'm a kid a lot of the times."

Becoming independent from her parents has not been a big issue for her in marking her progress to adulthood. She lived with her parents all the way through college, and enjoyed it. She has always gotten along well with her parents, except for a brief period in her early adolescence when she tangled often with her mom. "I think I had it bad with her probably sixth, seventh, and eighth grade[s]. But I went through it early, and then after that I was cake."

Her father travels around the world doing maintenance and repair on large ships and her mother is an optician. Solid middle-class jobs by most standards, yet Rosa sees their career paths as examples to avoid.

> I knew I wanted to be somewhere that I would grow as a person, and I don't see them growing as individuals. I mean, my mom is an optician, and you don't grow doing those things. That's why I kind of chose the high-tech path, because there's always new software to learn. And with my dad, I didn't want to have a job that beat up my body. I knew I wanted to be able to grow, and I didn't want to be broken by the time I was 40, you know. I think that's what I took from their jobs.

Although she has always had a good relationship with her parents, family life in their household has not always been easy. Rosa said her parents "almost divorced a few times" during her childhood. Her father resented her mother for working long hours and for making more money than he did; her mother complained that he drank too much. They get along somewhat better now, but it is hardly an ideal marriage.

There was additional tension in the household because of the problems of Rosa's brother, who is 18 months older than she is. "My brother and I have always hated each other," she said bluntly. "We don't really talk. We don't talk at all actually." He had various problems in childhood, then in high school "he went into the drug thing," she says. "I don't know. He got bent somewhere." She gets along much better with her sister, who is 8 years younger than she is. "My sister and I were never close until I moved out. Now I love her to death. She's 16 and she acts like it, but I love to be there for her. She's my baby sister."

Rosa sees the problems her parents and her brother have had as rooted partly in the unusual ethnic mix of Chinese and Mexican in the family. Each side of her parents' families regarded the other with suspicion and hostility, which generated conflict between her parents. Her brother was often ridiculed and beat up by other kids simply for looking Asian. Rosa has felt her own share of ethnic prejudice. When she goes to the mostly White suburbs, "I feel sometimes that we're looked at like, 'Why are you here?' Definitely like, 'There are too many of you here.'" It's not only Whites who look at her that way. "The Blacks too. And I sense a lot of hostility from Mexican people. I just don't have the connection. And I *am* Mexican! But I don't look like it."

Nevertheless, she has embraced her ethnicity with enthusiasm, especially her Chinese side. When she was young, her mother immersed her in Chinese culture, whereas her dad showed little interest in making her familiar with Mexican culture. "I grew up very Chinese. I grew up going to my grandma's sweat shop after school, I hung out in Chinatown, and I always saw my mom's family every weekend. My mom spoke Chinese to us." Rosa has always had mostly Asian friends, and her only two boyfriends have been Asian.

Now that she is in emerging adulthood, Rosa feels bad about letting the Mexican side of her background lapse. "I feel it's really unfair to my father. The only thing I know about my Mexican culture is that I'm Catholic, and I can cook the food. I'd like to learn more because I love my father to death." Her hope is that her children will have more of a Mexican identity than she does.

> I don't really know that much about my Mexican side and hopefully I'll learn, but I'm going to have my dad teach them their Mexican side. My dad already said, "When you have kids, they're going to call me 'Buppa,'" which is grandpa in Spanish. So hopefully he'll be able to pass on a lot to them. I just think it's a nice thing to know. You know, you're not just "an American." You have a beautiful, long history to your name.

However, the Catholic faith is one part of her Mexican heritage Rosa does not want to pass on to her children. Although she was raised "strictly Catholic," she now says, "I don't like Catholicism. I don't care for it at all. I don't think it applies to modern-day society at all. I'm not going to raise my kids Catholic." As an emerging adult she has become a deist, a person who believes in God in a general way, unattached to any specific religion. "I don't think my god has a religion—it's just God. There's just God. And that's the only thing I don't question. I know there's a God. I think it's the same God that Jews have, that Muslims have, they just all have a different name."

Perhaps influenced by her mother's Buddhist beliefs, she is inclined to believe in reincarnation. "I believe I was a cat before because I love to lay in the sun. Seriously! Every time I go home, I have my mom scratch my head or scratch my back." However, she adds that her focus is on this life, not the past ones or the next one. "I don't really give an afterlife much thought because it's not really that important to me. When I'm gone, I'm gone—I don't really care what happens to me when I'm gone."

For the future, Rosa has many dreams, of opening a bakery with her mother, of marrying Mark and having two children, of a lifetime of learning.

> If I was rich, I'd be a lifetime student. I love to learn. I wouldn't go back to school because I would require it for my future, I would just go back because I want it for myself. Like, I wouldn't mind going to law school, even though I don't see myself practicing law at all. Just for the fun of learning. I can really see myself going back for a Ph.D. in lit[erature] or something. I love to read, I love to write.

By the end of her life, she would like to be able to say:

> I experienced as much as I possibly could, and I spent as much time with my friends and my family as possible. And that people know how I feel about them. I tell my mom I love her every time I talk to her. And my dad. Just that I was happy and I tried to make the people around me happy. Those are the most important things. I just want to know that I made the most of my time. I can't just sit and watch TV. I believe in just taking life and choking it for all it's got.

Steve: "Who Knows What's Going to Happen?"

Steve, 23, flashes his ironic smile often, as if he wants to make sure you can see that he doesn't take himself too seriously. His brown eyes peer out from underneath dark eyebrows, which contrast with his short light-brown hair. When I met him for our interview in my office at the University of Missouri, he was wearing a green and maroon rugby shirt and casual light slacks.

Although he currently lives in Missouri, he lived in a variety of places in the course of growing up. His family moved often to follow his father's work as a contract engineer; every time his father got a new contract, they moved. He grew to dislike moving and vowed that he would put down roots somewhere once he left his parents' household. But as it turned out, he has moved around during emerging adulthood even more than he did with his family. "I always said that once I get out of high school and move away I'm going to stay in one place, but I've probably moved 15 times since I left home."

Missouri was one of the places his family lived for a while during his childhood, and he moved back there to go to the University of Missouri. However, he dropped out of school after a few semesters, feeling "kind of burnt out on it." Now, he waits on tables at a local restaurant. He is content with the money he is making. "I average about $16 an hour, so I mean, where else can I go right now and make that much money?" Nevertheless, he views his job, like he views many things in his life right now, as temporary. "I'm just kind of lazy right now. I'm just taking it easy."

While he was in college, Steve majored in fine arts because of his love of drawing. He continues now to do sketches and portraits, to make money in addition to his waiter job and because he enjoys it. However, he is doubtful that he could successfully make a career out of his artistic talents. "If I could wing it and be an artist I'd do it, but it's one of those things where you have to be great or you're working in advertising," and advertising does not appeal to him. "I'll probably end up doing art as a hobby," he says.

What course will he take, then, in terms of work? It's pretty clear that he doesn't know at this point. One moment he says, "I'll probably end up being an engineer. My dad's an engineer, so I'll probably end up doing that. I'm really good at math, and I know I could pick up on it real easy." Yet when I ask him a few minutes later what he sees himself doing 10 years from now, engineering has nothing to do with it.

> I'll probably be living in Colorado. I would want to say owning a restaurant, but probably in some kind of management position because I've been in the restaurant business for eight years so I know a lot about it. I cook, I've waited tables, I've bartended. I've pretty much done it all and that's what the criteria is to be a manager. I'm sure I could get a job, and just to be able to ski all the time would be great.

But right now he is doing little to bring this dream to fruition, unless you count the job as a waiter. "I'm just kind of 'treading water,' as my mom says."

With regard to love, Steve has been involved for about two months with Sandy, who is a waitress at the restaurant where he works. They get along well and spend most of their time together. They would like to live together but hesitate because of the objections of her parents, especially her father. "That's like his last little grip before he lets her go," Steve says resentfully. He'd like to move in with her for practical reasons, not because he feels nearly ready to marry her. "It would totally cut our expenses in half."

He is in no hurry to get married, to Sandy or anyone else. In his view, there is a lot less pressure to get married by a certain age today than in the past. "Nowadays, it's not even really an issue. If it happens it happens and if not, not. It's not as big of an issue as it was like in the '50s." He's still not sure what qualities he would like to find in the person he marries. "I haven't really narrowed it down yet. I guess when I find her, I'll know."

Steve is as uncertain and unsettled in his beliefs as he is in love and work. As he was growing up, his parents made little attempt to teach him a set of religious beliefs. He says they told him, "If you want to believe it, fine. But if you don't, that's fine too. We'll support you either way." Now, at age 23, he seems to have reached a few conclusions. "I believe in a Creator. Obviously, we couldn't have just sprouted from the earth." Reincarnation also seems plausible to him. "I always thought that there was obviously reincarnation." But as he talks further, it turns out that none of his beliefs are really so "obvious" after all. "I mean, none of us really know. There's no proof-positive to any of it. You have to have the facts and really I have none so I can't really make an educated guess yet."

Given his uncertainties about love, work, and beliefs, it's not surprising that he does not feel like he has entirely reached adulthood. "Mentally, I'm still trying to grab ahold of it," he says. He explains that what he means by this is that he doesn't yet accept the adulthood requirement of having to decide where his life is going. "I just don't look at it [from] an adult point of view. I just don't really buy into the whole system, you know. I'm like, 'I'm confused right now,' and everybody's like, 'You've got to make a decision,' and I'm like, 'Well, no, I don't.'"

Another thing that makes him feel he has not entirely reached adulthood is that he drinks more alcohol than he thinks an adult should. "I'm still in the party mode," he says. Still, his alcohol use has gone down from what it was a year or two earlier. "I don't really necessarily drink as much as I used to. Most of all it's because it's expensive to go out." He has grown tired of the local bar scene. "You can only go out to so many bars without them getting kind of boring." He has also grown tired of the effects of heavy drinking. "I don't like puking, and I don't like being hungover." Not to mention the insurance bills. "I got a DWI [Driving While Intoxicated], and I had a couple of rear-ends where I wasn't watching. I mean, my insurance is like $1,800 a year. Outrageous. That's why I kind of stopped drinking so much." But he still drinks enough to see it as a reason why he has not become an adult.

Nor do Steve's parents view him as having reached adulthood. "When I get a job, they will," he says. A job other than waiting on tables, that is. "We call it a 'real job.' 'When you get a real job.'" Nevertheless, his relationship with his parents has changed in recent years, to more of a relationship between equals. Now he is "a little more open with them, I guess. The way I talk to them and the way they talk to me, it's more on an adult level."

His parents have been successful in both their professional and personal lives. His dad has been successful as an engineer, and his mom, after devoting herself to raising Steve and his brother when they were young, now owns an antique store. Their marriage has been a relatively happy one. "I can't even remember them ever fighting once," Steve says. "They've got a pretty good sense of humor with each other, and they know how to communicate in kind of a funny way and still get the point across." They seem to have good relationships with their children as well. Steve says he was "very close" to his parents growing up, and it is clear that he remains fond of them.

Yet despite their success, and despite the unsettled quality of his life at age 23, Steve believes that his life will be better than his parents' lives have been. The reason for this is that he has been allowed to have an emerging adulthood with years of freedom to try out different possible paths, whereas his parents did not. "My dad, when he was 15, moved out and basically had to find a way to support himself and eventually his family, and I'm not having to go through that. My dad is in a position where he can help me out more than he got helped."

Eventually, Steve expects to have everything his parents have and more, all the best that adult life has to offer: satisfying and well-paying work, a happy marriage, a couple of children, living in an area he loves. For now, however, he is happy being "very nomadic. I've got so little stuff I can just move it around. I don't like to sign a lease, so usually I just try to do it month by month." He wants to be ready to hit the road in case a promising opportunity comes along. "Who knows when I'll find a job in Colorado? I've got to be ready to go! I don't want to owe anybody $1,000 on a lease when I'm not going to be living there. Who knows what's going to happen?"

Charles: "I'm Highly Portable"

You could tell by looking at Charles, 27, that there was something different about him, something out of the ordinary, even by San Francisco standards. His hair was in dreadlocks, and his black beard was trimmed short and looked striking against his brown skin. He wore a black T-shirt under a brown leather vest, and a silver earring. A black necklace with a gold pendant shone from his neck. But what was most striking about him were his eyes—large, alert, and intense, shining with energy.

He looked like he might be in the arts, and he is, a musician, songwriter, and singer, part of an a cappella band called the Jump Cats, which he described as "a rock band without instruments." He also works for an advertising agency, writing and editing advertisements, but even though he has been working there for a year he described himself as a "temp," meaning that he has an understanding with the agency that he can leave at any time, for short periods or long, as opportunities come up for the band. Right now, he and the band are recording a compact disc, so they have all taken temporary jobs to support themselves until the CD is finished and they can go on tour promoting it.

Charles graduated from Princeton, an elite Ivy League college, having majored in psychology, and he thought seriously about becoming either a psychologist or a lawyer. By then, however, he realized that "music is where my heart is," and he decided, "I didn't want to regret not going for something that would ultimately bring me more satisfaction" than psychology or law. His unfettered situation as an emerging adult has given him the opportunity to pursue his dream of devoting himself to music. "I'm single. I don't have a car or a house or a mortgage or a significant other that's pulling me in another direction, or kids or anything. I'm highly portable, and I can basically do whatever I want as long as I can support myself."

In the future, Charles sees himself pursuing other avenues of creative expression in addition to his music. Writing novels, plays, and perhaps screenplays. Designing games, like the card game he recently invented that has special cards specific to the game. He expects to have a full life and sees no reason why he should not be able to fit many different things into it. "I would basically like to set up my life in such a way that the things that I wish to do are the things that I'm doing and that they are not mutually exclusive. Now obviously, you can't do everything you want to do all the time, but you can work in ways so that you're able to consistently do pieces of things that you want to do."

Charles grew up in Shaker Heights, Ohio, a well-to-do suburb of Cleveland. His parents are attorneys, his mother in labor law and his father in personal injury. He got along well with them during childhood and adolescence, and he still does. Once or twice a year they "whisk me away," he says, for an exotic vacation—southern Spain, Belize, St. Martin.

Still, the privileges of his upbringing have not protected him from the wounds inherent in being an African American growing up in American society. He recalls, "The first day of first grade, a White kid hit me in the nose and gave me a bloody nose all over my new shirt." When Charles returned to school the next day, he gave the offending boy a bloody nose of his own, "with my parents' blessing. I told them about it, and my dad said, 'You can't let him do that to you.'" The following year, he heard for the first time the epithet that all Black children have thrown at them eventually.

> I was at a sports camp in the summer and a kid called me a nigger. I'd never heard the word before, so I went home and asked my parents, "What does this mean?" And they said, "He called you that?" And I said, "Yeah." My dad said, "If he calls you that again, hit him." So within two or three days, we were in tennis class, and he said it to me again, "Nigger." So I hit him in the head with the tennis racket, and he never called me a nigger again.

In adolescence, several times, Charles had the experience shared by many young Black men, of being pulled over for "Driving While Black." "My parents always had reasonably nice cars since I've been able to drive. And seeing a Black youth driving a nice car at night is grounds enough for many a police officer to pull that person over, regardless of whether or not there's any sort of violation."

However, these experiences have not prevented Charles from having many good relationships with Whites. His friends in high school were the smart kids, White as well as Black. Many of his friends at Princeton were White. He has dated Whites as well as Blacks and Asian Americans. The person at Princeton who persuaded him to be the leader of the a cappella group there that sparked his enthusiasm for music was an older White student who "took me under his wing," Charles recalls. And the Jump Cats are two Black guys and four White guys.

As an emerging adult, being African American is definitely part of his identity. "I'd be silly to try and say that none of my experiences have been at least somewhat based on or influenced by the color of my skin." He believes that opportunities in American society are restricted in some ways for African Americans. "It will be a hell of a long time before a Black person is ever president in this country," for example. "My parents told me at an early age that 'you're a Black kid, and you're going to be Black all your life. And that means you're going to have to work twice as hard to get half as much.'" Nevertheless, he believes that his talents and the advantages of his background will allow him to succeed at whatever he tries. Opportunities may not be entirely equal in American society, but "I think it's getting closer."

His parents, highly educated themselves, always encouraged him to excel academically. He says the message they gave to him was:

You are gifted with good genes and good brains because we gave them to you, and we know that you're bright. We know that you can make straight A's. We're not going to try and ride you and make you get straight A's because we don't think that's necessarily best for you. But we don't ever want you to think in any course you take that you can't get an A because that is bullshit.

The messages from his peers were more mixed. His best friends all did well in school themselves and supported each other in doing well. But he was aware that there were some Black kids who believed that "if you were in AP [Advanced Placement] classes, that was a strike against you" because most of the students in those classes were White. "Who you were in classes with determined who you would become friends with, so if you were in AP classes with almost all White kids and you were friends with almost all White kids, then they would say you're stuck-up." He also recalls that when he was accepted at Princeton, the reaction of one of his Black acquaintances was not "congratulations" but "I can't believe that, man. What the fuck is a nigger doing in the Ivy League?" However, Charles always easily shrugged off such views and never allowed his own pursuit of educational success to be affected by them.

He feels he has "definitely" reached adulthood, ever since he moved out to the Bay Area after college. He was alone, with no one to rely on but himself, and that made him feel adult.

> I had found my own living space, using my own contacts and my own initiative, and had gotten two jobs out here and was paying rent, you know, doing that whole thing. I felt that I had gotten off the ground in terms of starting a life out here. Not that it was my ideal life of what I wanted to be doing. I was working for a financial software company in a non-exciting capacity, and I was working at a nice restaurant in Berkeley, busing tables. But I felt that I had set my foot on the road, you know, "OK, I'm an adult now, and I'm walking."

Even though Charles is confident he has reached adulthood, his life shows a substantial amount of the exploration and instability that are two of the defining characteristics of emerging adulthood. In work, he has made a clear choice of pursuing a career in music, but the nature of that pursuit is still very much up in the air. He says that in 10 years, "I think I will still be doing music in some way, shape or form," but he adds, "I couldn't say exactly how." Perhaps with his current group, if they are successful, but perhaps as a guitarist or bass player, perhaps as a record producer, perhaps as a songwriter, perhaps some combination of these possibilities. Of course, there is also the writing of novels and plays to fit in, and the game designing. And then there is that Princeton degree to fall back on, perhaps leading to further education and a career in psychology or law. So, at this point, Charles is a young man full of possibilities, but it is difficult to predict which ones will be fulfilled in his future.

In love his future is even more wide open. He has been seeing his current girlfriend for three years. She is half Asian and half White. They share a love for music—they met at a singing competition—and a high level of education (she is currently a Ph.D. student in language and literature). Yet he says they both see marriage as something that is "not a realistic possibility any time soon." His musical career is likely to take him on the road for extended periods. She has at least two more years of graduate school, and after that there is no telling where her career opportunities might take her.

His beliefs about religious issues also seem not yet settled, still in the process of forming. Although he grew up going to an Episcopal church with his parents, by adolescence he was "bored with Sunday school and bored with the service." Also about that time, he said, he "realized that I was not being encouraged to think for myself." Even though the Episcopal church is relatively liberal in its doctrine, relatively tolerant of departures from orthodoxy, for Charles any organized religion is objectionable because it tells people what to believe rather than having them find out for themselves.

Now, he believes generally in a deity. "There's got to be something better than mankind in our universe, because we're too screwed up to be the best thing." However, he is more definite about what this deity is not than what it is. "I don't believe in a bearded White God or a bearded Black God or a nonbearded Black or White or Asian or Indian or Latino god or goddess sitting someplace, watching everybody." Buddhism appeals to him, especially the Buddhist belief in reincarnation.

> I like the Buddhist idea of rebirth and that in each subsequent life you make mistakes, but you're approaching perfection at which point you can achieve nirvana. There is something that really appeals to me about the idea that you get another chance because everybody makes tons of mistakes in their life. It'd be nice to have another shot with some benefit from the experience[s] you've been through.

However, he hastens to add, "I am not a Buddhist."

He is more certain about what he believes about this world, here and now, and the values he wants to live by. "In terms of how I conduct myself with friends and with people who aren't even friends, I try to treat them the way that I would want to be treated. To a certain extent that boils down to the Golden Rule, 'Do unto others . . .'" He also believes in being true to himself, following his heart and doing what he really wants to do with his life.

> It concerns me that of the many gifted people that I went to school with, so few of them are actually doing what they really want to do. And so many people say to me, "You are an inspiration to me because you are doing what you want to do. You have not yet sold out and said, 'I got a fancy degree from a liberal arts school. I'm just gonna go to business school or law school and get a degree and make lots of money.'"

Although Charles is 27 years old, an age when many of his peers are moving out of emerging adulthood into more settled lives, he has maintained his zeal for exploration, and he easily tolerates the instability that goes along with it.

Angela: "I Want to Get My Life in Order"

Angela, 21, has a job in landscaping, and you might have guessed that from looking at her. She is deeply tanned and her long hair is sun-bleached to a blondish light brown. She is quite tall, probably six feet, and quite slender. Her face is attractive and cheerful; she smiles a lot. You can see both vulnerability and hope in that smile, especially after you have talked to her for a while.

She returned to Missouri a year ago after spending two years at Michigan State, where she was majoring in horticulture therapy, which entails teaching people to cultivate plants as a way of dealing with their psychological problems. Going away to college was a key event in making her feel like she was reaching adulthood, because it meant "being away from my parents and everything and being independent." She loved being on her own, and she would have liked to finish her bachelor's degree at Michigan State. However, she decided she wanted to change her major from horticulture therapy to "just plain horticulture," and when university officials resisted she dropped out. She plans to finish her degree gradually at a local college. Meanwhile, she is working at her landscaping job.

Angela has known since high school that she wanted to pursue a career in horticulture. "I've always been an outdoors person, and I took a class in high school in horticulture. They had a greenhouse and stuff, and my teacher, I really liked her and she kind of showed me where some schools were and stuff, and that's why I went over there to Michigan State." She feels "a little bit disappointed" that she didn't graduate when she had intended, but she knows she is not alone. "It sounds like a lot of my friends aren't going to graduate, either. A lot of them have dropped out."

Toward the end of her time at Michigan State she was feeling exhausted from working full time in addition to carrying a full load of classes. "I was burnt out on school I think, so I'm kind of glad I took some time off." Now she can finish school gradually as she works in a job in her field. She is learning a lot about landscaping through her job. "We do all the planting and design of flowers and shrubs, and we do irrigation, we mulch, we cultivate, fertilize, all kinds of stuff. I enjoy it."

Although Angela is glad she chose horticulture and glad she went to Michigan State for two years, she is concerned about the debt she has taken on in order to finance her education. "I've got loans, and I'm worried about that. How am I going to pay off my loans? I'm in debt probably about $15,000 now." Her mother and father are both well-off financially, but neither of them supported her college education. "My parents could have helped me pay, you know. They say they can't afford it or something, but I mean, they both have nice houses and my mom has a condo down in Florida and on and on and on, and they didn't help me at all." Why didn't they? "I don't know why. I don't know if they were trying to teach us responsibility or whether they're just selfish or what. I don't know what the deal is." She feels burdened by her debts. "It's kind of depressing. I wish I could win the lottery!"

Angela's parents divorced when she was 4, and her mother remarried two years later, so she mostly grew up in the household of her mother and stepfather along with her older brother (now 24) and younger sister (now 16). Her mother is a medical technician; her stepfather is a professor of astronomy. She has always gotten along well with her mother, but she has never liked her stepfather. "I stayed away from him basically. He was just a jerk." His alcohol use was a source of conflict between him and her mother, and still is. "He gets to drinking and she says, 'Don't drink a lot,' and they start bickering back and forth. It's ridiculous." All the conflict made for a difficult environment to grow up in. "When I look back, it wasn't the best childhood, I think."

As for her father, he is a professor of medicine at a college in South Carolina, where he remained after her parents divorced, and Angela has seen him rarely since then. In fact, she hasn't seen him at all for the past seven years. Her reasons for why she hasn't seen him in so long sound more persuasive for explaining seven weeks than seven years. "It seems like there's never any time because he's busy all the time, and with me going to school and working I don't know when is the last time I had a vacation." But she talks to him a couple of times a month on the phone. "I don't know him as well as I would like to, but we talk about a lot of stuff."

With regard to her own love relationships, Angela got a late start because she was taller than virtually all of the boys. In high school, she says, "I went out with a few people but never dated anybody for a long period of time because I was tall and the guys were all short and they didn't want to ask me out. They were really intimidated. I was kind of paranoid about it." She still finds that some men are intimidated by her height, but her own view of it has changed in emerging adulthood. "It doesn't bother me now. It meant more what your friends thought then and it was more the peer thing that was so big, and you had to fit in."

At Michigan State, she dated a young man for two years. They shared a love for sports and the outdoors, and they got along well. But they broke up a year ago, shortly after he graduated. "He was wanting to get married, and I think that scared me off. I think that's why we broke up." At age 21, she doesn't feel anywhere near ready for marriage. "I just can't get married until I'm about 26 or so, because I want to get my life in order, like have a good job, be set financially. I don't want to depend on a man."

Angela met her current boyfriend shortly after returning to Missouri last year. It is clear she has a lot of reservations about their relationship. He drinks too much. "He's got a drinking problem, and I just don't want to deal with it." The difference in their educational levels makes it hard for them to understand each other. "Tom doesn't have a degree, so he does construction, and I think we just have two levels of thinking that just kind of conflict." He is older, 29, divorced, and has a son, and Angela thinks he is a poor father. "He has no patience. He just can't handle him, basically." Her boyfriend expects her to take over the childcare when the boy visits, which she resents. "I'm 21 years old. I don't want to be a mother right now."

How did she get herself into such an unpromising relationship? That's what she wonders. "I think I've been insane here for the last year. I lost my mind." She has noticed that her relationship with her boyfriend bears a disturbing resemblance to her mother's relationship with her stepfather, which alarms her. "My mom puts up with a lot of crap, and I don't know why she does, so I'm looking at my relationship now and I'm like 'Boy, this is the exact relationship as they have' and I'm going, 'What is going on?' I don't know how I got myself into this situation, but I need to get out of it!"

Despite Angela's concerns about her boyfriend, they are currently living together. "That's another thing I can't believe I did," she says regretfully. She moved in with him strictly for practical reasons. "I didn't want to live at home any more because they drove me nuts, and everybody else already had apartments, and some of my friends were living at home, and they didn't want to move out because they couldn't afford it. So I figured I might as well try it." But she doesn't plan to try it for much longer. "The lease is up here at the end of July and I think I'm going to say 'see you later' then."

Angela hopes to marry someone who shares her interest in the outdoors, as her former boyfriend did, but even more important is finding someone with the right personal qualities. "Someone sweet, honest, who can be my friend, who's not temperamental all the time, who can be happy. Because I'm a happy person, and I just want to have fun and have a good time and not worry."

She also looks forward to having children, eventually. "I think it'll be neat having a kid." She hopes that by waiting until at least her late twenties to marry, she'll improve her chances of having a successful marriage, unlike her parents. "I don't want to have kids until my upper twenties and I really don't want to be married until after 25 or 26. No hurry. Because my parents are divorced and it's just a pain in the butt."

If you look at Angela's life right now, as it is, you might not see much in her favor. She has dropped out of college, and she is working at a job she enjoys but that doesn't pay well and doesn't offer much in the way of long-term prospects. She is living with a boyfriend she doesn't respect and certainly doesn't want to marry. Yet she is reasonably happy with her life, less for what it is now than for what she believes it will be in the future. Ten years from now, she sees herself in a successful career doing something she enjoys. Ten years from now, she sees herself married to a man she loves, raising happy children with him. Although the fulfillment of these goals is far from imminent, she is confident that eventually she will be successful and happy. At age 21, even if she is currently adrift in many ways, all of her hopes are alive and well.

Conclusion: Themes and Variations

Four lives, each of them unique, each with its own history and its own prospects. Yet they share certain common characteristics as well, characteristics that are also common to many of their peers in this age period. In each of their lives we can see the themes laid out in the first chapter: emerging adulthood as the age of identity explorations, the age of instability, the self-focused age, the age of feeling in-between, and the age of possibilities.

All four of them are engaged in identity explorations in love and work. All have ideas about what they would like to do in their future work, although their ideas range in clarity from Charles's devotion to music to Steve's vague hopes of managing a restaurant. But none of them has settled into a definite work pattern yet. Rosa likes her job in the Internet company, but she views it only as a way of gaining a broad range of experience on the way to something else, although she is not sure what. Steve's position as a waiter is a long way from ownership of a restaurant, and he concedes that he is only "treading water" right now. Charles is committed to a career in music, but the precise form of that career remains to be determined. Angela loves horticulture, but she has not decided yet how this love will translate into a career. All of them are still exploring different career possibilities to see which ones appeal to them most and which ones will work out for them. All of them are still in the process of answering the questions "What do I enjoy most? What am I best at? How does that fit with the options available to me?"

In their love lives, the same process of exploration is evident. Steve, Charles, and Angela are all in relationships that seem unlikely to last. None of them has any desire to marry any time soon. Charles's first priority is his music, Angela and her boyfriend seem poorly matched, and Steve's life is too much up in the air to include commitment to anything right now, including his girlfriend. Rosa is the most settled of the four in terms of love, but even she wants to wait a while before entering marriage, and she wonders if it wouldn't be a good idea for her to explore her options a bit more. All of them are still pondering the question of who they should commit themselves to for life.

For all of them, the explorations of emerging adulthood go in tandem with instability. Exploring in love and work means that they may change direction at any time, as new possibilities come along. Steve is the extreme example of this, with his determination to sign only month-to-month leases so that he can take off on short notice. But none of them knows exactly what he or she will be doing a year from now, much less 10 or 20 years from now. With the possible exception of Rosa, none of them know who their intimate partner will be a year from now, much less 10 or 20 years from now. But instability doesn't trouble them much. They accept it as part of the process of exploring, as a reflection of the fact that they are still in the process of deciding what form they want their adult lives to take.

Their concentration on identity explorations makes emerging adulthood a self-focused time of their lives. Rosa is the most explicit about this, when she says, "I want to be a little selfish for a while," but it is an undercurrent for all of them. Steve and Charles don't want to commit themselves to love relationships because they want to be free to go where their wishes take them, on their own. Angela doesn't feel ready for marriage or children for many years yet, not until she has had enough time to focus on her own life and achieve self-sufficiency. All of them want to commit themselves to others eventually, but for now, during their emerging adult years, they want to focus on personal goals and self-development.

They are aware of being in a period of exploration, of not yet having made the choices that will provide the foundation for their adult lives, and this awareness makes them feel in-between, no longer in adolescence but not yet fully adult. They feel like they have reached adulthood in some ways, but in other ways they feel like they are "still trying to grab ahold of it," as Steve said. Of the four, only Charles feels he has definitely reached adulthood, and Charles also realizes that he is in a temporary period of being "highly portable," prior to taking on the responsibilities of adult life.

Although there is a lot of exploration and instability in their lives right now, all four of them are confident they will get what they want out of life. Everything seems possible for them, and their hopes are high. They expect to have happy marriages, and they expect to find meaningful work and to be successful in it. At this age, there is nothing to impede their dreams. Angela may have her career in horticulture, Steve may have his restaurant, Rosa may have her bakery, Charles may turn his musical ambitions into reality. All of them may find a lifelong love. Or maybe not. But here in emerging adulthood, no dreams have been permanently dashed, no doors have been firmly closed, every possibility for happiness is still alive. This is the glory of emerging adulthood, that it is the age of possibilities, the age of unvanquished hopes.

Not all emerging adults are like the ones profiled in this chapter. Some make enduring decisions relatively early and have settled lives by their mid-twenties. Others find their opportunities for exploration restricted by poverty, poor schooling, or family chaos. We will explore their stories, too, in the chapters to come. However, we will see that most emerging adults resemble Rosa, Steve, Charles, and Angela in having lives characterized by exploration and instability and in focusing on self-development as they seek to translate their possibilities into real life.

3

From Conflict to Companionship

A New Relationship With Parents

W**HEN I WAS A BOY OF** 14," Mark Twain famously remarked, "my father was so ignorant I could hardly stand to have the man around. But when I got to be 21, I was astonished at how much he had learnt in seven years." Although written nearly 100 years ago, Twain's wry observation is an apt description of the changes that take place today in relationships with parents as people move from adolescence to emerging adulthood. Conflict with parents tends to be high for adolescents, who often view their parents as ignorant and worse.[1] But in the course of emerging adulthood most people come to see their parents in a much more sympathetic and benevolent light, as persons and not merely as parents.

Twain's jest about how much his father had "learnt" in seven years is true in a sense because parents do change as their children move from adolescence to emerging adulthood. Although it is a popular cliché that adults often feel like they regress to age 15 when they return home because their parents still treat them like adolescents, this does not apply to most emerging adults. For the most part, their parents adapt to their growing maturity and treat them differently in emerging adulthood than they did in adolescence. Just as emerging adults come to see their parents as persons and not merely parents, so parents come to see their children as persons and not merely their children. These changing perceptions on both parts allow parents and emerging adults to establish a new relationship, as friends and near-equals.

Still, this change does not take place overnight but occurs gradually through emerging adulthood. The feeling of in-betweenness that so many emerging adults have, that feeling of being no longer adolescent but not yet fully adult, is rooted in the changes taking place in their relationships with their parents. Recall from chapter 1 that emerging adults see the three cornerstones for becoming an adult as *accepting responsibility for yourself*, *making independent decisions*, and *becoming financially independent*. Each of these criteria has connotations of independence specifically *from parents*. Learning to accept responsibility for yourself means taking over responsibilities that had previously been assumed by your parents and no longer expecting your parents to shoulder the responsibility for the consequences of things you have done. Making independent decisions means no longer having important decisions about your life made or influenced by your parents. Becoming financially independent means no longer having your parents pay some or all of your bills. Emerging adults are on the way to achieving independence in all three of these respects, but during emerging adulthood they are in-between, not there yet. They still rely on their parents in ways they expect will not continue once they become fully adult, especially for money but also for advice and emotional support.

In this chapter we take a look at the many facets of emerging adults' relationships with their parents. First we look at the changes that take place when emerging adults move out of their parents' households, as well as the experiences of emerging adults who move back in again and those who remain at home. Next we look at the shift that often takes place in emerging adulthood from a parent-child relationship to a new relationship as friends and near-equals. Finally, we look at the enduring repercussions of parents' divorces and remarriages—how emerging adults recall these events and how they believe they have been shaped by them.

Moving Out, Moving Back In, Staying Home

Moving Out

Despite the added responsibilities that come along with living independently, most emerging adults in the United States leave home in their late teens. Generally they move out at age 18 or 19, either to go away to college or simply to be independent.[2] In emerging adulthood, they may find it tough to run their own households and pay their own bills. They might miss having their parents take care of many of the annoying but essential details of daily life—the laundry, the grocery shopping, the toilet cleaning. However, for most of them, it is worth taking on these responsibilities in order to feel like they have control over their own lives, without their parents peering over their shoulders.

As long as they live at home, their parents are likely to be part of their lives every day, noting when they leave and when they return, inquiring in subtle or not-so-subtle ways about their jobs or their school progress or their love lives, offering subtle or not-so-subtle advice. Most emerging adults prefer to avoid this much involvement with their parents, if they can afford to live on their own. It's not that they stop loving their parents or that they do not value their parents' advice and assistance. It's just that by no longer living at home they have more control over how much involvement their parents have in their lives. They can call on their parents when they wish and see them when they like, but the rest of the time they are free to run their own lives. Carrie put it succinctly: "I don't have to talk to them when I don't want to, and when I want to, I can."

Perhaps because moving out means seeing their parents only when they choose, emerging adults tend to get along better with their parents after they leave home. Numerous studies have found that emerging adults who have moved out feel closer to their parents than emerging adults who have remained at home and have fewer negative feelings toward them. For example, in one study of 21-year-olds,[3] emerging adults who had moved at least an hour's drive away felt closest to their parents and valued their opinions most highly. In contrast, emerging adults who had remained at home had the poorest relations with their parents, and those who had moved out but remained within an hour's drive were in between the other two groups. In my study, Rich's comments were typical: "I don't live under their roof any more. They don't see me as often and I don't see them as often, so we're friendlier for the most part."

Apparently, absence makes the heart grow fonder toward parents, for many emerging adults. Although this may seem surprising at first glance, it makes sense upon closer examination. It's a lot easier to be fond of someone you do not see very much. Living with other people almost inevitably entails some degree of friction over household responsibilities and the collision of different habits and preferences. Moving out means avoiding all that day-to-day friction. Once they leave home, emerging adults can visit their parents for a day or a weekend, enjoy a few good meals, and leave while everybody is still smiling.

As long as they are still living at home, their parents might feel obliged to comment on how they eat, how they spend their money, and when they come home at night. Once they move out, their parents no longer know the details and so are less likely to meddle in things that emerging adults feel are none of their business. If absence makes the heart grow fonder, that's at least in part because ignorance is bliss. Lynn said she gets along much better with her parents now that "I don't let them know what I'm doing a lot of the times. The less they know, the better, because otherwise they'd bicker or talk to me and try to influence my life. I don't want to hear their advice. I want to be able to do what I want to do." Karen has found that she gets along better with her parents in emerging adulthood than she did in adolescence because she tells them less and they ask her less. "In high school, I went out of my way to avoid conversations with my parents because I felt that a lot of things they wanted to know about didn't concern them. I find now that my parents know less about my life because I'm not at home. They don't ask me as many questions, so I enjoy having conversations with them."

Although today's emerging adults generally expect to leave home shortly after high school, leaving home as early as age 18 or 19 is a new phenomenon in the United States.[4] Up until the 1970s, the most common reason for leaving home was marriage, which usually meant staying at home until one's early twenties. Young women, especially, did not typically leave home to live on their own before marrying. However, in recent decades, it has become uncommon for young people to remain at home until marriage. Now, the most common reason emerging adults give for leaving home is simply "to be independent." Also, more young people now than in the past attend college, so leaving for college has increased as a reason for leaving home. In combination, leaving home for college or to be independent have pushed the typical age of leaving home down to between ages 18 and 19, the lowest age ever.

For some, reaching emerging adulthood gives them the opportunity to liberate themselves from a family environment they find intolerable. Adolescents, because they are financially and legally dependent on their parents, do not have much choice but to live at home. Unless their parents' treatment of them reaches the extreme of abuse or neglect, they are legally required to remain in their parents' household. Some adolescents run away from home, of course. However, there are many others who would not take that drastic step but who nevertheless find their home lives unpleasant and look forward to leaving. Ron said that when he was in high school he and his mother fought "several times a day, seven days a week." Leaving for college came as a welcome relief. Time and distance have helped him understand his mother better, well enough to know that the best way for him to have a decent relationship with her is to see her rarely. "I've learned a great deal about my mother over the last four years, when I have not been at home. She can be sweet and kind of normal—you just have to stay away from her."

Moving out enabled Jill to escape a family situation that had taken a turn for the worse. Her parents got along "fairly well" as she was growing up. However, when she was 19, her father's sister committed suicide, and "he began drinking after that." He became an alcoholic, and the relationship between her parents deteriorated. But she was old enough that she could escape the worst of it by leaving home and being selective about when and how much she saw her parents. "I was old enough that I could go to college; I could get my own apartment; and I could choose the times I came back to visit. I could choose times that I knew would be good times."

But even for emerging adults who come from relatively healthy home environments, leaving home often improves their relationships with their parents. Parents and their emerging adult children value their time together more once they have to make an effort to have contact with each other. As Emily put it, "In high school they took me for granted because I was always around. Now I'm rarely around, so they appreciate me more." For Warren, the appreciation goes both ways. "Since leaving home for college last year, my relationship with my parents has been a lot closer because we miss each other more."

Sometimes emerging adults are surprised to discover the intensity of the attachment they have to their parents. While they were home, they may not have realized it in the course of daily life, or their love for their parents may have been buried under the petty conflicts and resentments generated by living at home. Especially when they have first moved away, emerging adults may realize more than ever how much their parents mean to them. Ellen, now a junior in college, recalled:

> My first two semesters away at school I was extremely homesick. I called my mom and dad every single day. I started to rely on their voices to make it through until my next break. I probably had more conversation time with my parents my first year at college than my entire high school career. I found myself telling them things I would never have dreamed about telling them, and they also shared many things with me.

Moving Back In

Moving out is not necessarily forever. Early in the 20th century, when marriage was the main reason for moving out and divorce was rare, young people usually did not return home once they had left. The rate of returning home was about 20% in the 1920s, which is as far as records go back.[5] Now, with leaving for college or for independence the main reasons for leaving home, moving home again has become quite common, experienced by nearly half of today's emerging adults.[6]

For those who left home for college, moving back home may be a way of bridging their transition to postcollege life after they graduate or drop out. It gives them a chance to decide what to do next, be it graduate school, a job near home, or a job in another place. For those who left home for independence, some may feel that the glow of independence dims after a while as the freedom of doing what they want when they want becomes outweighed by the burden of taking care of a household and paying all their own bills. Moving back in after an early divorce or a period of military service are other reasons emerging adults give for returning home.[7] Under these circumstances, too, coming home may be attractive to young people as a transition period, a chance to get back on their feet before they venture again into the world.

Emerging adults and their parents react in a range of ways when emerging adults "return to the nest."[8] For some, the return home is welcome and the transition is managed easily. Nancy, a social worker, recently moved back home while she is between jobs. She was apprehensive at first but pleasantly surprised when things went well.

> I was scared, not how they would react, but just what it was going to feel like for all of us. We talked quite a bit about it before I moved back, and they were very supportive. "Oh, move back home! We'd be happy for you to move back home while you look for a job." So I mean, they made it really easy, and they basically just let me do my own thing.

The key to a successful transition back home is for parents to recognize the change in their children's maturity and treat them as adults rather than as adolescents. Darren, like many college students, returns home for the summer and has found that his parents monitor him much less than they did when he was an adolescent.

> I still live at home during the summer, but the atmosphere is very different. In high school, they always wanted to know where I was going, what I was doing, when I was coming home, and so on. Now I have almost total independence even at home. I come and go as I please, and they don't question me. Because of the freedom they allow me, I feel closer to them. It's like they treat me as an equal even though I'm their son.

For others, however, the return home is a bumpy transition. Parents may have come to enjoy having the nest all to themselves, without children to provide for and feel responsible for.[9] Emerging adults may find it difficult to have parents monitoring them daily again, after a period when they had grown used to managing their own lives. After Mary moved home at age 22, she was dismayed to find that her mother would wait up for her when she went out with her boyfriend, just like it was high school all over again. They did not argue openly about it, but it made Mary feel "like she was sort of 'in my territory' or something." Annie moved home at age 20 as a single mother and has found that living at home makes her feel "like a kid with a kid. They boss me around, they boss her around, and then they tell me what to do with her, so it's like I'm her sister rather than her mother." Nevertheless, she appreciates the freedom that living at home allows. "Whenever [my daughter] goes to bed and if they're home, I can go do what I want. Eight o'clock comes and I'm at the mall!" For many emerging adults, moving back home results in this kind of ambivalence. They are grateful for the support their parents provide, even as they resent returning to the subordinate role of a dependent child.

Staying Home

Of course, there are also many cases of families who get along fine even as the emerging adults remain in their parents' households. This is true in the United States, and it appears to be even more common in Europe. In European countries, emerging adults tend to live with their parents for longer than American emerging adults do. For example, in Germany, the typical age of moving out is 22.[10] There are some practical reasons for this. European universities typically do not have dormitories or other on-campus housing, and for college and noncollege emerging adults alike, apartments are scarce and expensive. But also important is that European emerging adults are often able to enjoy the financial and emotional support of their parents within the household while maintaining independent lives of their own.

Italy provides a good case in point. Ninety-four percent of Italians ages 15–24 live with their parents, the highest percentage in the European Union (EU). Yet only 8% of young Italians view their living arrangements as a problem—the *lowest* percentage among EU countries.[11] This suggests that many young Italians remain at home contentedly through their early twenties, by choice rather than by necessity. Many young Europeans find they can enjoy a higher standard of living by staying home rather than moving out, and still live as they wish. Perhaps because European societies are somewhat less individualistic than American society, young Europeans may feel less compelled than young Americans to demonstrate that they can stand alone in emerging adulthood by living independently of their parents.

Several European societies have coined terms to describe young people in this extended state of living at home. In Sweden, the term is *mamboende*, roughly translated as "those who live with mama," applied to anyone who stays or returns home after age 18.[12] In Italy, the term is *mammoni*, which means "mama's boys," applied to men who live at home past their early twenties.[13] These terms have a pejorative, sarcastic connotation, as if it is somewhat socially disapproved to be an emerging adult living at home. At the same time, the prevalence of living at home during emerging adulthood in these societies suggests social acceptance of the practice. Maybe Europeans are ambivalent about it, believing it is best to leave home in emerging adulthood but also tolerating those who choose to stay at home.

In the United States, although most emerging adults move out of their parents' homes in their late teens, a substantial proportion (about 30%) stays home through their early twenties.[14] Staying at home is more common among Latinos, Blacks, and Asian Americans than among White Americans. The reason for this appears to be their greater emphasis on family closeness and interdependence, and less emphasis on being independent as a value in itself. Rosa (who was profiled in chapter 2) lived with her Chinese American mother and Mexican American father throughout her college years at the University of California–Berkeley. She enjoyed the way that staying home allowed her to remain in close contact with them. "I loved living at home. I respect my parents a lot, so being home with them was actually one of the things I liked to do most. Plus, it was free!"

For Latinos and Asian Americans, an additional reason for staying home is specific to young women, and concerns the high value placed on virginity before marriage. Some parents in these minority groups prefer to have their daughters stay home until marriage in order to reduce the likelihood that they will have opportunities for sexual involvements. Jenny, a 28-year-old Korean American who is now married, said that when she was single, "I wasn't allowed to go and live with roommates or friends. They basically said, 'You're living at home until you get married.'" Her brother, in contrast, never lived at home again after leaving for college. Although sexual issues were never discussed directly, it was clear to Jenny that sex was behind her parents' pressure for her to live at home. If she had decided to cohabit with a lover, she said, "I think my parents would have strangled me!"

Despite their parents' restrictions, many emerging adults from ethnic minority families view living at home as desirable, perhaps because of the values of family closeness they have learned in their cultures. However, there is considerable diversity in each minority group, and many emerging adults in minority groups leave home for reasons similar to Whites, especially leaving for college and for independence. In every ethnic group, these two reasons for leaving home have become more common in recent decades.[15] For Latinos and Asian Americans, the more generations their families have been in the United States, the closer their home-leaving patterns resemble those of Whites.

Is it possible to be an emerging adult while still living at home? If emerging adulthood is the period between dependence on parents and taking on new family obligations, does living at home imply remaining dependent on parents and therefore remaining in adolescence rather than entering emerging adulthood? It is certainly true that if you live at home, you are more dependent on your parents than you would be if you had moved out. However, if we consider the five criteria that define emerging adulthood—identity explorations, instability, self-focus, feeling in-between, and a widening of possibilities—there is no reason why they could not apply to young people who live at home. It is possible to live at home and still explore various possibilities in love and work. The instability of emerging adulthood, in the form of changes in love relationships, educational paths, and jobs, can take place while living at home as easily as while living independently—maybe even easier, because those who live at home are not as compelled to stay with an unsatisfying job just to pay the bills for rent and food. There is no reason why someone in their twenties could not be self-focused, feel in-between, and experience widening possibilities while living at home.

Also, like emerging adults who move back home, emerging adults who stay at home have more autonomy from their parents than they had as adolescents. Some parents feel obligated to keep close tabs on their children as long as the children are in their home, no matter how old they are, but most parents adjust to the new stage of life their emerging adults have entered by letting them lead their own lives with little interference. Belgians use the term *hotel families* to describe the arrangements between parents and their emerging adult children,[16] implying that in such homes the parents provide a room, food, and laundry services, but otherwise the young people go their own way. Many American emerging adults and their parents reach a similar kind of understanding. Aaron still lives at home, "but it's pretty much up to me. I go and do my own thing, and if I'm not coming home I'll call them so they know. They just want to know if I'm not going to be there for a day or two at a time."

From Parent and Child to Near-Equals

Adolescence is often a difficult time for family relations.[17] Conflict rises, as adolescents press for more autonomy while parents continue to feel responsible for protecting their children from potential harm. Closeness declines, as adolescents begin to have experiences, especially involving sexuality and romantic relationships, that they feel uncomfortable discussing with their parents and would much rather discuss with their friends. From age 10 to 18, adolescents spend an increasing amount of time with their friends and a decreasing amount of time at home.[18]

Things improve once the adolescent becomes an emerging adult and leaves home, as we have seen. No longer in the same household, emerging adults and their parents can avoid most of the day-to-day friction that results from living together. But there is more to the changes in relationships with parents in emerging adulthood than simply the effect of moving out. Emerging adults also grow in their ability to understand their parents. Adolescence is in some ways an egocentric period, and adolescents often have difficulty taking their parents' perspectives. They sometimes cast a pitiless gaze on their parents, magnifying their deficiencies and becoming easily irritated by their imperfections.

As emerging adults mature and begin to feel more adult themselves, they become more capable of understanding how their parents look at things. They begin to realize that their parents are neither the demigods they adored as children nor the clueless goofs they scorned as adolescents, but simply people who, like themselves, have a mix of qualities, merits as well as faults. Joseph, echoing the Twain quote that began this chapter, said, "I guess the old adage that 'the older you get, the smarter your parents get' is really true. The things they said and did make a lot more sense to me now than they used to." Gerard said he hated his father as a teenager, but as an emerging adult the problems he has faced in his own life have made him more sympathetic. "I feel profoundly more forgiving towards my father since I've seen how life actually can be difficult, and so I respect him a lot more than I used to because he's really persisted and got through a lot of his own struggles."

For some, this new sense of seeing their parents as persons leads to remorse for how they behaved toward their parents as teens. Lisa said, "I treat them a lot better now than I did when I was a teenager. I look back and I go, 'Man, I was terrible to them. Why did I treat them like that?'" Matt recalled, "In high school I was rude, inconsiderate, and got into many fights with my mom. Since coming to college I realize how much she means to me and how much she goes out of her way for me. I've grown to have a true appreciation for her." For Diana, the change has been especially dramatic.

> In high school, even starting in middle school, I had a terrible relationship with my parents. My mom and I rarely talked, and my dad and I were in conflict almost every day. Looking back, it's almost frightening to think of all the things I put my parents through. I went through a wildly rebellious time where I would do the most horrible things without thinking twice. Stealing, lying, sneaking out, taking the car, even getting a tattoo were just some of the things I felt compelled to do. I was kicked out, I ran away—everything was so dramatic!
>
> Then somehow I managed to control myself and make it to college. I slowly started to make attempts at reconciliation towards my parents. Somehow, in the course of four years, I've managed to get to a point where I can hang out with my parents and really love them. It's weird how time and age can just change relationships like that. My relationship with my parents is now on a loving, mutually respectful kind of level.

For other emerging adults, what they learn about their parents as persons is disillusioning. Carla grew up thinking her parents had a good marriage but discovered otherwise once she became an emerging adult. "They hid it very well until I got older and then when I started developing a friendship instead of a parent-daughter relationship, I found out the real business—divorce threats, affairs, all this stuff that I had no idea was going on at all." Helen had a similar experience. Growing up, she said, "I admired my dad a lot. I think he gave me a lot of the qualities that I have that people like." Now, however, she has learned that "parents aren't always perfect, you know. There's some things you find out." What she found out was that her dad has had a series of affairs for many years. This included sending money to his lovers while telling her he did not have enough money to give any to her when she needed it. As a result, "I almost hated him. And I had so much trouble dealing with it. It's still tough for me because it just makes me so upset." Doug now sees both his parents in a less flattering light.

> I guess just growing up I can see how fucked up they are. I think I've come to probably resent them a lot more. They have no fun, and they penalize themselves. My mom is like a big martyr, and my father is pretty solemn. When I was younger, I didn't really perceive their feelings too much, but now I perceive their feelings and also their personalities and some of their hang-ups and stuff.

Parents change, too, in how they view their children and how they relate to them. Their role as monitor of their children's behavior and enforcer of household rules diminishes, and this results in a more relaxed and amiable relationship with their children. Nancy said, "They're still my parents, but there's more—I don't know if friendship is the right word, but like I go out with them and just really enjoy spending time with them, and they're not in a parental role as much. It's not a disciplining role, it's just more of a real comfortable friendship thing." Parents become less inclined to issue commands and more inclined to take their children's point of view seriously. Paul said, "Now they look at me eye to eye, where before it was 'Do this, do that.' They give me a lot of leeway and a lot of respect and value my opinion a lot more." Similarly, Laurel observed that her parents "actually ask me what I'm going to do rather than tell me what I'm going to do, and that's sort of marked the change right there."

The changes in parents and their emerging adult children allow them to establish a new intimacy, more open than before, with a new sense of mutual respect.[19] They begin to relate to each other as adults, as friends, as equals, or at least as near-equals. Bonnie said that compared to her adolescence, her relationship with her parents now is "completely different. I talk to them and stuff now. I can just be more honest. There isn't any of that feeling that I'm hiding something. I can be more honest with them about who I am. I feel they actually like me for who I am, and I like them." Luke has especially changed in his relationship with his father.

> Over the past year, I have become very close with my dad. To sit down with my dad and have a beer and exchange dirty jokes has been a weird experience. We have also been able to relate to each other when it comes to work, school, women, etc. Before college, there was a definite parent-

Parents change as their children grow into emerging adulthood, and emerging adults relate to their parents differently than they did as adolescents. (© Lynn Johnston Productions, Inc./Distributed by United Feature Syndicate.)

child relationship with my father. Now he is more like a mentor or friend. Overall, the relationship between my parents and I has been a growing mutual respect.

Not all emerging adults reach a near-equal relationship with their parents. Darrell, who was living with his parents again after some time living on his own, said, "[They] treat me like a boy. 'You all right?' They worry about me. 'You're not getting into any trouble?' Just like parents. It's like when you go out or something: 'Where you goin'? You got money? You want a cold drink? You want this?' I'll be like, 'I got money, Mom.'" For some emerging adults, their parents' reluctance to let them go is mirrored by their own reluctance to take on the responsibilities of living independently. Sharon, a recent college graduate, said, "I'm not ready to accept responsibility for paying for my health insurance and blah, blah, blah right now. So I guess it's kind of like a double-edged sword thing. Like, I want them to think of me as being an adult and independent, but I also don't want to be fully independent." But these emerging adults are exceptions. For the most part, both parents and emerging adults are able and willing to adjust to a new relationship as near-equals.

The Multiple Legacies of Divorce

Americans, like people in most cultures, have a long tradition of extolling the joys of family life and idealizing the pleasures of the family home. "There's no place like home." "Home is where the heart is." As with most ideals, however, the reality of family life is much different and often falls considerably short of what we would like it to be. By emerging adulthood, many people have experienced one or more of the various tragedies that afflict families and change irrevocably the course of family members' lives. In the 300 interviews conducted for this study, we heard about many varieties of family tragedy. Parents lose their jobs and/or their money, as a result of bad decisions or simple misfortune. A parent becomes injured or falls victim to a chronic illness. A parent dies young. A sibling dies in an accident. A parent goes to jail. A parent suffers a psychological illness such as manic-depression. A parent slides into the mire of alcoholism or drug abuse.

But the number one affliction of family life, affecting more families than all of the others combined, is divorce. No account of the family lives of emerging adults would be complete without a discussion of their responses to their parents' divorces. With a divorce rate of nearly 50% in the United States, many people have witnessed the demise of their parents' marriage by the time they reach emerging adulthood.

Overall, experiencing parents' divorce is related to an increased risk of a wide range of problems in childhood, adolescence, and emerging adulthood.[20] Compared to young people in nondivorced families, young people from divorced families have higher rates of using alcohol and other drugs. They are also more likely to be depressed and withdrawn, especially in the first year or two following the divorce. They tend to do less well in school and are less likely to attend college.

Nevertheless, the responses of emerging adults to their parents' divorce are complicated and various, and perhaps for this reason their responses have been the subject of dispute among scholars. There has been a vigorous debate in recent years about the long-term effects of divorce on children, with some scholars arguing that the damage of divorce is evident into the twenties while others argue that most children recover from divorce after a few years and lead reasonably contented and successful lives by emerging adulthood.[21]

However, argued in this polarized way, the debate misses the truth about the effects of divorce in the lives of emerging adults. Anything that happens to half of the population will not be experienced in only one way but in a wide variety of ways, as the experience takes a specific form according to a vast range of circumstances. Some emerging adults recall responding to their parents' divorce with shock and sorrow, but others remember relief or even happiness, because the divorce finally brought an end to years of conflict and tension in the household. Some of them have no memory of the divorce, because it happened when they were very young, and they grew up with their parents living apart. For others, their parents divorced in recent years, after they had reached emerging adulthood and left the household, so they were little affected by it in their daily lives.

Thus the circumstances of the divorces vary tremendously. It matters how much conflict there was between the parents before the divorce, how old the children were when the divorce took place, how well or badly the parents got along following the divorce, how much the noncustodial parent remained in the picture, when and whether the parents remarried, and so on. As a result, there is not just one legacy of divorce but multiple legacies, with all of the different circumstances filtered through the different personalities of the persons who experienced the divorce. Let's examine those multiple legacies, focusing first on negative legacies, then on positive legacies, then on the further complications that parents' remarriage can bring.

Negative Legacies: Divorce as Tragedy

For some emerging adults, their parents' divorce is a wound that has never quite healed. Years later, they still vividly remember the pain of it, and they see it as a source of problems they have as emerging adults. Ray said his parents fought a great deal, but for him their divorce when he was 10 years old was a turn for the worse. "I lost all will. I figured I don't have what the others have now. They got the mother, they got the father, they got the sisters. I just had my mother. That kind of made me feel that I lost my better half. You know? So, I didn't strive for the things I wanted. [If not for the divorce,] I wouldn't have got in a lot of stupid things I got in."

Like Ray, Holly has compared her divorced family to nondivorced families and has felt distressed—then and now—at what she feels she has missed.

> I was always jealous. My little cousin, I used to go stay with them, and her dad would come home. She would run into his arms, you know, and yell, "Daddy!" and I was just so jealous when I'd go over there. And I'd see them, you know, they'd all cook dinner and all that kind of family stuff, and I had never seen anything like it, because me and my mom would always have McDonald's or something and eat in front of the TV, every night. I was always jealous of that atmosphere, which I still am when I go over there. I mean, I can't wait to someday have that.

Christopher Lasch, who was a trenchant observer of American family life, argued that because of the decline in the stability of the family, children growing up today learn "a certain protective shallowness, a fear of binding commitments, a willingness to pull up roots whenever the need arises, a dislike of depending on anyone, an incapacity for loyalty or gratitude."[22] Although it is by no means true for all emerging adults from divorced families, this effect is evident in the comments of emerging adults such as Jerry, whose parents divorced when he was 11. Because his parents divorced:

> I grew up on my own. I mean, my mom was there, but when you deal with things, you have to take care of yourself, and for a good number of years I didn't really feel like anybody cared about me. I went through a lot of counseling, and it wasn't until the past year or two that I actually [learned to] trust people. . . . I always know that I can count on myself, and that's what it comes down to. You've got to be able to count on yourself, and then you can count on others.

Melissa has also grown more protective of her self-interest in the decade since her parents' divorce when she was 17.

> It's not my problem, it's theirs. They got divorced. I'm not going to have two birthday parties, and I'm not going to have two Christmases. It's their problem, and if they want to come to my birthday and if they want to

come to my Christmas, they can come, and that's how I see it. That's how I've always seen it. And I know some people think that's really rude, but it's not my fault they got divorced and it's not my problem.

Negative Legacies: The Fading Father

After divorce, the father's role in the children's lives usually diminishes sharply. Even in nondivorced families, the father is usually less important in children's lives than the mother is. By adolescence, the father is often on the margins of the family's emotional life, a "shadowy presence" in the family, as one pair of scholars puts it.[23] But when parents divorce, the father's role in his children's lives usually becomes even more removed. At five years after divorce, over one-third of fathers see their children little or not at all.[24]

There are a number of reasons why divorce pushes most fathers further out of their children's lives. Most obvious is that in about 90% of divorces the mother retains custody of the children and the father leaves the household.[25] As a result, he may see his children only every other weekend, an occasional holiday or vacation, and perhaps much less if one parent moves to a different area after the divorce. But perhaps even more important is that the children's sympathies and loyalties tend to be with the mother rather than the father.

This imbalance exists even before divorce, as one reflection of the greater emotional closeness between mothers and children, but divorce skews it further. Despite the legal rhetoric, few divorces are "no-fault" in the eyes of the family members experiencing it. Perhaps because marriage is the most intimate of relationships, divorce nearly always generates emotions that are fierce and deeply painful.[26] Ex-husbands and ex-wives each tend to see themselves as the injured party, and their children are under implicit or explicit pressure to side with one or the other. Because they are already closer to the mother before the divorce, most children tend to side with her. Christy recalled that after her parents divorced, "There was a lot of resentment there. My poor mother had to pretty much raise her children while her ex-husband was finding himself. I listened to her crying a lot at night, wondering who was going to pay the heating bills and the food bills. There was a lot of bitterness there." Now, although she says she and her father "get along fine," she also says, "His wife is only three years older than I am. I mean, there's tension there, and I don't choose to be involved with that family, and that really hurts his feelings." The hurting is quite deliberate on her part. Although she is now 27 and the divorce took place when she was 16, she is still punishing him for "the way he pretty much shoved us all away and took this other woman into his life and created another family. He can't regain the things that he lost. And I know that bugs him and deep down I think I really want it to bug him. I want him to know the consequences of his actions."

The remarks of Christy and others show how the reverberations of divorce continue in emerging adulthood even when the divorce took place years earlier, especially in relationships with fathers.[27] Theresa, recalling her reaction to her parents' divorce when she was seven, said:

> I was like, "Why did you leave my mom?" I went through a very angry stage. I'm just now working through the anger with my father. He's one subject that's really hard to talk about. We don't have any [problems with] each other, but I can't see myself sitting down and having a father-daughter talk with him at all. I don't feel like he can say anything to me because he was never there.

Divorced fathers who try to reconcile with their emerging adult children may find a reluctant audience for their overtures. Corey's parents divorced when he was 5, and he saw little of his father until he was 20. In the past five years, his father has tried to develop a relationship with him, but Corey feels it is too late. "When I needed a father growing up, he wasn't there, and now it seems like I really don't need him any more. It's kind of hard to forgive."

The question of whether or not to forgive their fathers for the divorce is a key issue for emerging adults from divorced families, one that is not easy for them to resolve. Forgiving the father can seem like betraying the mother. Bob's parents divorced when he was nine. Every summer for the past 15 years he has gone to San Francisco to live with his father. But he still harbors anger toward his father for being unfaithful to his mother and for leaving them both, and he is reluctant to relinquish this anger, despite his father's entreaties.

> He has kind of reached the point where he thought, well, I should have totally forgiven and totally forgotten all this. But I couldn't do that and I told him as much, and we had severe fights about it because I could not just completely block that out. I really believe when that sort of thing happens, you should forgive, but not forget, because forgetting is stupid.

Some emerging adults are more open to reconciliation with their fathers but find it difficult to recover the lost years. Cleo was just 3 when her parents divorced, and she did not see her father from age 5 to 18. He was "a drug addict, and he sold drugs. He was a basic idiot. He was a loser, and my mom didn't want me around him." Now that she has reached emerging adulthood she has begun to see her father again, and they have grown quite close, although both mourn the years they have lost.

> He'll feel bad about it, and he'll be like, "Why didn't your mom let me see you?" I told him, "You'd lie to me. You wouldn't come through on things, and my mom was sick of me being disappointed. So I couldn't see you. But I loved you every day. I thought of you every day." He may not have been there physically, but his spirit was there.

Despite the sadness of growing up without her father, Cleo understands and supports her mother's decision to cut off contact. "If I had kids and that was the situation, I'd do the absolute same thing."

Not all emerging adults have experienced a fading relationship with their fathers after their parents divorced. For some, the mandatory time together in their biweekly visits resulted in more time actually doing things together than when the father was still at home. Leah said, "Actually I became closer to my father afterwards because, it's ironic, but I spent more time with him after they got divorced than when he was living in our house." Calvin echoed Leah's comments: "I actually saw my father more when they were divorced. I spent the whole weekend with him so I saw him more." Other emerging adults with divorced parents lived with their fathers rather than with their mothers after the divorce and now feel closer to their fathers. Still others had difficult relationships with their fathers after the divorce but managed to reconcile with them in emerging adulthood. Nevertheless, the most common pattern is that emerging adults with divorced parents recall the divorce as a crucial turning point—for the worse—in their relationships with their fathers, and in emerging adulthood they continue to feel ambivalent about them.

Positive Legacies: Divorce as Relief

Divorce may be a tragedy when placed next to the ideal of a happy, stable family, but it looks quite different when the alternative is a household full of chaos and conflict. It is the latter that typically precedes divorce; after all, if the parents were happy with each other, they would not be divorcing. In the months or perhaps years preceding most divorces, the parents' unhappiness with each other is often displayed vividly before their children in frequent battles, to which the children respond with anguish and distress as they find themselves unable to stop the fights and unable to escape them.

When this is the case, the parents' divorce may come as a relief to their children because the daily fighting in the household finally comes to an end. Chalantra, whose parents divorced when she was 11, recalled, "I was very happy. Because I got tired of the noise waking me up every day, and I am the type of person that'll cry and get emotional, so me and my brother would hide in the closet together until they stopped fussing. So I was happy they got divorced." Like Chalantra, Sally was fed up with years of fighting by the time her parents divorced. "They had been fighting for 20 years, and it was just a relief to get it off. In fact, when my mother said, 'Your dad and I are splitting up,' all I said was 'Good,' and that's the last thing I said about it." Similarly, Tammy recalled, "My parents were divorced when I was 12, and up to that point, it was kind of a 'stay out of the way of flying objects' kind of thing. It was horrible, pretty much. I really am glad they got divorced, because they were just killing each other, they really were."

Sometimes, when their parents' divorce does not take place until after they have left home, emerging adults are able simply to shrug it off as something that is more their parents' business than their own. Barry, whose parents divorced when he was 18, said, "I guess I was happy for them because I think they were happier people. And I was gone by that time, so its effects on me, I think, are subtle. I think there may be nostalgia for the way things were or a sense of loss in a way, but I don't feel traumatized or anything like that." Keith also took it in stride. "I thought it was a good thing. I wasn't really spending a lot of time at home, so when they were apart, it really didn't make any difference to me either way. I'm just like, 'OK, you do what you have to do.'"

But for some who experience their parents' divorce in emerging adulthood, the blend of thoughts and emotions that results is more complicated, more ambivalent. Allen's parents are in the process of divorcing after separating for the third time, and he views it with complex feelings—detachment, because he is no longer living with them; happiness, because he believes they will be happier apart; and wistfulness, because they will no longer be together.

> It's very odd, you know, 'cause I'm so far away from the whole situation.
> It's not in my face like it was before. And my dad, he's a lot happier and

in many senses I'm happy to see him happy, and I know my mom will be fine. So in that sense it's almost a relief in a way. It's just kind of twisted 'cause, you know, I want to see my parents together. I don't want to see my parents getting divorced, but I want to see them happy.

Doug experienced similar ambivalence when his parents announced their divorce just after he left for college.

I had just arrived at Stanford, and I was like totally detached. It was my first time out of New England, and I was so psyched to finally be at the college I wanted to be at, and meeting all these great people and doing these things. And so at first I was like, "Gosh, you know, maybe if they're happy it's fine with me. I'm happy, so hopefully they can be happy."

As his first semester went on, however, and his college experience became more stressful, he regretted not having his former family home to go back to. "I came home for Christmas and I needed to take some time off and needed my parents to be together, like I would really have liked them to be on some kind of united front. They were both going through a lot of difficulties. And so when my life like kind of fell apart for a second there, it really hurt. You know, it was too bad that they weren't together."

In sum, parents' divorce can leave a "positive" legacy in the lives of emerging adults, in the sense that many of them feel it as a relief from the alternative of living in an unhappy household where conflict or the threat of conflict was a constant presence. Also, the more they come to see their parents as persons, the better they understand and accept that their parents would wish to leave an unhappy marriage and the more they support their parents' wishes to pursue happiness by dissolving the marriage. Nevertheless, for some emerging adults at least, there remains a sense of wistfulness, a certain ambivalence, as they reflect that even after they have reached their twenties, left home, and established their own independent lives, there are times when it is "too bad that they weren't together."

Out of the Frying Pan: The Multiple Legacies of Remarriage

As complex as the legacy of divorce is, for most children it is not the end of the changes in their family situation. About 70% of persons who divorce remarry,[28] and consequently most children who experience their parents' divorce also experience the remarriage of one or both parents. For emerging adults from divorced families, this means that their current relationships with their parents are affected not only by the lingering legacy of divorce but often by the enduring complexities that result from remarriage.

Like divorce, parents' remarriage happens to many children, and they respond in a variety of ways.[29] Some emerging adults describe their parents' remarriage with pure enthusiasm and approbation, and their stepparent as someone they like and value. Theresa said, "My stepfather is wonderful. I'm probably closer to him than I am [to] my father." Rachel said her father's remarriage "has actually been probably the best thing for him. And it helped me a lot too because during that time, I was living in his house when he got married. Since Dad was really strict, [my stepmother] made it a lot easier. She could be kind of like a go-between. Everybody got along a little bit easier." Tory's mother remarried when he was 17, and he says of her new husband, "He's great. He's probably the best thing that's happened to her. He's really nice." His own relationship with his stepfather is described with similar enthusiasm. "I love him. He's a great guy. I mean, it's more like a friend, not really a stepfather. I talk to him about everything. And he knows that he's more than welcome to come over or call me or whatever."

More commonly, however, relationships between stepparents and stepchildren are fraught with difficulty and bad feelings.[30] For a variety of reasons, the deck is stacked against the likelihood of a happy relationship between them. The stepparent may be viewed as a usurper, as someone taking the role that rightfully belongs to the displaced parent. This is especially likely if the stepparent had an affair with the parent prior to the divorce. Also, the remarriage may bring to an unpleasant end any fantasies the children may have harbored that their parents would reunite.

There is also the blunt fact that the decision to marry the stepparent is made by the parent, not by the children. Presumably, the parent chooses the stepparent because they love each other and get along reasonably well, but the children come along for the ride without ever signing up for it, whether they want to or not. Doug put it succinctly: "There's people that you get along with and there's people that you don't, and my dad just happened to marry somebody I don't get along with." Stepparents may, in turn, view their stepchildren as an annoyance, an unavoidable but regrettable part of marrying their new spouse.

But by far the biggest issue of contention between stepparents and stepchildren is the extent of the stepparent's legitimate authority.[31] Stepparents, especially stepfathers, often feel compelled to take a role of authority in the household, setting and enforcing rules and exercising discipline just as they would if they were a "real" parent. However, with no history of mutual affection and attachment between the stepparent and the children, and with possible resentment and dislike for the reasons just described, stepparents' attempts at exercising authority are often fiercely resisted by their stepchildren, especially if they enter the household when the children are in or near adolescence. Terry, whose mother remarried when she was 12, recalled that during her teen years, "When I'd get in trouble, he'd yell at me, and I'd get mad, like, 'You're not my dad,' you know." Joel said that when he was 14 years old and his stepfather moved in, "He set down a bunch of stupid rules. I had to be home before dark if I went to a friend's house. I couldn't go out with my friends unless it was a weekend." The result was a kind of cold war within the household. "He would say something to me and I'd ignore him because I felt he didn't have the right to tell me what to do." Leanne had difficulty accepting her stepfather's entry into the household when she was 10 years old—"It had just been me and Mom all that time, and I didn't like somebody else coming in"—and resisted his attempts to assert authority.

> For a while he tried, I always call it "tried to be my dad," you know, but it wasn't in a good way, it was in a bad way. I felt like he was trying to boss me around or something, and I didn't feel he had any right to. So I guess right from the beginning, as soon as he started acting like that, we just never really got along. We kind of avoided each other as much as possible.

The silver lining in the generally dismal relations between stepparents and stepchildren is that things often improve once the children reach emerging adulthood. Just as with their parents, emerging adults often get along better with their stepparents once they no longer live with them and no longer have to rub shoulders with them on a daily basis. And just as with their parents, emerging adults often come to see their stepparents in a different light, as persons rather then merely as stepparents. Sheila said that when her mother first married her stepfather, "I resented him because he tried to be my father and he wasn't. But now, I love him." Eventually, his patient good will won her over. "I was a terrible teenager. I was absolutely terrible, and he loved me and stood by me no matter what. Yeah, we've had our fights, you know, the 'I hate you' kind of thing, but he's loved me and supported me through everything, regardless of whether it was right or wrong. So we're very close."

Lillian recalled that in the years following her mother's remarriage when she was nine years old, she and her stepfather were in constant conflict. "It was a hard time. Boy, we did not get along well at all, and it was very stressful for my mom, and it was very stressful for me. I didn't like him very well for a long time." She deeply resented the new rules he and her mom laid down for her and her brother. "They were very, very strict. I mean, we couldn't have sleep-overs. There were very set curfews. I had a bedtime of 10 [o'clock] even when I was in high school." But now, from the perspective of her twenties, she sees things much differently. "It's all worked out very well now. I very much appreciate everything they did. But I was horrible in high school to them, and I apologize all the time. But they never missed a basketball game or a volleyball game or anything I ever did. They were always there, which I look on now and think, 'Wow. That's really amazing.'" Her view of her stepfather has changed dramatically from adolescence to emerging adulthood.

> He's a very wonderful man. He always has been, but we just didn't appreciate him. But I think that would be the same for any kid. Really, I don't know that you appreciate your parents until you're older and can look back and think, "Wow. They were pretty incredible."

Conclusion: The Enduring Importance of Parents

Becoming independent from parents is a key issue for emerging adults in American society. The process begins in adolescence, but it accelerates during emerging adulthood. When they move out of the household, emerging adults experience a dramatic shift in the balance of power in their relationship with their parents. No longer do they inevitably see their parents every day. No longer do their parents know the details of their daily lives—what they eat, what they wear, how much they spend, whether they come home drunk after a party, and so on. Instead, they can see their parents as much, or as little, as they wish. They can tell their parents as much, or as little, about their lives as they wish them to know. As a result, typically they get along with their parents much better than they did before moving out. What their parents do not know cannot become an issue of contention.

Although emerging adults are more independent than they were as adolescents, in some ways they become closer to their parents. The hierarchy of parent as authority figure, child as dependent and subordinate, fades away. What remains, in most cases, is the mutual affection and attachment they have for one another on the basis of many years of shared experiences. They learn to see each other as persons, as individuals, rather than being defined for each other strictly by their roles as parent and child. They talk about a wider range of subjects than they did before, and they do so more openly, more as friends. Still, there is a limit to their openness, and a limit to the extent that their transformed relationship is like a friendship. One of the reasons they get along better is that emerging adults withhold information that might be a source of conflict, and parents learn not to inquire too much.

For those who have experienced their parents' divorce, emerging adulthood is a time for reassessing the legacy of that experience. Some move toward reconciliation with a parent from whom they have long been estranged. Some continue to feel bitter and resentful toward the parent they believe was in the wrong, usually the father. Some see their divorced parents or their stepparents in a new and more benevolent light, now that they have greater insight into human relationships than they did in childhood or adolescence. In any case, for most emerging adults, the experience of their parents' divorce and perhaps remarriage has left an enduring legacy that has helped to shape their personalities, their identities, and their own approach to intimate relationships. This is a topic we will return to in chapters 4 and 5.

Whether their parents divorced or not, whether their family life growing up was happy or unhappy, whether they have stayed at home or moved away, for virtually all emerging adults their relationships with their parents remain emotionally charged. The nature of the emotions varies tremendously—love, with roots all the way back to infancy and childhood; gratitude, from a new perspective of appreciation they have gained in emerging adulthood; acceptance, as they relate to their parents on a new level as one adult to another. And there are darker emotions as well—resentment for how they believe their parents have failed them in one way or another; disillusionment, when they come to realize in emerging adulthood that their parents have flaws that had been concealed from them; wariness, as they strive to keep their parents from meddling in their lives; even outright hatred, especially as the residue of a bitter divorce. Emerging adults' relationships with their parents involve different blends of these emotions, but the emotions are nearly always among the strongest they have for anyone in their lives. For better and worse, their parents have contributed mightily toward shaping the persons they have become in emerging adulthood.

4

Love and Sex

CONSIDER THIS LETTER, WHICH appeared in the Ann Landers advice column recently:

> Dear Ann:
>
> Two years ago, I met the most wonderful guy in the world. We are both in college and plan to marry. "Darryl" is saving up for my engagement ring. The problem is, he is my first and only boyfriend. All my dating experience has been with him. My friends and family members have said, "Don't marry the first guy you date. You need to have fun and get more experience." They ask, "How do you know it is love when you have nothing to compare it with?"

The letter goes on, but this much is enough to illustrate that the expectation for emerging adults today is that they will have a number of love partners in their late teens and early twenties before settling on someone to marry. With marriage delayed for most people until at least their late twenties, the late teens and early twenties become a time for exploring their options, falling in and out of love with different people, and gaining sexual experience. They clarify for themselves what kind of person they would like to marry by having involvements with a variety of people and learning what they *don't* want in a relationship as well as what they want most.

In fact, as the letter suggests, finding a love partner in your teens and continuing in a relationship with that person through your early twenties, culminating in marriage, is now viewed as unhealthy, a mistake, a path likely to lead to disaster. Those who do not experiment with different partners are warned that they are limiting their options too narrowly by staying with one person and that they will eventually wonder what they are missing, to the detriment of their marriage. Emerging adults believe they *should* explore different love relationships, that such exploration is both normal and necessary in order to prepare for committing one's self to a marriage partner. But most emerging adults don't need to be encouraged—they are eager for the opportunities that emerging adulthood provides for having a variety of love relationships.

Like emerging adulthood itself, the current norm of pursuing variety in love and sex before settling down to marriage is a new phenomenon. Early in the 20th century, the main pattern of middle-class courtship in American society was "calling."[1] A young man would call on a young woman, at her invitation, by visiting her at her home. There he would meet her family and then the two young people would be allowed some time together, probably in the family parlor. They would talk, perhaps have some refreshments she had prepared for him, and she might then play the piano. All of this seems innocent enough, even superficial, but the underlying meaning of it was entirely serious. A young man did not call on just any girl, or on a variety of girls. Calling was considered a statement of serious intentions, potentially leading to marriage.

Needless to say, very little sex went on in that parlor. There was a strong taboo on premarital sexual relations. A young woman's virginity was her highly prized "jewel," a "treasure" she would bestow on her beloved only on her marriage night.[2] The pressure on men to remain chaste until marriage was not as intense, and some men had premarital sex with a prostitute or with a woman who did not observe the taboos. Nevertheless, for both young women and young men, courtship was highly structured through the custom of calling, and sexuality was highly restricted until marriage.

Norms changed dramatically in the 1920s, as calling declined and dating arose.[3] In contrast to calling, dating meant *going out* to take part in a shared activity. This moved the location of courtship out of the home and into the public arena—restaurants, theaters, dance halls, and so on. It also removed the young couple from the watchful eyes of the girl's family and gave them opportunities for sexual experimentation in the "rumble seat" of the automobiles that were now widely available. The 1920s are sometimes called a period of "the first sexual revolution," because the strict taboo against premarital sexual activity faded, and it became acceptable to engage in necking and petting before marriage. However, this premarital sexual experimentation was supposed to stop short of intercourse, and usually did.

From the 1920s to the 1960s the norm continued to be dating and sexual experimentation up to intercourse. The most notable change during this period was that the age of marriage declined, especially among men.

For men, the median marriage age declined from 24.6 in 1920 to 22.8 in 1960; for women, from 21.2 in 1920 to 20.3 in 1960.[4] The consequence of the drop in the marriage age was that dating became more serious at an earlier age. By the 1950s it was not uncommon for young people to become engaged in high school and marry shortly after graduating.

For the increasing proportion of young people who attended college, the college campus became the setting not only for education but for finding a mate. Few young people remained unmarried past their early twenties. Although premarital intercourse became somewhat more common—about 40% of college students at midcentury reported having sexual intercourse at least once[5]—the majority of young people continued to save intercourse for marriage.

The period that set the stage for love and sex as emerging adults experience it today was the 1960s and early 1970s. Dating became much less formal as distinctions in gender roles came under fire and the traditional dating pattern—where the young man asks the young woman out, chooses the event, and pays for everything—began to be viewed as sexist. A new sexual revolution took place, and previous restrictions on sexual activity before marriage now seemed repressive. The invention of the birth control pill made it easier for young women to have premarital sex without becoming pregnant.

By the mid-1970s, the proportion of American college students who reported having premarital sexual intercourse rose to 75%, close to today's 80% figure.[6] The typical marriage age reversed its decline and began to rise, beginning a steady ascent that has continued through the turn of the 21st century, so that today the typical age at marriage is about 27 for men and 25 for women.[7] With so many years stretching between the time they first begin dating and the time they marry, few young people now give much thought to marriage in high school or even college. Instead, through their teens and early twenties they pursue a pattern of what sociologists call "serial monogamy"—a series of love relationships, usually including sex.

Although serial monogamy may be the norm for emerging adults today, marriage is the ultimate goal for virtually all of them. In my research, over 90% of emerging adults who are not married plan to be married eventually.[8] But "eventually" may be a year, 5 years, or even 10 years or more down the line. Meanwhile, they gain experience through a variety of romantic and sexual relationships.

In this chapter we examine many aspects of love and sex in the lives of emerging adults. First, we look at the ways that emerging adults meet potential love partners. This includes a discussion of the role that ethnic background plays in love choices. Then we look at sexuality, including emerging adults' reflections on their first episode of intercourse and their views of the circumstances that make premarital sex acceptable. Finally, we look at the ways that the fear of AIDS shapes the sexual consciousness of emerging adults, and at the experiences of emerging adults who have contracted sexually transmitted diseases.

Meeting Someone

Emerging adults meet potential love partners in a wide variety of ways: through friends and relatives, at bars, parties, and church functions, and in the workplace.[9] School is an especially fertile setting for love. Schools place young people of similar ages in close proximity on a daily basis, which gives them plenty of opportunities to meet, get to know each other, and arrange to see each other later. Many emerging adults met their current love partner in college or graduate school—at parties, in dormitories, or in classes. Perry's experience is a little unusual, but nevertheless provides a good illustration.

> To tell you the truth, we met in a graveyard. It was during what we called "the summer field exercise" with the geography department. The new grad students, we got out into the field and did some field geography. I was on the same team as her, and we were looking at the cultural geography of the area by looking at names on tombstones. That's where we met.

Once they are out of school, meeting someone becomes a little more challenging for emerging adults as they are no longer in a setting where there is a concentration of other people their age. But most of them manage, one way or another. Friends or coworkers introduce them to someone. They keep their eyes out: Tracy met her boyfriend when "I was driving down the street and he was the passenger in the car next to me. He asked me to pull over and I did." They go to bars and nightclubs, most of which are filled mainly with people who are young and single, looking for love or something like it. However, emerging adults tend to regard the people they meet in these settings as potential partners for flirtation and perhaps casual sex rather than as potential love partners.[10]

Most of the ways that emerging adults meet someone have been around for a long time. School, friends, work, and family have long been sources of connections to potential love partners. One new method is through the Internet. Although only a handful of the people we interviewed mentioned this as the way they met their love partner, it is worth mentioning because it is becoming increasingly common, as Internet use becomes more widespread. Katy met her current boyfriend when "we started talking through e-mail. We chatted back and forth for about a week and finally said, 'We've got to meet.'" Ian met his girlfriend in a similar fashion.

> I was fiddling around on the computer and I got on the Internet and met her. And I drove up just to meet her. There was a whole bunch of people that I'd talked to on the Internet and that she'd talked to and we were all going to meet. The rest of them couldn't make it, and I'm like, "Well, I can still make it." So I went up. She was in Des Moines. [He was in Missouri.] The wonders of technology!

Some emerging adults, like Ian, meet potential dating partners just in the course of "fiddling around" on the Internet, but in recent years there has been a boom in Internet dating services. Web sites such as Matchmaker.com, Match.com, and Kiss.com have more than 40 million subscribers and are adding tens of thousands more every week.[11] There are also sites designed for specific groups, such as Asian Americans (AsianFriendFinder.com), Catholics (Catholicsingles.com), Jews (Jdate.com), and gays and lesbians (PlanetOut.com). Some sites are free, but most charge about $20 a month. Subscribers provide personal information such as educational background, hobbies, and what they are most looking for in a partner. Some sites have the option of including a photo. The site's computer then matches the subscriber up with persons who have similar characteristics, and the dating adventures begin.

Does this work any better than the old-fashioned ways of meeting? Because Internet dating is such a recent phenomenon, there is little research yet to indicate how well it works or fails to work. Certainly Internet dating services provide emerging adults with an easy way to meet new people. However, although the technology is different, the basic idea behind Internet dating is not really new. Internet dating services offer little more than a high-tech personal ad, with all of the advantages and liabilities of personal ads: yes, it's a way to meet a lot more potential love partners than you are likely to meet in the course of everyday life, but chances are high that you will meet a lot more frogs than princes or princesses, however royal they may have appeared in their Web self-descriptions. Even with photo included, most people are likely to make themselves appear a lot more appealing and wartfree in cyberspace than they are in real life, so the great majority of meetings through Internet dating services are likely to begin with great expectations and end in disappointment.[12]

Another recent change in emerging adult dating patterns is that young women are more likely to take the initiative, to do the "asking out." In the old days of "calling," women did the asking; a man would have been seen as rude and unmannerly if he asked to call on her. When calling declined and dating arose, men became the initiators—they did the asking, the arranging, and the paying. A woman could not ask a man out without appearing too aggressive, too forward, potentially "loose."

Most of the onus is still on boys and men to do the asking, arranging, and paying, but the rules are not as rigid as they used to be. It is no longer frowned upon for young women to do the initiating, so many of them do. Tina met her husband at a dance, where "we started dancing and we just danced the rest of the night, and I got his phone number and I called him the next day, and the rest is history." Brock recalled that he met his girlfriend when "I had her in a class and she came up during class and asked me out." Corey and his girlfriend met at the liquor store where he worked. "She used to come in and flirt with me a lot, and I'd flirt back with her, and a lot of times she'd ask me to go out and finally I decided to go ahead and go."

Another way the rules of courtship have become less rigid for the current generation of emerging adults is that often young men and women become friends first, then gradually move toward love.[13] They may not even "date," per se, but just do things together, perhaps as part of a group of friends, and gradually become intimately involved. For example, Mandy and

Most people make themselves seem more appealing in cyberspace than they are in real life. (© Hilary B. Price. Reprinted with special permission of King Features Syndicate.)

her boyfriend "started doing stuff together just on a friendship basis, going to church and having dinner and stuff like that. And then eventually it became more."

Becoming Partners

After they meet, what is it that leads two emerging adults to fall in love? Sexual attraction is certainly at the center of it.[14] Even when emerging adults such as Mandy have been friends with their love partner for a long time before dating, they usually say they were attracted to their partner from the beginning. Beyond sexual attraction, similarity between the two partners often forms the basis for love.[15] Opposites rarely attract; on the contrary, birds of a feather flock together. A long line of sociological studies has established that emerging adults, like people of other ages, tend to have romantic relationships with people who are similar to them in characteristics such as personality, intelligence, social class, ethnic background, religious beliefs, and physical attractiveness.[16] Sociologists attribute this to what they call *consensual validation*, which means that people like to find in others a match, or *consensus*, with their own characteristics. Finding this consensus reaffirms, or *validates*, their own way of looking at the world. The more similar your love partner is to you, the more likely you are to reaffirm each other, and the less likely you are to have conflicts that spring from having different views and preferences.

Similarity also brings potential love partners together in settings that give them the opportunity to meet and initiate a relationship. Students taking the same class may have a common interest in the subject that reflects other common interests as well. Emerging adults attending the same church, temple, or mosque are probably similar in their religious views. There were numerous examples in our interviews of this kind of similarity bringing two emerging adults together. For example, Charles (who was profiled in chapter 2) met his girlfriend at a singing showcase in which they both competed, reflecting their similar interests in music. Arthur, a 25-year-old Chinese American, met his girlfriend in a college class on Asian American films. He confessed that his motivation for taking the class "was not purely educational!"—that is, he'd taken it for the purpose of meeting girls with an ethnic background similar to his own.

Similarity of ethnic background is one of the most influential determinants of whether two emerging adults will become involved. The long troubled history of race relations in the United States continues to cast its shadow on this generation of emerging adults. Up until fairly recently, marriages between persons of different racial backgrounds were actually forbidden by law in many states. It was only in 1967 that the Supreme Court ruled that such laws were unconstitutional, forcing 16 states to rescind them.

In some ways, the United States has come a long way since those days. The number of interethnic marriages surged from 300,000 in 1970 to 1.4 million in 1998.[17] It is no longer unusual to see interethnic couples on the streets of most American cities. Nevertheless, for the most part, people still choose love partners from within their own ethnic group. Only about 5% of the married couples in the United States include spouses of different ethnic groups. However, there is substantial diversity among ethnic groups in their rates of intermarriage. Native Americans have the highest rate of marrying outside their ethnic group, at just over 50%. Asian Americans are close behind, at about 40%. Then the rates drop considerably, to Latinos at 17% and African Americans at 9%, with Whites lowest at 3%.

One reason that emerging adults tend to date and marry within their ethnic group is that they often find love partners from their social network, and their social network usually consists mainly of people from their own ethnic group. Figure 4.1 shows that, in my study, a majority of emerging

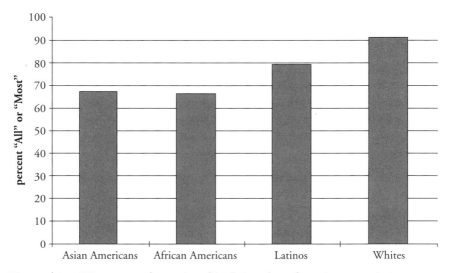

Figure 4.1. "How many of your close friends have been from the same ethnic group as you?"

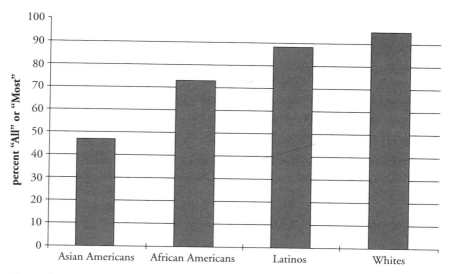

Figure 4.2. "How many of your dating partners have been from the same ethnic group as you?"

adults in all four major ethnic groups said that "all" or "most" of their friends come from their own ethnic group.

This corresponded to their choices in dating partners, as Figure 4.2 shows. For all ethnic groups except Asian Americans, a majority of emerging adults said that "all" or "most" of their dating partners come from their own ethnic group. Notice how these findings concerning dating partners match the patterns from national statistics on interethnic marriage, with Asian Americans most likely to find partners outside their ethnic group, Whites least likely, and African Americans and Latinos in between.

Even though a majority of emerging adults in every ethnic group stated that it was not important to them to date within their ethnic group (see Figure 4.3), in their actual behavior they usually did. Latisha, a 20-year-old African American, put it like this: "If I met a really nice guy that wasn't [Black] I wouldn't like shun him or anything. I guess I just [date Black men] because those are the people that seem to be around, like if I go to a party, those are the kind of people that I meet. So it just kind of happens like that." Just as emerging adults with a particular interest in music, religion, or the outdoors are likely to seek out groups of other people with similar interests and may find love partners from within those groups, so emerging adults with a common ethnic background tend to form groups of friends and then find their love partners within those groups.

A second reason for finding a love partner within one's own ethnic group arises from an awareness of cultural differences between ethnic groups and a feeling of being more comfortable with what is familiar. Rhonda, a 26-year-old African American, said she prefers to date African American men "because we have the same background and the same ideas and goals. It's not that I have anything against people who are not African American, but we tend to have the same outlook on things. And it's easier to communicate with someone who you're in sync with." Arthur, the Chinese American who met his girlfriend in a college class on Asian American films, said he prefers Chinese women because "I want to be with someone who can understand me without me having to go through an entire explanation of why I think that way about a certain thing. Without having to educate them. I feel like I do that enough with just people at large, and I don't want to do that with the person I'm going to spend the rest of my life with." Emerging adults also usually believe that their parents will be more comfortable with someone from within their ethnic group, especially if the parents are immigrants who speak limited English.

Racism stops some from dating and marrying outside their ethnic group. No emerging adults in my study admitted to such views themselves, but many of them freely admitted that their parents had made their prejudices clear in conveying to them that they should not marry outside of their ethnic group. Sophie, a 21-year-old Chinese American, said her parents had explicitly told her:

> This is the order: Chinese American, Chinese, and then any Asian, and then White, but I don't think they would want me to marry an African American or Hispanic person. [*They wouldn't? Why's that?*] Because of what they see in the media—how they're always in trouble, how it seems like whoever's getting arrested is African American or Hispanic.

Cleo, a 23-year-old African American, said that if she became involved with a White man her mother would "flip her lid" and her father "would disown me." Becky, a 22-year-old White American, said she had once dated an African American man, a "wonderful man" with whom she "just clicked and everything was there." But when she told her mother about him, "my mom said, 'Now don't you go liking him.' Because he was Black! I mean, she was being a racist saying that. I said, 'Mom, I can't believe you!'" Becky's relationship with him did not last long, in part because of her mother's opposition. As shown in Figures 4.3 and 4.4, Asian Americans and Whites see it as far more important to their parents than to themselves that they date or marry within their ethnic group.

In these examples, we can see evidence of the transmission of the American history of ethnic antagonism to a new generation of young people. Still, it should be mentioned again that in all ethnic groups in my study, a majority of emerging adults stated that dating within their ethnic group was not important to them. They stressed, instead, that it is the qualities of the person that matter most, not their ethnic background. For example, Leonard, a 20-year-old African American, said that to him a prospective love partner's ethnic background "doesn't matter. . . . It's the person, the heart, not the skin color. I'm not prejudiced. I mean, everybody's American, everybody's human." Amelia, a White 22-year-old, summed it up this way:

> If I really loved someone it wouldn't bother me. I mean, I think I realize that it might make my life harder in some ways because not all people are accepting of, you know, that type of thing. But I also think in order to overcome that type of thinking in our society we need to get beyond that, and if I really want to do something I'm not gonna think, "Well this might make my life hard so I'm not gonna marry someone who I love and think is a great person."

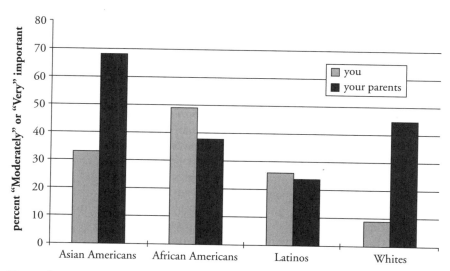

Figure 4.3. "How important is it to you/your parents for you to date people who are in your own ethnic group"?

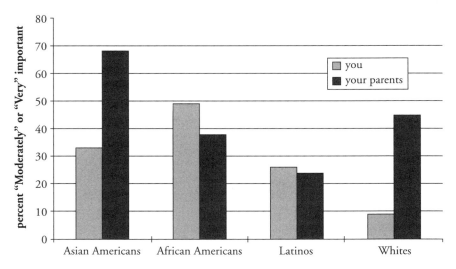

Figure 4.4. "How important is it to you/your parents for you to marry someone who is in your own ethnic group"?

It may be, then, that a generational change is occurring and that this generation of emerging adults will be more accepting of interethnic relationships than their parents' generation has been. In my study, both White and Asian American emerging adults reported themselves to be much more accepting of interethnic relationships than their parents are. Of course, this is easy to say, and in saying it a person can count on being credited for tolerance and broad-mindedness. Whether people may harbor different thoughts within themselves or whether a person would translate such noble sentiments into action is difficult to know on the basis of what they say in an interview. Still, the rise in interethnic marriages indicates that today's emerging adults are more likely than previous generations to be open to interethnic relationships.

Sex: New Opportunities, New Problems

The sexual revolution of the 1960s demolished what was left of the long-standing expectation that young women would remain virgins until marriage. That expectation had been under pressure since the earlier sexual revolution of the 1920s, when some degree of sexual experimentation before marriage became common. But between the two sexual revolutions, sexual intercourse remained the boundary that young people, especially young women, were not supposed to cross. Young lovers learned to enjoy each other within what the novelist John Updike described as the "large and not laughable sexual territory . . . within the borders of virginity, where physical parts were fed to the partner a few at a time, beginning with the lips and hands."[18]

Since the 1960s, virginity until marriage has ceased to exist as an ideal for most emerging adults.[19] Nor does American society promote it strongly. On the contrary, it is now widely accepted that young people will have sexual relations, including sexual intercourse, before marriage. Angela reflected the norms of her generation and her times when she observed, "I mean, I don't know anybody who waits for marriage any more. I think that's probably gone out of style."

We can see how American society has become more liberal in its views on premarital sex by looking at changes in the policies of American colleges.[20] Until the late 1960s, college officials were expected to act *in loco parentis*, "in place of parents." This meant monitoring students', especially female students', behavior closely and enforcing rules that discouraged sexual activity. The rules included curfews in women's dormitories, every night of the week. Repeated violations might prompt a letter from college officials to parents or the threat of expulsion from the school. Even in daylight hours, most colleges allowed no young men in the women's dormitories. Those that did stipulated that the young woman's door must remain open at all times while she had a male visitor.

Today's emerging adults would find it hard to imagine such restrictions. They are intent on making their own decisions without adult interference, including decisions about their sexual behavior. Nor would today's adults wish to play the role of enforcing restrictions on emerging adults' sexual behavior, as adults did in the past. They, too, believe that by the time young people reach their late teens and early twenties they merit a wide scope of personal autonomy that adults have no right to infringe upon.

The old rule about remaining a virgin until marriage is passé, but it's unclear exactly what the new rules are. It's OK to have sex before marriage, but at what age is it OK to begin? It's OK to have partners other than your future spouse, but how many partners? There are no clear guidelines in American society for answering these questions, so young people must muddle their way to the answers as best they can.

One thing that is clear is that views of sex in emerging adulthood are somewhat different for men than for women. For example, in a national survey of unmarried 20–29-year-olds, 65% of men but only 41% of women agreed that there are people they would have sex with even though they have no interest in marrying them.[21] Both men and women seek a soul mate in marriage, almost unanimously, but prior to marriage young men often have a more recreational attitude toward sex whereas young women are more likely to enjoy sex if it is in the context of an emotionally intimate relationship. Jessica, now engaged, looked back at her previous relationships and observed, "Maybe it's my Catholic roots, but the sex I could have done without. It wasn't until finding a man I truly loved and trusted that I felt comfortable enough to learn about myself physically." Of course, some women also have a recreational attitude toward sex in emerging adulthood, but in general they are more likely than men to prefer the combination of love and sex.

"Too Young": Recalling the First Time

The question about when it is OK for young people to have their first sexual intercourse is especially problematic. Americans' mixed attitudes toward this question were reflected in a national survey of 18–59-year-olds.[22] In this survey, only 20% of respondents agreed that "premarital sex is always wrong." However, 60% agreed that "premarital sex among teenagers is always wrong." So, at some point between the time young people cease to be "teenagers" and the time they enter marriage, usually in their late twenties—sometime during emerging adulthood, in other words—it becomes acceptable for them to have premarital sex, according to a majority of Americans. But when, exactly? Young people trying to discern some kind of acceptable sexual morality from the society around them would be understandably confused.

The results of the two survey questions imply that Americans generally believe that premarital sex is a mistake for adolescents but acceptable for emerging adults. Generally, the emerging adults in my study supported this view. Most of them had intercourse for the first time when they were adolescents, usually during the period from age 14 to 18. This is consistent with other studies; most Americans have had intercourse at least once by the time they leave high school.[23] However, over 70% of the emerging adults in my study now believed that their first intercourse had taken place when they were "too young."

Their feeling of being too young that first time is due to a belief that premarital sex is "wrong" for teenagers, but not so much in a moral sense as in a psychological sense. They regret their teenage premarital sex because they realize now that they were too immature at the time to appreciate the significance of what they were doing. Jake thinks his teenage sex was a mistake, now that he realizes how complicated sex is emotionally.

> I'm sure I was too young. It's a big responsibility. Not only that, it causes a lot of problems between people. When you get that close to somebody, it's never the same again. Never. I don't care how casual it is, it's never the same. You can't just be friends with them any more. You can't. There's jealousy involved on one side or the other every time. I've never met anybody that you could just have sex with and be like, "Oh, OK, whatever you want. No big deal."

Emerging adults don't believe that in adolescence they were capable of making such a profound decision wisely. Learning to make independent decisions is something they view as an important part of becoming an adult, as we have seen, and when they look back to adolescence they shake their heads at what they now see as foolish sexual decisions. Mindy had sex for the first time at age 14, and at 25 she feels that was "way too young." The basis of her decision to have sex seems immature to her now. "I was just curious, I think that's why I did it. I was curious to know what it was like, and I don't think that's why you should do it. I was just too young to make that decision."

Some see their unreadiness for making the decision to have sex reflected in their failure to appreciate the possibility of pregnancy and the necessity of contraception. Leah, who had sex for the first time at age 17, now recalls: "I wasn't even in tune with my own body, you know, and I was terrified. It didn't hit me until afterwards, then 'Oh my God! What if I get pregnant?' That never even crossed my mind. I was just young and stupid." Similarly, Jean, who also had sex for the first time at age 17, says now: "I think I was probably too young because I didn't prepare for it the first time. After that I was prepared, but the first time I didn't prepare for it. It was with my first boyfriend, and I don't think I was making logical decisions at that time in my life." Larry had a similar view, from a male perspective, of his first sex at age 15: "It was too young for me, I think. I mean, you tell yourself you know what you're doing, but you don't. You know, you're not mentally ready for all the implications, like what if she got pregnant? You'd be like, 'Oh my God, I'm 15 years old, and she wants to keep it!'"

In contrast, the emerging adults who have no regrets about their teenage sex tend to recall themselves as making the decision in a more mature, careful manner. When Martin and his girlfriend had sex for the first time at age 18, they decided on it together and bought condoms so they would be well prepared. "It was a very rational decision, because my girlfriend and I had discussed it for about two or three weeks prior, and we finally set it up and went out."

Also important to having good memories of that first episode of intercourse is that it took place in the context of a loving relationship. For example, Gabriella said she had no regrets about her first partner because "he was a good guy, and I really cared about him. I felt like I was old enough to handle it, and I felt like he was the right person for it to be with." Similarly, Christy had sex for the first time at 17 and now believes that was "probably about the right age." Then she adds, "I don't think the age was so much the issue. I was in a relationship that was healthy, and I was with someone that sex wasn't just sex. It was emotional, and that was really important to me." But age does matter, because the older people are when they have their first episode of intercourse, the more likely they are to make a reasoned decision about it and to be prepared for it emotionally and contraceptively. Although the majority of the emerging adults in my study believed they were too young when they had their first intercourse, no one who waited until past age 18 expressed regrets.

Having their first intercourse within the context of a loving relationship is especially important to young women. In a national survey, one half of women said their main reason for having intercourse the first time was love for their partner, compared to only one fourth of men.[24] For young men, including the emerging adults in my study, their first intercourse is more likely to be recalled as an adventure, a rite of passage. Curiosity, the desire to see what it would be like, is usually their main motive, according to national surveys; love often has little to do with it. Rocky glowed with nostalgia as he described his first time:

On my 16th birthday. First day with my license. In my first car. That was a big day! A friend threw me a party and I walked in the room and a girl grabbed my hand. I had no idea who in the hell she was. I wasn't even there long enough to get drunk. It was more like, I walked in, people say, "Happy Birthday," she grabs my hand, and we go out to the car and drive off to have sex! It was a trip!

Contrast this with the experience of Mindy, who had her first sexual intercourse at age 14 with a neighbor boy she knew but did not love. Because it was loveless she regretted it so much she became depressed. "I never felt like committing suicide, but I felt really bad about myself." She also swore off sex for some time afterward, because of the unpleasantness of the experience. "I hated it. I thought, 'This is not what it is on TV. I don't want to do this any more.' And I waited until after I was out of high school to even try sex again." These two experiences reflect the general patterns. Studies indicate that boys generally respond to their first intercourse with feelings of excitement, pride, and happiness, while girls are usually much more ambivalent, much more likely to feel guilty, worried, and regretful.[25]

Other young people wish they had saved the first time for their true love, the special person they intend to spend the rest of their life with. Although the majority of emerging adults sees no problem with premarital sex as long as the persons involved are mature enough, there are some who still maintain the traditional belief that sex should take place only in the context of marriage. This belief is nearly always grounded in religious principles. Many emerging adults believe that sexual intercourse is best reserved for a special relationship, but only those with conservative religious beliefs think the special relationship must be marriage. However, this is not an insignificant portion of the American population; various surveys have found that 20–25% of Americans have conservative religious beliefs.[26] This proportion is consistent across age groups, including emerging adults (as we shall see in chapter 8).

For example, Nate is "still a virgin" at 25 and says this is due to "my religious beliefs. I believe in commitment and that really sex is a gift for marriage." Nancy said, "I have a real strong feeling about not having sex until I'm married. It's because of my religious beliefs and my upbringing that I feel that way." Now 28, as she has passed through her twenties she has felt increasing pressure on her beliefs, from boyfriends as well as from society at large. "It's hard, it's really hard now. There was a time when it would be easier to say, 'This is what I believe and this is how I'm going to lead my life,' and it wasn't as hard to follow through with it." However, she has a group of friends who share her beliefs and who have provided mutual support, and now she has a boyfriend who also values virginity before marriage. "Fortunately, I think I've found one of the few guys out there that shares the same belief and is the same age. It's been really refreshing to find someone who shares that belief because in at least a couple of my relationships that's been a problem." Not all emerging adults with conservative religious beliefs stay virgins until marriage, of course, but they are more likely to believe that virginity until marriage is an ideal worth striving for.

The Specter of AIDS

Because they are more independent of their parents than adolescents are, and because there is no social stigma against them having sex the way there is for adolescents, emerging adults have less reason to be furtive and anxious about sex. Most of them passed through the awkwardness of their first experiences of intercourse during adolescence, and as emerging adults they are more comfortable with their sexuality, more knowledgeable about the emotional and physical experience of sex. They more or less assume that sex will be a part of any love relationship they become involved in.

However, one source of acute anxiety surrounding sex for emerging adults is the threat of sexually transmitted diseases (STDs), especially HIV/AIDS. Sexual experimentation takes place for emerging adults under the specter of potentially becoming infected with a deadly virus for which there is no cure.

Today's emerging adults are not the first generation of young people to face such a grim threat in relation to their sexuality. Syphilis carried a similar threat for centuries, until the development of penicillin in the 1940s, and syphilis was contracted much more easily than HIV. However, strict social codes against premarital sex made the prospect of syphilis remote for most people. In contrast, AIDS has arisen at a time when the taboo against premarital sex has faded, in the aftermath of the sexual revolution of the 1960s. Emerging adults today grow up in a society in which the normative expectation is that they will have a series of sexual relationships before marriage. But this freedom to engage in sexual experimentation now collides with the terrible prospect of contracting a deadly disease.

Emerging adults respond to this situation in a variety of ways. Some view AIDS as a threat to other people but not to themselves. Brady dismissed AIDS by remarking, "I don't know anybody who has it, so I don't really think about it." Jake said, "I'll admit that I never thought something like that would happen to me. That's not very smart, but I just never did." Casey said his reading had convinced him that "the odds of me getting AIDS from a woman are so incredibly remote. I can get AIDS from another man, and I can get AIDS from a needle. Those are two of the highly possible ways. So I think technically, doing what I do, the odds are incredibly low for me, anyway."

Some young men view AIDS as a legitimate threat, but accept that threat as the price of pursuing sexual pleasure. Benny admitted that although he is aware that unprotected sex leaves him at risk for AIDS, "I haven't been careful at all. I guess you could say I've been rolling the dice. It's kind of hard to say, but putting on a rubber is like turning on the cold water, you know, it just don't happen. And I want [sex] to happen enough that I would even blow off all the worries and scariness about it and end up doing the deal." Keith sometimes worries about AIDS, but the threat of it "hasn't stopped me. I've always been willing to suffer the consequences of my actions. If something like that ever came about, I mean, I'm sure I would be quite upset because I was going to die—who wouldn't be?—but all you can do is say, 'Well, I got what I deserved. I took my chances and knew what the possibilities were. Tough luck.'"

Most emerging adults, however, say that fear of AIDS has become the framework for their sexual consciousness, deeply affecting their attitudes about sex and the way they approach sex with potential partners. Bridget insisted that her boyfriend get tested before she would have sex with him. "I was like, 'We're not going to do it until we find out.'" He resisted, but eventually agreed when she held firm. "He had problems with it, but it was kind of like, 'If you don't want to wear your raincoat, you can't play in the rain,' you know. So I was like, 'It's your choice, buddy.'" Sam took a similar view: "Today, you basically want the blood test before you go to bed with somebody." Gabriella asserted, "I don't think I would ever have unprotected sex, meaning without a condom. I've always known a lot about AIDS. I certainly wouldn't want to put my life in jeopardy for something like that." Bruce said his "awareness and consciousness" of AIDS is "really intense." A rock musician, he often has sexual opportunities when on the road that he passes up for fear of AIDS. "I don't want to roll the dice with somebody I don't even know."

Even for many emerging adults who have been on the conservative side in their sexual behavior, AIDS is part of their consciousness. Helen has been with the same boyfriend for the past five years. "I know I don't have anything," she said. Yet:

> I do think about it sometimes. You know, when you cut yourself or something and I always think, "Well, if it doesn't scab up right away . . . " And if something popped up on my body that's kind of weird-looking, [I would] think about AIDS a lot of times. I'm glad I know the symptoms so I can look out for those.

They realize that even if they have been careful in their sexual behavior, their partners may not have been, and that puts them at risk. Vernon said,

"One of the girls I dated, I found out she had sex with one of these [male stripper] guys. And I started doing the math and I was like, 'Holy cow! I had sex with California just now!' And that made me nervous, you know."

Other studies confirm that young people's sexual behavior has changed since the rise of AIDS. Use of condoms has increased sharply since the late 1980s among both high school and college students.[27] Among college students, most now say they talk to their sexual partners about HIV prevention, and they name fear of HIV infection as their main motive for using condoms consistently.[28] The increased concern with practicing "safer sex" is reflected in declines in the consequences of unprotected sex. Throughout the 1990s, there were steady declines in unintended pregnancies, abortions, births to unmarried mothers, and STDs among young people.[29]

Still, although most young people are quite responsible about their sexual behavior, a substantial proportion of them take at least occasional risks. Recent studies show that from one fourth to one third of college students have had unprotected sex at least once in the past year.[30] An opportunity comes along, the mood is right—often enhanced by alcohol—and they take their chances. Most of them, especially young men, say condoms reduce their sexual sensations, and they dislike using them. They are sometimes inhibited from talking about contraception by embarrassment or by fear that doing so will break the mood. It may seem ironic that two people could be unembarrassed enough to have sex with each other yet too embarrassed to talk about contraception, but that is often the way it is between emerging adults.

Few emerging adults match Bridget and Sam in requiring a clean blood test from their partners before having sex. The typical pattern is to use condoms in the early phase of a relationship, then switch to reliance on birth control pills after a few months. The switch to birth control pills is usually not inspired by any mutual certainty that neither has HIV or any other STD, or even by a conversation about STDs, but simply by knowing each other better and trusting each other more.[31] As their relationship develops and they become more committed to each other, they each decide that their partner is "not the kind of person" who would have HIV. Wilson put it this way:

> I've had a girlfriend for a while, and I've never been tested but I don't feel the need to be safe. I trust her and she trusts me. I know that's sort of unsafe, but now we're both only having sex with each other and that's it. So I think we're doing all right.

HIV/AIDS is the most formidable source of anxiety in the sex lives of emerging adults because it is incurable and deadly, but other STDs also present a risk during an age period where people typically move from one sexual partner to another for several years. The most common STD among young people is chlamydia.[32] Symptoms include pain during urination and pain during intercourse, although sometimes there are no symptoms at all. It can be treated effectively with antibiotics, but if left untreated in women it can lead to pelvic inflammatory disease (PID), which in turn causes infertility; in fact, chlamydia is the leading cause of female infertility. It is also highly infectious; 25% of men and nearly three fourths of women contract the disease during a single episode of intercourse with an infected partner.

That was Holly's unfortunate fate. "I slept with this one guy one time— one guy, one time—and we actually didn't use anything, and I don't know why. We were both being stupid." She had no symptoms afterward, but about a month later she had her annual pelvic exam. "They called me and said I was positive for chlamydia. That just shook me up because I couldn't believe that would happen to me." She was treated immediately, but the experience made her realize that "it could happen. Anything could happen." She won't forget the experience. Nor will her friends. "My two good friends, they say, 'You know, every time we hear that word *chlamydia*, we think of you.' And I'm like, 'Thanks.'"

Herpes is another common STD among emerging adults. Like chlamydia, it is highly infectious; 75% of persons who have unprotected sexual contact with an infected partner contract the disease.[33] Symptoms usually appear from one day to one month after infection. First there is a tingling or burning sensation in the infected area, followed by the appearance of sores. The sores last three to six weeks and can be painful. Other symptoms include fever, headaches, and fatigue. Treatment within four days of infection reduces the chances of recurring outbreaks of sores, but there is no cure for herpes. Once people are infected, the virus remains in their bodies for life, and the chance of another episode is ever present.

This can't be an easy thing to break to a prospective lover, as Freda has found out. She contracted herpes at age 17, from the first person she ever had sex with. She noticed his sores, but she did not recognize them as symptoms of herpes. "I remember a day when he had a sore or something, and I didn't even think about it. I remember going, 'Oh, what's that?' and he said, 'Oh, nothing.'" When she found out she was infected, the news devastated her. "It affected me a lot. A lot. It just really threw me for a loop. I was just like, 'OK, scarred for life.'"

She has had only two episodes in the four years since then, and she has learned to live with it. But she dreaded having to tell her current boyfriend about it when they became involved. Herpes is most infectious during an episode of sores, but it can also be transmitted through repeated unprotected sex over a long period of time. So, she had to tell him that she was infected and that there was a risk to him of becoming infected unless they always used a condom. "It was very difficult for us. I had to be so honest and try to be careful about not freaking him out to the point of no return, you know. I was just kind of like, 'Well, I have to tell you this.'" He did not take it well at first but eventually accepted it. At least it wasn't AIDS. "He was pretty freaked out, but I think he started to realize that there's worse things you can get." Still, she continues to resent her misfortune in getting herpes. "I feel really cheated somehow, but at the same [time,] I'm going to have to live with it. That's just the way it is."

Conclusion: The Perils of Freedom

Emerging adults today have unprecedented freedoms in love and sex. Unlike previous generations, they are not constricted by gender roles that prescribe strict rules for how they may meet and get to know each other. A man may take the initiative and ask the woman out, or a woman may take the initiative and ask the man out. They may share time together as friends and get to know each other well before they decide whether to cross the border from friendship into love, without anyone tut-tutting that they are doing something improper by spending time together.

Also unlike previous generations, they are not forbidden to fall in love with someone from a different ethnic background. Prejudices still exist, of course, but they are not inviolable—or illegal—as they once were. Today, rather than interethnic love relationships being stigmatized, it is the prejudice against such relationships that is now stigmatized and widely viewed as intolerable. Most young people still find their love partners within their ethnic group, partly for reasons of shared social networks and shared cultural backgrounds, partly because of the lingering effect of ethnic prejudice. But more than ever before, emerging adults find love partners across ethnic borders.

Sexually, too, emerging adults today have freedoms that would have seemed unimaginable a half century ago. Most of them have a series of sexual partners from their late teens until they get married. For the most part, their sexual partners are not people they have just met and barely know but people with whom they have an ongoing intimate relationship. Few Americans see anything wrong with a young woman and a young man in their twenties having a sexual relationship in the context of their love relationship, even if they are unmarried, even if they have no intention of getting married. The new norms are especially striking for women, who in the past would have been scorned and ostracized if they were known to be sexually active before marriage, even with someone they loved.

Yet the new freedoms of emerging adulthood are accompanied by new fears. Although they are allowed and even encouraged to have a variety of sexual experiences before marriage, the spread of AIDS has added an undercurrent of anxiety to their sexual freedom. Few emerging adults will ever contract AIDS, but for virtually all of them AIDS has become part of their sexual consciousness. The threat of other STDs, nonfatal but nevertheless traumatic, also casts a shadow on their sex lives.

There are perils in their pursuit of love as well. They may be freer than generations past to seek a love partner without the restrictions of courtship or dating rules and without prohibitions against crossing ethnic boundaries, but that does not mean that finding the right love partner has become any easier. This is especially true when emerging adults begin looking for a love partner for life, someone to commit themselves to in marriage. It is to this topic that we turn in the next chapter.

5

Meandering Toward Marriage

To look at the titles of some of the books popular among emerging adult women, you might think that most of them could do without marriage. *Why Dogs Are Better Than Men*. *One Hundred and One Reasons Why a Cat Is Better Than a Man*. Even *Why Cucumbers Are Better Than Men*. As for emerging adult men, the cliché is that they are terrified of commitment, especially of the marriage variety. Humorist Dave Barry, in his *Complete Guide to Guys*, offers women a number of "relationship-enhancement tips," including

> *Do not expect the guy to make a hasty commitment.* By "hasty," I mean, "within your lifetime." Guys are *extremely* reluctant to make commitments. This is because they never feel *ready*. . . . A lot of women have concluded that the problem is that guys, as a group, have the emotional maturity of hamsters. No, this is not the case. A hamster is much more capable of making a lasting commitment to a woman, especially if she gives it those little food pellets.

Yet few young women remain sufficiently satisfied with cats, dogs, or cucumbers in the long run, and few young men fear commitment so much that they stay single past their twenties. About 85% of Americans get married, 75% by age 30.[1] Today's emerging adults spend more years single and dating than young people in previous generations, but the great majority of them eventually make their way to the altar.

In the course of emerging adulthood, young people change in a number of ways that make them increasingly ready for marriage. Emerging adults become more capable of enduring intimacy. They come to appreciate the rewards of staying with one person for a longer period of time and developing a deeper emotional closeness. They also come to desire more security and commitment in their relationships. Eventually, it grows old to move from one partner to the next every few weeks or months and start all over. Most emerging adults come to desire the stability and comfort of developing a long-term relationship with a person who seems to fit them just right.

For nearly all of them, this means thinking about marriage and trying to find someone who will make a good marriage partner. They may wish to wait for marriage until they have finished school, or become settled into a career, or had sufficient opportunity to live on their own and focus on their own development and desires for a few years. But they expect to commit themselves to marriage once they feel ready, and most of them, even the "guys," eventually do. They fear some things about marriage, but the dream of a true, lifelong love outweighs those fears.

In this chapter, we first look at the qualities that emerging adults hope to find in a marriage partner. Then we look at how they decide when they would like to marry, including the widespread sense, especially among women, of having an "age 30 deadline" for marriage. Next, we discuss issues of commitment, and examine different motives for cohabitation. Finally, we look at how the fear of divorce shapes marriage expectations.

In Search of a Soul Mate: Finding a Marriage Partner

When they talk about what they are looking for in a marriage partner, emerging adults mention a wide variety of ideal qualities. Sometimes these are qualities of the person, the individual: intelligent, good-looking, or funny. But most often they mention interpersonal qualities, qualities a person brings to a relationship, such as being kind, caring, loving, and trustworthy. Emerging adults hope to find someone who will treat them well and who will be capable of an intimate, mutually loving, durable relationship.

In addition to looking for ideal qualities, emerging adults also seek a marriage partner who will be like themselves in many ways. Just as they look for similarities when considering another person as a potential dating partner, they look for similarities when considering potential marriage partners. Mindy thinks that marriage prospects look good with her boyfriend because "we have the same interests, we like to do the same things, we can talk about things on the same level. . . . We both want pretty much the same thing out of life."

Similarity is more important for marriage in this generation than in the past, because married couples today usually expect to spend most of their leisure time together. Gone are the days when men would spend their evenings with other men at a pub or a men's club—clubs such as the Elks, the Lions, the Masons, and so on have all declined steeply in membership over the past 30 years.[2] Nor do today's young women have much use for women-only groups—garden clubs, bridge clubs, and so on. Young couples often expect to find their main leisure companions in one another, and this makes similarity in leisure preferences a key quality to look for in a marriage partner.

It is not that they expect to do *everything* together. They just want to have enough common interests so that they can enjoy shared activities. Perry said he'd like to find someone who "likes to do some of the things that I do, but then won't mind if there's some things I like to do and she doesn't. Just somebody that does have enough similar interests so that we can spend a lot of quality time together." Most emerging adults want to strike a balance and find someone whose companionship they will enjoy when doing things together but who will also allow them some time for independent activities.

Even more important than shared activities are shared beliefs and values, a similar way of looking at the world. Those who have strong religious beliefs emphasize the importance of finding someone who shares them.[3] Andrea said she's looking for "somebody who's got the same religious beliefs as I do, and values and all that." When emerging adults who are members of ethnic minority groups emphasize finding a marriage partner with the same ethnic background, it is often because they believe that similarity of ethnic background means similarity of world view. Gloria, a 22-year-old Latina, put it this way:

> It would have to be someone who was of the same religion that I was and also the same ethnicity as me. And sometimes when I say that people take it that I'm prejudiced or something. But it's not necessarily that, because I have a lot of traditions and customs that I grew up with, and I want someone who understands the same traditions and everything. So I've always looked for someone who was Latino. And I've always looked for someone who was Catholic because I'm Catholic.

The importance placed on interpersonal qualities and the importance placed on similarity of interests, beliefs, and values together make up the ideal of compatibility that emerging adults envision when they think about marriage. The ideal marriage partner would be someone who is your "soul mate"—someone with whom you will have a loving, lifelong relationship, someone who sees life as you do and enjoys the same things as you. When Annie thinks of her future husband, she imagines "someone you'd like to share your life with, your soul mate, the one you share everything with." Annie's dream is extremely common—in a national survey, 94% of single Americans in their twenties agreed that "when you marry you want your spouse to be your soul mate, first and foremost."[4]

Add physical attraction and sex to this soul mate, and you have a powerful ideal—but an elusive one. Ideals are not easy to find walking around in the flesh. Those who find their soul mate plus passion in their marriage are fortunate, but many will find that this is more than marriage can deliver. Given the loftiness of the ideal, many real marriages will seem inadequate in the long run. But before marriage, when emerging adults are still imagining whom their future spouse will be, their hopes run high that they will be one of the lucky ones to find their soul mate. In the same national survey that reported that 94% of single Americans in their twenties hope to marry their soul mate, 88% agreed that "there is a special person, a soul mate, waiting for you somewhere out there."[5]

Deciding When to Marry

Nearly all emerging adults want to get married eventually, but when? In the past, the answer was relatively clear. Men married when they became financially capable of supporting a wife and children, usually by their early twenties and rarely later than their mid-twenties. Women married when they were mature enough to assume the responsibilities of caring for a husband and children, often in their late teens and rarely later than their early twenties. Any woman who remained unmarried past her early twenties was relegated to the dreaded status of "old maid," applied to a woman who was viewed as past marriageable age and who would never marry.

Emerging adults today have much greater freedom to decide for themselves when they should marry. The norms for what is considered the "right" age to marry have weakened.[6] Some young people still marry in their late teens or early twenties, but most wait until at least their mid- to late twenties, and it is no longer unusual for them to wait until their thirties. It is not just that the average marriage age has risen steeply since 1970 for both men and women, but that the whole range of when people marry has become spread out. Young people can marry in their early twenties, their mid-twenties, their late twenties, or their early thirties and still be considered "normal."

This is an important new freedom for emerging adults, since they may now marry according to the timing they feel best fits their individual personalities and circumstances rather than rushing to get married because of the pressure of social expectations. However, like the other freedoms of emerging adulthood, this new freedom comes with a cost. Instead of being able to follow a clear cultural norm for when to marry, now the responsibility for deciding when to marry is on the emerging adults themselves. And it may not be easy.

In the views of many emerging adults, the early twenties are clearly too early. Marrying that early would cut off their opportunity to experience the independence and spontaneity that are so attractive about the emerging adult years. It would restrict their possibilities during a time of life when they have unparalleled opportunities to do what they want to do when they want to do it. Roy described it this way:

> It would kind of bum me out to be married. One day I was at work and my friend called me up from Florida and said, "What are you doing?" I'm like, "Just working," and he said, "Can you come down?" I'm like, "When?" and he's like, "Tomorrow," and I'm like, "Well, let me see what I can do." So I took a week off all of a sudden and went down to Florida. And I know I'd never be able to do that if I was married.

But emerging adults also wish to delay marriage for more substantial reasons. They want to get their own lives in order, as individuals, before they commit their lives and fates to another person. Some of this project is practical and concrete—finishing education, establishing financial stability, settling into a stable career. Other aspects of it are more intangible and internal. To judge their readiness for marriage, emerging adults look within themselves and ask themselves if they feel ready, if they feel mature enough, if they feel they know themselves well enough.

Financial reasons are often involved as well. In a national survey of 20–29-year-olds conducted by the National Marriage Project,[7] 86% agreed that "it is extremely important to you to be economically set before you get married." However, in focus-group interviews with 20–29-year-olds conducted as part of the same study, the researchers observed that emerging adults "believe that [you] have to take time to 'work on yourself and your own happiness.' Postponing marriage gives you time to grow up, experience life, and 'be happy with yourself.'" These results indicate that both economic preparation and identity explorations are important as precursors to marriage for emerging adults.

In Erikson's theory of human development across the life course,[8] after the challenge in adolescence of forming an identity, the next challenge is intimacy versus isolation, that is, finding someone to commit to for a life-long intimate relationship, usually in marriage. Only after forming a definite identity is a person ready to take the psychological and emotional risks involved in intimacy. Emerging adults sometimes seem to be ordering their lives in the way Erikson described, waiting until they feel they have resolved identity issues before considering marriage as the next step. Bonnie has been living with her boyfriend for a year and a half. He would like to get married, but as for herself, she says, "I don't know. . . . I'm not sure. There's a part of me, I think, that still needs to find some things. Not that I couldn't if I was married, but I don't know if this is it, and if I'm ready. Because there's times I guess I just feel it would be too soon, right now. There's things I don't want to lose, and I'm not sure what they are."

Staying unmarried allows emerging adults to keep their options open, not just in terms of whom they might marry but in terms of whom they might become and what they might decide to do with their lives. What if you decide you want to move across the country to train to be a helicopter pilot, as Carl is thinking of doing? What if you decide you want to join the Peace Corps and move to another part of the world for a while, as Maya is thinking of doing? As long as you remain unmarried, those kinds of choices continue to seem possible.

The Age 30 Deadline

Although there may be no "right" age to marry for emerging adults, age 30 comes up a lot as the age by which they would like to be married. For some, 30 is the age by which they imagine that they will be finished with their identity explorations and ready to commit themselves to someone else. Scott chose age 30 as the upper limit for marrying because "I'd like to be focused by 30, be settled down and working in my long-term job or what-ever. I'd just like to be focused by that age." Sheila also thought she would be done with her independent explorations by age 30 and ready to marry.

> I hope to be married by the time I'm 30. I mean, I don't see it being any time before that. I just think I have a lot of life left in me, and I want to enjoy it. There's so much out there, not that you couldn't see it with your

husband, but why have to worry "Is he going to get mad at this?" Just go out and enjoy life and then settle down, and you'll know you've done everything possible that you wanted to do, and you won't regret getting married.

For many emerging adults, especially women, age 30 is the deadline age because it fits with their Plan for the rest of their lives. If they get married by age 30, that gives them 2 or 3 years to establish intimacy with their spouse and still have time to have a child or two before they pass their prime child-bearing years. Nancy, who will be 28 in two months, said she'd like to get married to her boyfriend "ASAP!" but by age 30 at the latest, because "I feel very strongly about being married several years before starting a family, just in terms of getting to know each other, which much past 30 puts you into your mid-thirties to start a family and that concerns me, I guess." Sandy voiced similar sentiments: "I'd like to be married before 30, but definitely by 30 because I'd like to have time to spend with my husband before we have kids, just to get to know each other better before the family thing. And once you get to a certain age, you just don't really have time for that."

So, in theory, they can get married whenever they want, whenever they decide the time is right, but in practice age 30 is for many people a deadline age. It is the age by which they want to get married, and it is also the age by which they feel that other people expect them to get married. Emerging adults start to feel the pressure of these expectations as they cross into their late twenties. Often the pressure comes from parents. Sometimes this pressure is mild, as for Wendy, whose mother, "hinting around about grandchildren," helpfully suggested, "You should go to Alaska. There's a ratio of like 2 to 1 men to women."

Sometimes the pressure from parents is more intense, especially for Asian Americans. Because Asian American parents are less individualistic and more collectivistic in their values than most other Americans,[9] they feel fewer qualms about telling their emerging adult children what they should be doing. They often tell them explicitly that they have an obligation to keep the family line going. Greg, a 23-year-old Chinese American, said his parents tell him, "They really want to see grandchildren. I think it would provide them more of a sense of accomplishment if they saw that they had not only taken care of me but that they also provided for a new generation. And so they can rest assured that 'our family moves on. It doesn't stop here. All that hard work paid off.'"

Asian American immigrant parents also sometimes bring traditional beliefs from their home countries about gender roles, specifically the belief that women should focus on finding a husband and having children. Vanessa, whose parents immigrated from Taiwan, said her mother "doesn't understand why I'm working so hard to get a master's degree. She thinks a husband is the most important part in your life. If you can find a nice husband to marry, even though you only graduated from elementary school, that would be enough."

Sometimes pressure to get married comes from friends. Emerging adults whose friends are marrying may find themselves the object of unwanted expectations. Tory said he and his girlfriend "went to nine weddings this year. We're the last ones left. So yeah, there's a lot of pressure. And she gets really mad when everybody goes, 'Well, when are you guys going to get married?' It's to the point now where she's tired of hearing it." Melissa, who has been with her boyfriend on and off for several years, said, "Our friends are getting married and that kind of puts pressure on you because everybody says, 'Well, you'll be getting married next.' And then it'll be 'When are you having kids?'"

Of course, then there are emerging adults such as Brock, who says, "To be honest with you, I look at all my friends who have gotten married and think they've made the hugest mistake of their life." Most emerging adults would probably agree with Kwame:

> It's not when you get married, it's who you marry. That's the whole thing. If you find your happiness early, that's great. If you find your happiness later, that's great, too, 'cause the whole thing about it, you gotta make sure you're happy for yourself. Don't feel like you've been forced into any situation.

So, some emerging adults may feel pressure to get married, but most of them are intent on deciding for themselves when the time is right.

Commitment: His and Hers

Young men and women are more similar than different when it comes to deciding about marriage. Both want to find someone who is similar to themselves in key ways and who is easy to live with. Both want to have a period of years in emerging adulthood to learn to stand on their own, to make independent decisions, and to explore the possibilities available to them before committing themselves to marriage. Both get more serious about finding a marriage partner once they reach their late twenties and see the age 30 deadline looming only a few years off.

Less rigid gender roles than in the past make it possible for men and women to meet on more equal ground in their love relationships. Young women no longer need to feel that they have to marry as soon as possible in order to have a man to support them and in order to have a legitimate, respected role in their society. They no longer have to fear being stigmatized as an "old maid" if they pass age 25 without a wedding ring on their finger. Young men no longer need to worry that in order to marry they must first be capable of being the sole "breadwinner" for a wife and, very soon, children. Young men and women can now, more than any time in the past, anticipate a marriage in which they will be equal partners and have a relationship as soul mates plus sex.

Still, it is unmistakable that women feel more pressure than men to find a marriage partner before age 30. They feel this pressure partly because they believe they face a biological deadline—if they wish to have children, as most of them do, they want to have them no later than their early thirties, because the risk of infertility and prenatal development problems rises substantially by the late thirties. But part of the pressure is also social and cultural—they fear that by the time they pass age 30 they will have missed their chance to marry because men their age will prefer younger women. The term "old maid" may be used rarely today, but the stigma it represents still lingers. Jake was quite blunt in assessing the issue from a man's perspective.

> I think men have a great advantage over women in that they can be at an older age when they get married because it's acceptable for a man to marry someone of a younger age. Like, I could be 35 and marry someone who's 23. I mean, I've got all the time in the world.

This difference between men and women in how their attractiveness as a potential marriage partner changes with age sometimes results in tension within couples who are in their late twenties and serious about each other but not engaged or married. She, believing that her time is running out, is often eager to marry, although she realizes she has to be careful about seeming too eager—it is no longer acceptable for women to be seen as trying to "catch" a husband. He, on the other hand, may feel like he has "all the time in the world," as Jake put it. He wants to stay involved with her, but he sees no need to hurry the decision about whether to marry her.[10]

The views of Jean, 26, and Trey, 28, illustrate this difference. They have been seeing each other for two years and living together for a year and a half. Jean says, "I'd like to be engaged before Christmas." If not by Christmas, well, then, at least "within the next year to two years." If not within the next year or two, OK, but "it would be nice to be married by the time I'm 30," even though "it's not going to kill me if I'm not."

Talk to Trey and you get a much different perspective. It becomes clear that Jean can forget about getting engaged by Christmas, and it's a good thing it's not going to kill her if she's not married by age 30. Trey says he might get married—"possibly someday." He is well aware that "my significant other would probably like it to be soon," but he says, "I'm not quite ready for that." Originally he thought he would be married by age 25, but "that's past. And then it was 30, and that's approaching and I don't think I'll feel too bad if that goes by either." For now, he has decided, "I'm not ready to settle down. I'm more on the side of 'I've got plenty of time yet.'"

Jean was taking the delay in her marriage hopes pretty well at this point, but other young women express frustration at the difficulty they face in getting their young men to make a commitment to marriage. Twenty-seven-year-old Christy and her boyfriend have been seeing each other for three and a half years, and for all but the first year of that period he has been in medical school. She has been supportive of him during the stresses of his medical training. "I've been understanding. I've pretty much helped him through med school emotionally." But three months ago, he suddenly told her, "I don't think I'll ever get married." Surprised and dismayed, she told him, "'Well, I'm sorry, but I'm going to leave you now,' and we didn't talk for three weeks."

Then he called her and said he had reconsidered. He agreed to marry her—sort of. "He said, 'I will marry you,' so I did get a verbal agreement from him," she said, sounding like someone trying to coax a reluctant potential client into signing a contract. He has told her they will talk about becoming officially engaged when he finishes medical school in a year and a half. Although she remains skeptical of his commitment to her, she figures, "I will only lose about 18 months at the most if I wait it out." She is telling herself to be patient, because "men think of it differently. They don't want to feel like there's a time limit, where they're feeling like they're being coerced or rushed." But if he doesn't come through when medical school is over, "I'm fully prepared to leave, although it would be very hard."

I want to emphasize again that men and women are more alike than different in how they view marriage. Most people, men and women both, feel ready to enter marriage by the time they reach their late twenties. Like Joel, they "get tired of going home every night and looking at four walls by myself." Like Joseph, they anticipate that it will be nice "not to have to worry about who I'm going to be sleeping with or worry about what they've got or who they've been with, or even have to mess with the dating thing." Nevertheless, when there is a difference between partners in their feelings of readiness for marriage, it is usually the woman who feels ready and wants to get on with it while the man is reluctant and is dragging his feet.

One Foot In: Cohabitation

For emerging adults who do not feel ready to marry but who want to have many of the benefits of marriage—daily companionship, shared expenses, more frequent sex—there is the alternative of cohabitation. This is an alternative that was not as readily available in previous generations. Figure 5.1, adapted from a national study, shows how the proportion of young people who cohabited with at least one person prior to marriage changed in the course of the past half century.[11]

As the figure shows, for the generation that reached their twenties in the 1950s and early 1960s, cohabitation was extremely rare. Nearly every-

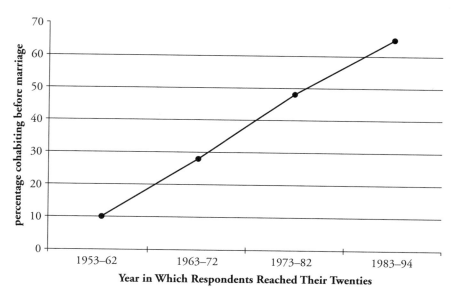

Figure 5.1. Historical Changes in Cohabitation

one waited until marriage before living with a romantic partner. Even for young people in the late 1960s and early 1970s, the generation of the much-discussed Sexual Revolution, cohabitation remained relatively rare, practiced by less than one-third of young people. This was an increase from the previous generation, but cohabiters were still a minority. However, by the 1980s and 1990s, cohabitation was the norm, and today two-thirds of emerging adults live with a romantic partner before marriage.

Although the rise in cohabitation has been dramatic, placing all cohabiters into one category is a bit misleading. There are three distinct kinds of cohabitation, very different from each other. The two most common types are what I call *premarital cohabitation* and *uncommitted cohabitation*.[12] In premarital cohabitation, the two emerging adults have firm plans to marry. They may be officially engaged and may even have set a date for their wedding. In uncommitted cohabitation, however, the two emerging adults have made no long-term commitment to each other. One partner or the other may be hoping their relationship will lead to marriage eventually, but the fact that they are living together does not signify that marriage between them is imminent or even likely in the long run.

Premarital cohabiters often want to test their compatibility before they enter marriage.[13] Pete and his wife lived together for about a year before they married recently, and he's glad they did. "I don't see how people can do it without that. I wanted to make sure she doesn't throw her socks on top of the sink and if she puts the top back on the toothpaste and stuff. All those little things." Mindy and her boyfriend have been living together for five months. They are engaged, but before they married, "we wanted to try it out and see how we got along, because I've had so many long-term relationships. I just wanted to make sure we were compatible. And he'd been married before, and he felt the same way."

As Mindy's comments suggest, premarital cohabiters often decide to live together in the hope that doing so will make it less likely that they will divorce. Indeed, in a national survey of 20–29-year-olds, 62% agreed that "living together with someone before marriage is a good way to avoid eventual divorce."[14] Emerging adults who have experienced their parents' divorce are especially likely to mention this as a reason for cohabiting. They have seen divorce up close, and they want to avoid it themselves if at all possible. By living together before marriage, they hope to improve their odds.

Jackie and her fiancé both have divorced parents; his mother has been divorced three times. Burned by divorce and wary of marriage, they decided to live together during their engagement to try to make sure it would work.

"I'm not going to marry somebody and maybe have children and then have him walk out or me feel like this was a big mistake," she said. Unfortunately for Jackie and young people like her, the likelihood of divorce for young people who live together and then marry is higher, not lower, compared to their peers.[15]

Premarital cohabiters also may have practical reasons for moving in together. He or she has a lease ending and cannot or does not want to find a new roommate; he or she wants to escape a current roommate; they both want to save on their expenses. They will be getting married soon anyway—why not just move in? But even if they have practical reasons as well, premarital cohabiters are motivated to live together mainly because they are committed to each other and the momentum of their relationship is toward marriage.

In contrast, uncommitted cohabiters almost always move in together mainly or solely for practical reasons, because their relationship lacks a shared understanding that they are headed toward marriage. For Amelia and her boyfriend, their decision to live together was motivated primarily by high rental prices in San Francisco. They talk about marriage only "in an abstract sense, more like in a someday type of thing or jokingly like, 'Oh yeah, we'll get married when I'm old,' you know, stuff like that." Living together is seen by both of them as likely to be temporary. "We both want to go back to school and want to do a lot things so it's sort of like . . . you know, there's a good chance we're gonna be apart for a while, too, and so like we'll take that as it comes. But getting married right now? I don't feel like I'm ready to make that type of decision yet."

The third type, which I call *committed cohabitation*, is essentially a stable—if often impermanent—substitute for marriage. Partners in this type of cohabitation are committed to each other, as premarital cohabiters are, but like uncommitted cohabiters they have no intention of ever entering marriage. Leah has been living with her boyfriend for a year and says, "I don't expect to get married to him or anybody. I don't view marriage as being very important. I mean, I basically consider myself to be married to Brad. There's just not a legal document that says that we're married. I just don't believe that you need to have a piece of paper that ties you up with somebody like that."

In the United States, this view is unusual among emerging adults. Even among the uncommitted cohabiters, nearly all of them eventually want to get married—to someone, if not to their current partner.[16] However, committed cohabitation is growing in the United States and is already quite common in northern Europe. For example, in Sweden, 53% of children are born to cohabiters, and only about half of cohabiting parents have married five years after the birth.[17] But even in Sweden and other northern European countries, cohabiting relationships are less "committed" than marriage is—that is, cohabiting relationships are more likely than marriages to dissolve, and marriages are more likely to end in divorce if they are preceded by cohabitation.[18]

What makes marriage different from cohabitation? Why don't more emerging adults take the committed cohabitation path of Leah and Brad and simply "consider themselves married" without obtaining the legal document, especially if they already live together? Marriage is different precisely because it requires the legal document, the ceremony, the public declaration of the intention to remain together "'til death do us part." This makes marriage not only a private commitment between two people but a social commitment, backed up by the expectations of society, by the power of tradition, and by the force of law. And marriage really is different from cohabitation in terms of the effects it has on the people involved. According to a substantial body of research, marriage has a variety of positive effects on psychological health, financial well-being, and emotional well-being that cohabitation does not.[19]

Each partner gains from marriage a sense of security, a promise that their partner is serious about staying with them for life. This may seem ironic, given that nearly half of all marriages in the United States end in divorce. But almost no one who enters marriage expects to end up among the half who divorce. Upon entering marriage, partners at least have from one another a declaration of their intention to remain together permanently.

The relationship between Mike and Laurie illustrates some of these issues. They have been married for a year, after living together for five years. Talking about the past year, Mike first says, "Being married wasn't a big change other than I have a ring on my hand now and a piece of paper that says we're married." But then he adds:

> I take that back. It does make the relationship a little more comfortable to know that the escape hatch isn't standing open just waiting for you to walk out. Once you're married, it kind of forces you to at least try to work things out before somebody packs up and goes.

For Laurie, the five years of living together were more fraught with anxiety, and marriage has been more of a relief. "I think during that time I was really stressed, because I didn't know exactly whether or not I was going to be with him or if I was wasting that much time in my life." She felt that, as a woman, she was risking more by living with someone for so long without the commitment of marriage. "I think it's always a major thing for a woman, whether or not they're going to find somebody." To her, living together unmarried, even for as long as five years, meant that they were "not really committed. You could leave at any time. There's always a chance that the other one is going to leave." Now that she and Mike are married, she feels liberated from that anxiety. "Once you [get] married, there's no turning back. You're bound for life."

We can see, then, that marriage is different from cohabitation not just legally but *psychologically*. The two partners are still living together after marriage, just as they were before. There is still the possibility that they will split up eventually, just as there was before. But once they move from cohabitation to marriage, it *feels different*. Whatever the future may actually hold, when they enter marriage they believe and hope they are making a lifelong commitment, that they are "bound for life."

In addition to the desire for this psychological sense of permanence, what moves emerging adults from cohabitation to marriage is social pressure, especially from parents. Although there is no longer a deep social stigma attached to having premarital sex or cohabiting in American society, there are many parents who have mixed feelings about it or who oppose it, especially when their own son or daughter is involved.[20]

Few emerging adults have any moral qualms about cohabiting. For them it is normal, typical, and perfectly acceptable, something that most people their age do at some point.[21] But for their parents, who grew up at a time when cohabiting was considered daring if not scandalous, the prospect of seeing their own child move in with a lover may not be something they welcome. Especially when the cohabitation is uncommitted, many parents are adamantly opposed to it. Grandparents, remembering a time when cohabitation was known as "living in sin," also sometimes register their opposition.

To avoid confronting their parents about the issue and facing their opposition directly, many emerging adults adopt a strategy I call *semi-cohabiting*, in which they maintain two residences even though they essentially live together at one or the other. When I asked Steve if he and his girlfriend were living together, he said, "Lease-wise, no," meaning, "I have my own place and she has her own place, but we basically spend most of our time together." Semicohabiting is a necessary strategy for them because her parents have told her she cannot move in with him. But it is a source of great irritation and unnecessary expense in his eyes. "We're paying two rents and two utilities and two of this and the other, and it doesn't make any sense to me."

It is interesting to note that semicohabiters may respond no to a simple yes-no question about whether they are cohabiting, as Steve did at first. This suggests that the proportion of emerging adults who cohabit before marriage may be even higher than the two thirds reported in surveys, because the surveys may miss those who are semicohabiting. It seems reasonable to count the semicohabiters as people who are cohabiting, since they are living together for all practical purposes except "lease-wise."

Besides stating their opposition to cohabiting, parents can also obstruct it by withholding resources from their emerging adult children. Leslie and her boyfriend, Rich, are 20-year-old college students at the University of Missouri. She says, "I think we both would prefer to live together, but his parents don't approve of that, and they won't help him with school if he does." Rich says they have made this known to him "very blatantly." So he and Leslie are semicohabiting as long as they are still in school and he is financially dependent on his parents.

However, parents' power to obstruct cohabitation diminishes as emerging adults move into their mid-twenties and become less dependent on their parents financially and more intent on making their own decisions. When Ginny told her parents that she and her boyfriend were going to move in together, her mother threatened her "by just saying things like, 'Oh, you're not going to get any money from us.' You know, making it clear that money was directing a lot of her orders."

But Ginny was 24 by then and no longer depended on her parents financially. It was difficult nevertheless to defy her parents, but she was able to do so because she did not need the money they threatened to withhold. "I had always done everything they told me to do, and now I made my own decision. I said, 'You know, I really can't do what you want me to do this time because this is too important to me. This one I'm not going to compromise on.'" Financial independence allows emerging adults to make their own decisions about cohabiting even if it means overriding their parents' objections.

"A Horrible Alone Feeling": The Shadow of Divorce

Although nearly all emerging adults eventually want to get married, and although they often have high hopes for the kind of marriage they will have, they realize that today in American society marriage is often a temporary rather than a permanent bond. The ship of hopes they send out on their wedding day amid sunshine and celebration may, some years later, end up being dashed against the rocks. Divorce looms before them as the thundercloud on the horizon, carrying the storm they may already have seen claim the hopes of their parents, siblings, or friends.

The fear of divorce, and the desire to avoid it, has contributed to the rise in the marriage age that has made emerging adulthood a distinct stage of life. True, most emerging adults postpone marriage until at least their late twenties so that they can be free to pursue opportunities in school, work, and leisure, and free to have a variety of intimate relationships. But for some of them postponing marriage also has fear as a motivation, fear of divorce and the desire to be as certain as possible that their marriage will succeed.[22]

We have already seen how fear of divorce can be a motive for cohabiting. But even for many emerging adults who do not cohabit or who do so for other reasons, fear of divorce is often part of their thinking about marriage. It leads them to be wary of marriage and to delay it until they feel as confident as possible that they are making the right choice with the right person. Dana and her boyfriend have been seeing each other for five years and living together for two and a half years. They are engaged to be married this summer. They might have married years earlier, but "we wanted to make sure that we were doing what was best for both of us. I mean, we didn't want to get married and then get divorced two years later. We wanted to be sure." Wesley is 22 and doesn't see himself being married for many years yet. "I want to wait until I'm older because I know a lot of people who get married young and then there's a lot of fights and stuff. Personally I think I'd rather wait until I know myself a little bit better and probably the person I marry a little bit better so we're more secure with each other." Sheila thinks her parents divorced because they married young and her father "felt trapped." So for herself, she wants to finish her emerging adult explorations before she thinks about getting married, in the hope that she'll be less likely to divorce when she does marry.

I think everyone should experience everything they want to experience before they get tied down, because if you wanted to date a Black person, a White person, an Asian person, a tall person, short, fat, whatever, as long as you know you've accomplished all that, and you are happy with who you are with, then I think everything would be OK. I want to experience life and know that when that right person comes, I won't have any regrets.

As Sheila's comments suggest, emerging adults with divorced parents often take their cues from their parents in learning what *not* to do in a marriage. In the course of witnessing the breakup of their parents' marriage, they observed their parents behaving in ways they hope not to repeat themselves. For Dana, her parents' divorce comes to mind whenever she and her live-in boyfriend have a disagreement, as a model of what to avoid. "When I see myself saying or doing something that I remember them saying or doing before they got divorced, I try to stop myself and back up."

Emerging adults are especially motivated by a desire to spare their future children the pain they experienced. Melissa, who has been living with her boyfriend for the past two years, said that before they decide to get married, "I think we both want to be really sure because his parents are divorced and mine are, too. I don't want to go through what my parents did, and I don't want to have kids and put them through what happened, and he wouldn't either. So I think we're both real careful about that." Dan said that witnessing his parents' bitter divorce and problematic remarriages has made him "scared to death of divorce. It's hell. Divorce is so painful for everybody, you know, and when you get some kids involved, that's a big deal. So I've been really careful, and I know what I want, and I wouldn't settle for anything."

Samuel Johnson wrote centuries ago that "remarriage is the triumph of hope over experience." For today's emerging adults, especially those with divorced parents, even a first marriage often represents such a triumph. But, with such hopes and such determination about making their marriages last, how could it be that emerging adults whose parents have divorced have an even higher likelihood of divorce than those with nondivorced parents? What happens to the emphatic resolutions of people like Melissa to be "really sure" before they enter marriage? Why don't the experiences of people like Dan, which have made them "scared to death of divorce" and vow to be "really careful" about marriage, make them any less likely to become divorced eventually themselves?

The explanation seems to be that even though witnessing parents' divorce is often horrifying and deeply painful, it also makes divorce seem more acceptable as an option when a marriage is unhappy.[23] Rob's parents divorced recently after 25 years of a marriage that was not satisfying for either of them. After hesitating for a long time to marry his girlfriend, his parents' divorce inspired him to become engaged to her, because now he has "the knowledge that if it doesn't work out, you know, divorce is a way out of it, and it's acceptable. You're not trapped. I think their divorce now, for me, says, 'Well, if you don't get along, it's OK. You can get divorced. It's not going to be the end of the world.'" Similarly, Jake saw his parents divorce when he was in high school, after years of being unhappy together, and he concluded:

> I don't think divorce is such a bad thing because I don't think you should spend your time with somebody that you're not enjoying. It just doesn't make any sense. I think that's why divorces happen more often now, because people realize they should be happy, you know. It's not their job to make somebody else happy. I just don't think that's right.

It works the other way, too: Emerging adults whose parents have had long, reasonably happy marriages see divorce as a less acceptable option. Maya said her parents' long marriage has taught her that "I don't feel like you can choose to get married and then choose to end it. I think you need to decide before you get married, and I think that if I married someone, even if I wasn't necessarily perfectly happy, I wouldn't divorce him." Terrell said his parents have impressed upon him that his marriage, like theirs, ought to be for life. "I was always raised to believe that when you get married, you stay married. So when you get married to somebody, you better know it's the right person. It's a lifetime commitment."

Even emerging adults whose parents are still together cannot help but witness many examples of marriages that have failed—brothers, sisters, friends, uncles, aunts, cousins, coworkers. Although they fervently hope their own marriage will last for life, they are all too aware of how common it is for once-hopeful couples to end their marriages in acrimony and divorce. Holly has been talking to a coworker who is in the process of divorce, and now the thought of divorce "just scares me to death, because I even asked him, 'Well, there must have been something good there once, a long time ago?' and he's like, 'Well, I thought there was.' Well, everybody thinks there is. Nobody goes into it going, 'Someday we'll hate each other's guts.' So it just scares me to death." They try to keep their hopes up even as they shudder to think what divorce would be like. Gabriella's comments sum it up: "I think it would be a horrible alone feeling. When I think of divorce, I think of loneliness. I think it would be really hard to start all over again. Hopefully I'll find somebody that I will be with forever."

Conclusion: Marriage Hopes, Marriage Fears

Just as with love and sex, when it comes to marriage emerging adults today have greater freedoms than the young people of the past. There are no longer any rigid expectations about the right age to marry that push young people to rush into marriage before they feel ready, with someone about whom they may have serious doubts. Most emerging adults want to marry by age 30, but that gives them the entire decade of their twenties to meet people, have different relationships, and find someone with whom they wish to commit themselves to a common future. Even for emerging adults who do not marry by age 30, their marriage prospects are by no means over. Twenty-five percent of young people are still unmarried when they reach 30, so emerging adults who are in that group have plenty of company and plenty of people left to choose from.

Flexible expectations for when to marry allow emerging adults to time their decision on when to marry according to what fits best with the individual circumstances of their lives, rather than according to what other people are doing. For some, that means waiting until they have finished an extended period of education or attained financial stability, or until they have tried various career paths and settled upon one they believe suits them well. For others, it means waiting for less tangible changes, until they know themselves well enough and have a clear enough identity that they feel ready to commit themselves to another person.

For many, it means waiting until they find someone who at least approximates the ideal they imagine: a marriage partner who will be kind, loving, attractive, and similar to themselves in what they like to do and how they look at the world. Until they find their soul mate or someone close to it, they can have other relationships that involve love and sex. They are also free to cohabit with someone if they wish, in order to have daily companionship and save on their expenses without the binding commitment of marriage.

Yet, as with love and sex, the freedoms of emerging adults in their marriage decisions are tinged with fear and anxiety. It may seem like an advantage to have various love partners without being bound by the commitment and restrictions of marriage—unless you are the one who would like to have the commitment. You may be in love with someone, having sex with them, even living with them, and yet they may feel no long-term obligation to you. You may have given yourself to them, body, heart, and soul, yet they could walk out any time. Young women, especially, sometimes fear that they may use up their twenties in a relationship or a series of relationships that do not lead to marriage, only to find themselves at 30 feeling that their marriage prospects are sharply reduced.

For young men and young women alike, divorce lurks among their marriage hopes as a potential disaster. They are well aware that divorce is prevalent in American society. They do not need the statistics to tell them, because they have seen it happen to the people around them, if not to their parents then to siblings, other relatives, friends, or coworkers.

They do what they can to try to avoid the same fate. Cohabiting is not just for convenience or companionship, but to see what it is like to live with that person, to try to detect any major problems so that an unhappy marriage and an unhappier divorce can be avoided. Waiting until at least their late twenties to get married is not just to allow years for exploration during emerging adulthood, but to allow them to reach a level of maturity and judgment they hope will lead them to make the right choice in marriage.

Even then, of course, there is no guarantee they will make a choice they will not regret and that their marriage will work out as they wish. As Holly observed, nobody goes into marriage thinking, "Someday we'll hate each other's guts." Emerging adults look ahead to marriage as they look ahead to much of life, wary but optimistic, aware of the hazards before them but confident that they have it within their power to shape the future into something resembling their dreams.

6

The Road Through College

Twists and Turns

THESE DAYS, IT IS WIDELY RECOGNIZED that you have to have a college education in order to get a good job in American society. As numerous studies have shown, number of years of college education is positively related to a variety of good things in adulthood, such as higher income and occupational status.[1] Emerging adults may not know the studies or the statistics, but they know, from what they have seen friends, neighbors, and family members experience, that a college education opens up a wide range of job possibilities and that those who don't have one face more limited, less promising employment options. So, as they leave high school, 9 out of 10 young Americans expect to continue their education by attending college.[2] About two thirds actually enter college in the year following high school.[3]

Although schooling now continues after high school for most young Americans, the significance of school changes from adolescence to emerging adulthood. With some exceptions, most American adolescents don't take high school very seriously. They find it boring, except for the fun of seeing their friends.[4] They are rarely engaged in what is taking place in the classroom, and they rarely do much homework.[5] They don't really expect to learn anything important in high school. Few adolescents expect their high school education to provide the basis for what they will do as their adult occupation. In my study, only 35% of emerging adults agreed with the statement "My high school education prepared me well for the workplace."

In emerging adulthood, school takes on an entirely new significance. Now you have to think about how your education will prepare you for the workplace. Instead of simply going to your local high school, you have to choose from a wide range of possible colleges. And once you enter college, it's not so easy to just show up and shrug your way through it, as you may have in high school. If you are not engaged in the classroom and you don't do your homework, your college professors are less likely simply to pass you through, as your high school teachers did. In college, you have to develop enough self-discipline to get yourself to class and do the work required, or you may find yourself flunking out. The stakes are also higher in college because somebody, probably you or your parents, is paying real money for you to go, money that will be wasted if you don't pass your classes. Thus school, like love, becomes more serious in emerging adulthood, more focused on laying the foundation for adult life.

Because a college education has become a requirement for obtaining the best jobs available in the economy of the 21st century, attending college has become the typical experience for young people in American society. By age 25, nearly 70% of emerging adults have obtained at least some college education.[6] This percentage is considerably higher than in most other industrialized countries. Figures in Canada and Japan are similar to the United States, but in most countries in Europe and Asia the availability of higher education is more restricted.[7] These countries also tend to be better at preparing young people for work at the high school level, through apprenticeships and school-to-work programs, so that there is less need for them to obtain higher education in order to develop skills useful in the workplace.[8]

No other country in the world has a system of higher education as open and extensive as the United States, with more than 4,000 colleges, universities, and community colleges. In this way American society supports an extended emerging adulthood, in which young people have abundant opportunities to obtain higher education that will allow them to explore a wide range of possible occupational futures. Young Americans are able to keep their work options open for a long time as they try out different college majors before choosing a specific direction. In Europe, young people who attend university must enter with their major already decided; they do not take general education classes for a year or two while they decide on a major, as college students do in the United States, but take classes only in the area they have chosen to study before entering.

The percentage of today's American emerging adults in higher education is not only higher than in other industrialized countries, it is also higher than at any time in American history.[9] Until the middle of the 20th century, higher education was mainly for the elite. In 1900 only 4% of 18–

24-year-olds had attended college, and by 1940 that proportion had risen only to 16%. But the percentage rose steadily through the second half of the twentieth century, as Figure 6.1 shows,[10] and college has become an experience shared by the great majority of emerging adults in the early 21st century.

In fact, the spread of college education has been an important influence in creating a distinct period of emerging adulthood in American society. Emerging adulthood is characterized by identity explorations in love and work, and attending college allows young people to explore various possible educational directions that would lead to different occupational futures. Because of the extensiveness and openness of the American system of higher education, young people in the United States are more likely than young people in virtually any other country in the world to have the opportunity for an extended period of educational exploration. College is also a prime setting for love explorations, because it brings together in one place a large concentration of people who are mostly emerging adults and mostly unmarried.

In this chapter, we examine a variety of aspects of emerging adults' college experiences. First, we look at how emerging adults chart their course through college, including choosing a college major from among the many options available to them. This section also contains a look at emerging

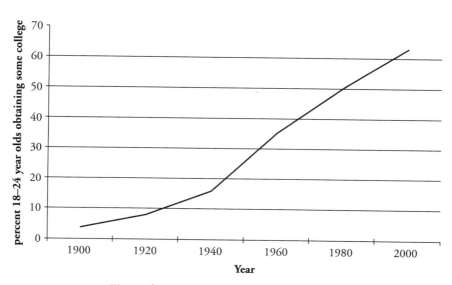

Figure 6.1.   College Enrollment, 1900–2000

adults who succeed in college and those who flounder, and some reasons for the differences. Then we will take a critical look at the American system of allowing such widespread access to higher education and compare it to the European system, looking at the pros and cons of each. In the second half of the chapter, we look at what undergraduates have to say about their college experiences, for better and worse.

Charting a Course Through College

As they enter college in the fall following their graduation from high school, most emerging adults have only the most general idea of what they want to study when they get there.[11] They know that they want to get a college degree. They know that attending college is important for their future, because a person with a college degree is likely to make considerably more money than a person without one. They may look forward to the nonacademic pleasures of college life: meeting a variety of new people, dating a variety of new people, falling in love, making new friends, getting drunk, running their own lives independently of their parents. They may have made a tentative decision about a field of study. But few of them have made a definite choice of an occupation that they will be preparing themselves for as the purpose of their college studies.

College in the United States is for finding out what you want to do. Typically at four-year colleges, you have two years before you have to make a definite decision and declare a major. During those two years you can try out a variety of different possibilities by taking classes in areas you think you might want to major in. And even after you declare a major, you can always change your mind—and many emerging adults do.

Their college meanderings are part of their identity explorations. In taking various classes and trying various potential college majors, they are trying to answer the question "What kind of job would really fit me best, given my abilities and interests?" Many are waiting for something to click, searching for that "aha!" moment when they know they have found their true calling. Some find it, some do not. But college at least gives them the opportunity.

Many emerging adults have complicated tales to tell about their search for a college major that fits with their developing identity. For example, Barbara has changed her major four times since entering college six years ago.

I started out in chemistry actually. I wanted to go into pathology or radiology. And then I went through a stage where I wanted to be in pharmacy school and do some drug testing in space. Then I decided that that probably wasn't going to be realistic. I kept changing my mind. I went back to chemistry. And then I got into the business end of it, into accounting, but I decided that I did not want to sit in an office all day long. I wanted to be out seeing more people every day.

Now, she is majoring in "administration of athletics" and plans to get a job arranging advertising and promotion for athletic events. She grew up in an athletic family—her father was a professional athlete, and all of the children were involved in sports—and athletics feels like the right fit to her. "I've just always enjoyed sports. It was just a love of sports more than anything" that eventually led her in this career direction.

Ken also followed a twisting road during college, through four different degree programs.

The first major I got into was in communications/public relations, but I didn't really care for that one. So I switched to educational counseling psychology, leaning more towards teaching social studies. And then I went into physical education and was going to be a teacher/coach. Finally I ended up taking a physiology class and really liking it. Then one thing led to another, and I ended up getting a degree in exercise physiology.

It took him seven years to graduate, but he has no regrets about it. "I think when I finally ended up graduating, I had 140 to 150 hours of class work just because I'd changed so many times. There were a lot of things I enjoyed in terms of class work."

Some emerging adults, especially the younger ones, are still looking, still waiting for something to click. Elaine is about to enter her third year of college, but she still has not decided what she wants to study.

I don't have a major right now. I'm undecided. And I have absolutely no idea. I mean, I have a lot of interests—that's the problem. I can't decide on just one to stick with for the rest of my college career. I'm interested in psychology. Also in sciences, like, any of the sciences. I guess [I lean] mainly toward biology. I'm kind of interested in law. Law is kind of overwhelming thinking about it, but law. And arts. I love drawing. I'm not very good at it, but I think I'm kind of good at, like, designing things. I

thought about maybe going to fashion school. Everyone I know is majoring in business, but it's not my thing. So I don't think I'm going to get
into that.

So, she has narrowed it down to the arts, the sciences, psychology, law,
or fashion design—pretty much anything but business! Clearly she still has
a long way to go in her school explorations before she finds the right fit,
but she remains hopeful. "I guess to me the important thing is to be able to
actually find that little niche and get there and be able to make lots of money
and be happy and still have time for myself."

In general, the late teens and early twenties, the years that are the heart
of emerging adulthood, are the main years of educational exploration for
most people. Few people are still bouncing from one possible path to another by the time they reach their late twenties. In both love and work, most
people make a transition by their late twenties from the explorations of
emerging adulthood to the more settled choices of young adulthood. They
may obtain more education later in their twenties or beyond, but it is likely
to be in the field they have already chosen.

Some emerging adults enter college with a major influenced strongly
by their parents, only to discover that it does not fit at all with their own
identity. Rob was a pre–veterinary medicine major during his first year in
college, following in the footsteps of his veterinarian father. However, he
soon realized, "I really wasn't that interested in the chemistry and biology
that I was taking." Trying to figure out what he really wanted to do, he
thought about how "I've always been mathematically inclined," and he
decided to take a few courses in accounting. It clicked, and he changed his
major to business.

For Cindy, the influence from her parents was more explicit.

> I have Asian parents, so every Asian parent's dream—especially if they've
> immigrated here—they want to live their dreams through their children
> because they never had the chance to go through education. So my par-
> ents' dream was always for us—there's three girls in my family—to pur-
> sue being a doctor or a lawyer. So I remember when I was little, my little
> sister said, "I'll go be a doctor," and I said, "Then I'll go be a lawyer."

She stuck with this resolve through childhood and entered the University
of California-Berkeley, intending to prepare herself for law school. But two
years into her college studies, she still had not declared a major. Her advi-
sor gave her a book with descriptions of 80 majors and told her to pick one

by the same time next week. "So I looked through the whole book," Cindy recalled, "and I thought, 'What do I really like doing?' I mean, I know my mom wants me to go be a lawyer, but I only live once, and I really want to do something that I really like doing. So I thought, 'There's something about being on stage that I really like,' and I'd done a lot of shows as a model." She decided to major in dance—about as far away from law as it is possible to be. Now graduated from Cal, she is a model and actress, and her dancing is one of the skills she has to offer as an actress.

Succeeding and Floundering

Although two thirds of American emerging adults enter college following high school, this does not mean that all of them follow a direct path to a college degree four years later. Quite the contrary. For most emerging adults, entering college means embarking on a winding educational path that may or may not lead to a degree. One fourth of college students drop out in their first year.[12] Among 25–29-year-olds, less than one third have obtained a bachelor's degree.[13] Even for emerging adults who do get a bachelor's degree, for most of them it takes at least five or six years to get a "four-year degree."[14]

There are many reasons why students often sputter in their educational progress once they enter college. With some emerging adults, it is clear that they were not ready for college when they entered. They didn't really know why they were there, they were not committed to it, and consequently they floundered. They may have come to college simply out of inertia, because it seemed like the thing to do, or because all of their friends were doing it and their parents expected them to do it, too. Cecilia went to college for a year and a half, but did poorly and dropped out. "I just wasn't ready. I wasn't really sure what I wanted to do. I wasn't studying." Instead, she spent her time "watching TV, going out, just anything but studying." Now, she is working as a cashier in a bookstore and trying to decide what to do next. She has a vague desire to enter a medical profession, but she says, "I'm not good at math, and there's a lot of classes like chemistry where you have to do lots of math." She admits she has "no clue" what she will be doing in 10 years.

Some enter college because of their parents' wishes rather than their own, and fail as an act of defiance. This was the case with Danielle. "My mom made me come to the university, and I didn't want to be there, so I was like, 'Well, I'll blow off school if I want.'" She was soon expelled for poor grades and spent three years drifting between low-wage jobs before she decided to reenter college—her own decision, this time. Now she is studying to be a nurse.

Some enter college and find they lack the self-discipline to get themselves to class and do their course work. They may enjoy the freedom of being away from home so much that they are easily distracted by the pleasures of the moment, which usually do not include studying. Jake nearly flunked out during his first two years of college, because he was too undisciplined and too busy with activities that diverted him from his school work. "I slept too much, played too many computer games, partied too much—all that stuff." Eventually he did get his degree, in psychology, and he now works as a bank teller. Looking back, he now thinks he lacked the maturity to make the most out of his early college years. "I wasn't ready. I should have gotten a job for maybe a year and then decided what I wanted to do. I think I would have gained some perspective."

This is a common sentiment among emerging adults in their mid-twenties, that they were too immature at age 18 or 19 to apply themselves to educational goals in college, and consequently their early college years were wasted. They got caught up in what education critic Murray Sperber calls the "beer and circus" of college life—the parties, the drinking, the social life, the sports events.[15]

Not that there is anything wrong with these things in moderation, but for many emerging adults moderation is not the standard they live by in their early college years. On the contrary, the pursuit of excess may be part of the fun of college life, part of what students view as the full college experience. This is especially evident with regard to alcohol use. College students drink more than emerging adults who are not college students, and in national studies nearly half of college students in their late teens and early twenties report drinking five or more alcoholic drinks at least once in the past two weeks.[16]

All of their lives, until they left home for college, their parents were around to exercise control on their behalf. Their parents made sure they got up in the morning to go to school; their parents kept track of how they were doing in their school work; their parents knew what they were doing after school and what time they came home at night. Sure, they were able to conceal some things from their parents, but they were always aware that their parents were keeping track of them. Once they leave home for college, their parents are no longer around to make sure they do things they are supposed to do—get up on time in the morning, go to class, do their

The academic demands of college sometimes come as a shock to emerging adults. (© Lynn Johnston Productions, Inc./Distributed by United Feature Syndicate.)

homework—or to discourage them from doing the things they are not supposed to do—go out drinking several times a week, stay out long past midnight, lie around with a hangover half the next day.

Many college students manage to handle their new freedoms well. By the time they leave for college, they have developed enough self-control that they no longer need to have their parents monitoring them in order for them to behave responsibly. They manage their own schedule, they get their school work done, they pass their classes. Although they may drink to excess, as long as they restrict their binges to the weekends they can still manage to get to class and do their school work. But for many others, the freedoms of college life prove to be too much for them to handle. With no one around to exercise control on their behalf, their own resources of self-control and self-discipline prove to be inadequate for the challenges of college life. They blow off their classes, they fail to do their course work, they drink too much too often, and eventually they drop out or get kicked out.

The cost of college is another reason why many students drop out before obtaining a degree. Since the 1980s, tuition costs at most colleges have risen at a steep rate, in part because financial support from state and federal governments has declined. During this same period, the focus of financial aid shifted from scholarships to loans, so students got whacked with a double whammy: higher costs, and less financial help to pay them. As a consequence, nearly 60% of students now hold a job while they go to school, and one fourth of students work full time.[17] Despite working, many students go deeply into debt during their college years. According to the most recent figures, the average student has accumulated about $15,000 in college debt by graduation.[18]

Imagine a student attending college as well as working 20, 30, even 40 hours a week, under constant pressure from juggling school and work, and sliding more deeply into debt with each semester. In this light, it does not seem surprising that many of them decide to give up school before finishing their degree. Especially for emerging adults who are undecided about a career path, staying in college may come to seem pointless under these conditions.

College dropout rates are higher among African Americans and Latinos than among Whites.[19] This may be partly because African Americans and Latinos tend to grow up in poorer areas and go to poorer schools than Whites, which makes them less prepared for the academic demands of college. However, it is also because the financial strain of college tends to be greater for African Americans and Latinos. The poorer a student's family, the more likely he or she is to drop out of college,[20] and African Americans and Latinos are more likely than Whites to have grown up in poor families.

In my research, ethnic differences in financial support for college were sharply evident in response to several of the items on the questionnaire, as shown in Figures 6.2, 6.3, and 6.4.

It is clear from these responses that in terms of their financial support for college, most African Americans and Latinos live in an entirely differ-

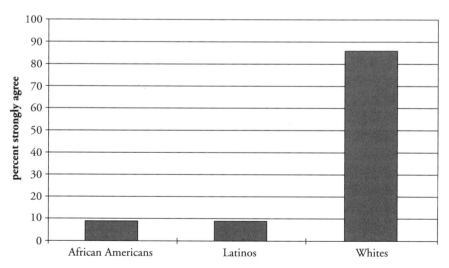

Figure 6.2. "In high school, I knew that if I wanted to go to college, it would be possible for me to find financial support either from my family or from scholarships, loans, or other programs." *Note*: This item was not included on the Asian American questionnaire.

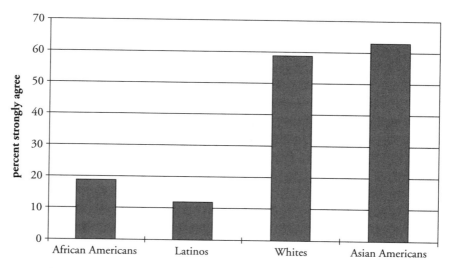

Figure 6.3. "For as long as I wished to continue my education, it would be possible for me to find financial support either from my family or from scholarships, loans, or other programs."

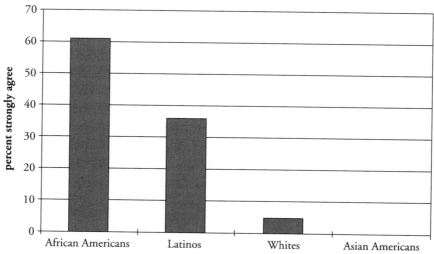

Figure 6.4. "It has been difficult for me to find the financial support to get the kind of education I really want."

ent world from most Whites and Asian Americans. For the most part, Whites and Asian Americans can assume that if they wish to go to college, the money will be there, one way or another, to allow them to get as much education as they need and want. In contrast, for most African Americans and Latinos, going to college is likely to be a financial struggle, and many of them are discouraged from getting as much education as they would like by their lack of financial resources.

This problem is evident in the life of Nicole, an African American emerging adult. She is one of four children of a single mother with psychological problems who was on welfare for most of the time Nicole was growing up. Since she was very young Nicole has had high educational goals, but so far those goals have been difficult for her to reach. She left home after high school after concluding, "I needed to experience living out of my mother's home in order to study," and has attended two junior colleges. But she has found it hard to make progress in her education while also working full time as a medical receptionist to support herself and to provide money for her mother. She has taken classes at night and is close to finishing an associate's degree, but "this semester, I took off. I said, 'I gotta get my funds together.' Hopefully by the time I'm 26, 27, I will have enough saved to go to school full time." She remains determined to achieve her ultimate goal of getting a Ph.D. and becoming a talk-radio psychologist, but the obstacles before her are formidable. We will hear more about Nicole's life in chapter 9.

Some emerging adults know from an early age what kind of work they want to do, and they enter college already firmly established on a path toward their career goal. For them, no period of exploration is necessary in their first year or two of college to allow them to find the kind of work that best fits with their identity. The purpose of college is to obtain the skills and the credentials that will enable them to do the work they know they are cut out to do. Gloria is studying to be an elementary school teacher because "I just really like children, and I've always wanted to work with them." Maya said, "I knew since I was five that I've wanted to do science," and now she is studying chemistry, planning to go to graduate school and eventually to become a chemistry professor. Arnold remembers, "I was very, very strong in math, ever since the third grade. I took an accounting class in high school and everything just started to click—the numbers started to flow and everything was fine." He majored in accounting in college and now works in an accounting firm.

Emerging adults like Gloria, Maya, and Arnold go straight through college in four years, because they know what they want to do when they enter college and they do not spend any time searching for the career direction that will fit them best. But they are the exception, not the rule. The influences that lead emerging adults to take a long time to finish their degrees are the same ones that lead many of them to drop out—uncertainty over what to study, too much "beer and circus," financial struggles.

Emerging adults are mixed in their feelings about taking five, six, or more years to finish their undergraduate education. On the one hand, many of them are frustrated by it. They expected to get their four-year degree in four years, and when it turns out to take longer than that, they feel a sense of inadequacy, like they have failed to meet the standard set out for them. In response to the interview question "Are you satisfied with what you have achieved by this age?" the most common source of dissatisfaction stated by emerging adults in their mid-twenties was that they had not yet completed college.

Casey entered college intending to major in business, but soon discovered that he did not like it at all. "The accounting and the marketing and the econ[omics] classes, I just did not enjoy them. I was just like, 'This isn't right.' It was a chore to get up and go to class." He dropped business and floundered for a year and a half, uncertain of what direction to pursue next. Then he decided to major in education, with the goal of being a math and science teacher in a high school and coaching the high school baseball team. Now age 24, he loves the area he has chosen and feels he has found the right fit, but he regrets that it took him so long to find it. When I asked him if he was satisfied with what he had achieved, he said, "No, I'm not satisfied at all. I'm very disappointed in myself. Just because of the education thing. I would have liked to have shown up in college and known what I wanted to do and graduated in four years."

More typically, however, emerging adults see their education as something they expect to continue through their twenties or even their thirties, combined or interspersed with work. The idea that college is mainly for persons aged 18–22 is rapidly fading. By the turn of the 21st century, nearly half of undergraduate students were more than 25 years old,[21] and one third of the persons obtaining undergraduate degrees were entering graduate studies the following year.[22] According to one national survey of college undergraduates, only about one fourth said they planned to end their education when they obtained their bachelor's degree. Nearly 40% planned to get a master's degree, and nearly 30% planned to get a Ph.D., a medical degree, or a law degree.[23] And they are backing up their goals with their actions. From 1970 to 1999, according to the National Center for Education Statistics, there was an 80% increase in the number of advanced degrees awarded.[24]

The fact that the pursuit of formal education often continues through the twenties and beyond helps explain why "finish education" ranks so low when emerging adults indicate the criteria they believe are most important for marking adulthood.[25] Many emerging adults expect their education to continue long past the time when they have come to feel they have reached adulthood.

There are a variety of reasons why so many emerging adults intend to continue their education through their twenties and thirties. First, they recognize that continued education is a way of improving their income. In most fields, the more education you have, the higher the salary you can command. A related incentive is that more education carries higher status. Being able to tell others you have a bachelor's degree, a master's degree, or a Ph.D. is something to be proud of in American society. But some emerging adults wish to obtain more education simply for the joy of learning. They like the classroom environment, they like learning new things, and they don't ever want that process to stop.

Evaluating the American System

In sum, most young Americans spend the early years of emerging adulthood taking college courses and using those courses to help them clarify what career path they want to pursue. Some succeed in their college courses and establish a clear direction to follow, others flounder and drop out, but for nearly all of them a college degree is one of their eventual goals, whether it takes them four years or far longer. The openness and flexibility of the American system of higher education makes it possible for emerging adults to take college courses on and off through their twenties and beyond if they wish, often in combination with a part-time or full-time job.

Is this a good system? Is it better to allow young people to take their time and explore various possible career directions in their late teens and early twenties, or would it be better to encourage or require them to decide while still in high school what career direction they will take? These questions arise because the European educational system is so much different than the American system. In most European countries, young people separate into different schools by age 14 or 15, with some entering schools that will prepare them for college and others entering schools that will prepare them for a trade, such as electronics or auto mechanics. Those who go to college must decide before entering what they will study. Once they enter college, all of their courses are in the field they have chosen.

So, which system is better? There is probably no simple answer to this question. In truth, each system has strengths and weaknesses. The strength of the European system is that many young people leave secondary school well trained for a well-paying job in a respectable trade. They devote their late teens and early twenties to making progress in their chosen profession rather than searching for a profession during those years, as Americans typically do. But the weakness of the system is that many young people may not be ready at age 14 or 15 to make a decision about what career path to follow for the rest of their working lives. It is difficult for them to change their minds in their late teens or their twenties and pursue a different career path. The European system does not possess that kind of flexibility.

The strength of the American system is that young people have a longer period to try out different possible career directions. During emerging adulthood, they try out various jobs and college classes in the course of clarifying for themselves what they really want to do, what job would really fit them best. But the weakness of this system is that for some emerging adults this is more freedom and flexibility than they can handle. Rather than using their late teens and early twenties as a period of systematic exploration, some American emerging adults drift through that period, paying little attention to their college courses, drinking a lot of alcohol, learning little. They may find themselves in their mid-twenties with no college degree but with a large load of debt from their indifferent efforts to obtain one.

Maybe it is because I am American, but it seems to me that the American system offers young people more of an opportunity to find the educational and occupational path that will be the right fit for them. It is difficult for me to believe that most people can know themselves well enough at the age of 14 or 15 to make a decision about what career path to follow for the rest of their lives. It would be like asking them to decide at that age whom they want to marry—absurd! Most people simply have not developed their identity well enough by that age to make a permanent decision about love or work. Self-understanding is required for those kinds of choices, and for most people this quality develops gradually through their teens and early twenties, partly as a consequence of experiencing different possibilities.

Educational psychologist Stephen Hamilton, in comparing the American and European systems, makes a useful distinction between *transparency* and *permeability*.[26] Transparency is his term for how clearly the path is marked through the educational system leading to the labor market. In a transparent system, the educational and training requirements for various occupations are clearly laid out and young people are well informed about them from an early age. Permeability refers to how easy it is to move from one point within the educational system to another. A permeable system makes it easy to drop one educational/career path and move to another.

Thus the American system is low in transparency and high in permeability. Even in emerging adulthood most Americans have only a limited understanding of how to obtain the education or training that will lead to the job they want, but it is easy to enter college and easy to switch paths once they get there.[27] In contrast, the European system is high in transparency but low in permeability. European adolescents know which path of education and training leads to which job, but once they choose a path—as they are required to do at the age of just 14 or 15—the system makes it difficult for them to change their minds.[28]

Some critics of the American system have argued that we should move closer to the Europeans. Most notably, Barbara Schneider and David Stevenson of the University of Chicago claim that "adolescents need help in developing coherent life plans" while still in high school, so that by the time they leave high school they can "commit to a course of action to achieve specific goals."[29] But why is this necessary or good? Essentially, it is an argument for eliminating the kind of free exploration that is at the heart of emerging adulthood. But it is through these explorations that emerging adults have the opportunity to find the path that will suit them best.

Most emerging adults have no intention of marrying and having children until at least their late twenties. Before they enter those obligations, they are responsible for no one but themselves. If it takes them several years of trying different college courses, different college majors, going back and forth between work and school, before they find the direction that fits, well, why not? There is no good reason why they should rush to make a choice while still in their teens. It seems likely that by taking their time, exploring different possibilities, and waiting until they have a more fully formed identity, for most of them the choice they eventually make will be the basis of a more satisfying adult work life than a hurried choice in their teens would have been. It is true that leaving college with $15,000 or more in debt is a great burden, but that fact is more of an argument for better financial support for students and colleges than for ceasing to use emerging adulthood for educational explorations.

The College Experience

What kind of experiences do emerging adults have in college? What kind of an education do they get? What sorts of things do they learn, and fail to learn, at college? How do they change during the course of their college years? These questions have been the target of considerable research and growing concern over the past 25 years.

At the outset, it should be noted that the college experience is many different things to many different people. The colleges that emerging adults attend vary widely, from enormous research-oriented universities with tens of thousands of students, to small liberal arts colleges with a few hundred students, to community colleges whose students are mostly people who work as well as go to school. The nature of the college experience also depends on the goals and attitudes of the students themselves, as we will see in the next section.

Four Student Subcultures

One useful way of characterizing young people's college experiences was developed in the 1960s by sociologists Burton Clark and Martin Trow, who described four student subcultures: the collegiate, the vocational, the academic, and the rebel.[30] The *collegiate* subculture centers around fraternities, sororities, dating, drinking, big sports events, and campus fun. Professors, courses, and grades are a secondary priority. Students in this subculture do enough school work to get by, but they resist or ignore any encouragement from faculty to become seriously involved with ideas. Their main purpose during their college years is fellowship and partying. This subculture thrives especially at big universities.

Students in the *vocational* subculture have a practical view of their college education. To them, the purpose of college is to gain skills and a degree that will enable them to get a better job than they would have otherwise. Like collegiates, students in the vocational subculture resist professors' demands for engagement in ideas, beyond the requirements of the course work. But vocationals have neither the time nor the money for the frivolous fun of the collegiate subculture. Typically they work 20–40 hours a week to support themselves and help pay their college tuition. Students who attend community colleges are mostly in this category.

The *academic* subculture is the one that identifies most strongly with the educational mission of college. Students in this subculture are drawn to the world of ideas and knowledge. They study hard, do their assignments, and get to know their professors. These are the students whom professors like best, because they are excited about and engaged with the materials their professors present.

Students in the *rebel* subculture are also deeply engaged with the ideas presented in their courses. However, unlike academics, rebels are aggressively nonconformist. Rather than liking and admiring their professors, they tend to be critically detached from them and skeptical of their expertise. Rebels enjoy learning when they feel the material is interesting and relevant to their lives, but they are selectively studious. If they like a course and respect the professor, they do the work required and often receive a top grade, but if they dislike a course and find it irrelevant to their personal interests, they may slack off and receive a low grade.

Clark and Trow described these student subcultures in the mid-1960s, four decades ago. Do the same subcultures still apply to today's emerging adults attending college? Observers of higher education think so,[31] and from my experience as a professor I would agree that their description still rings true. All of these subcultures are likely to be familiar to anyone who teaches college students. But it is important to emphasize that these are types of subcultures, not types of students. Most students are blends of the four subcultural types, to different degrees, although most identify with one subculture more than the others.

To put it another way, the four subcultural types represent different kinds of goals that emerging adults have for their college experiences. As collegiates they pursue fun; as vocationals they pursue a degree; as academics they pursue knowledge; and as rebels they pursue an identity. Most students hope to make all of these things a part of their college years, but they vary in which one they make their top priority.

Is College Worth It? What the Students Say

Critics of American higher education have long deplored the way undergraduate courses are taught at most colleges.[32] Especially in their first two years, students often find themselves in classes of several hundred students. The professor is merely a speck on a stage who knows few if any of the students by name and who is far more devoted to research than to teaching. Class periods are devoted almost entirely to lectures, and students sit there passively (if they come to class at all), scribbling occasional notes, struggling to stay awake. Research confirms that students learn much better in smaller classes that require active involvement, and that they enjoy those classes much more.[33] But most students experience few small classes in their first two years of college, especially at large universities.

Given these criticisms and given the research indicating that students generally dislike the large classes that are often their only option, it is surprising that a large majority of students respond favorably to survey questions about the education they are receiving. In a national survey of more than 9,000 students,[34] Arthur Levine and Jean Cureton found that 81% indicated that they were "satisfied with the teaching at your college." Also, 65% indicated that there were faculty members at their college who took a special interest in students' academic progress, and more than half had professors who had "greatly influenced" their academic career. More than half also had professors to whom they felt they could turn for advice on personal matters. In all respects, students' satisfaction with their academic experiences in college has increased compared to earlier surveys that Levine and Cureton conducted in 1969 and 1976.

Do the results of the survey by Levine and Cureton mean that the educational critics are wrong, and that everything is fine with American higher education? Not exactly. Although students are generally satisfied with the education they receive, they tend to be more satisfied at small colleges with small classes than at large universities where the classes are often enormous. In the *Princeton Review*'s annual survey of students at 300 American colleges of various sizes,[35] small colleges consistently rank highest on almost all positive measures, such as "professors make themselves accessible," "professors bring material to life," and "best overall academic experience for undergraduates." In contrast, big research universities dominate the top rankings for all of the negative items, such as "professors suck all life from material," "professors make themselves scarce," and "class discussion rare."

The responses of my students at the University of Maryland to questions about their satisfaction with their college experiences show how students can be satisfied overall even as they are dissatisfied with some aspects of the education they have received. Most have had some professors they found impressive and inspiring, even if others were disappointing. Kayla complained about having professors who were "not challenging, engaging, or even remotely human," but also said she'd had "some wonderful, memorable, and influential professors." Some students have goals that are primarily vocational, so their satisfaction is based on the prospect of getting a degree. Timothy said, "I don't feel I have learned as much as I anticipated," but nevertheless he is pleased that "I am achieving a college degree, which is very satisfying," and he expects his degree to be "a great deal of help when I am looking for a job."

But the most common theme, when I have asked them to write about whether they are satisfied or dissatisfied overall with their college experiences, is that their satisfaction is based mainly on what they have experienced in terms of *personal growth*. This theme could be seen as a combination of the collegiates' search for fun and the rebels' search for identity, with an additional element of becoming more organized and responsible. Sherry said she had some classes where she "didn't learn much" and other classes where she had "extremely smart professors and have had a great experience with them." However, what makes her "very satisfied" with her college experience is that she has "learned a lot about myself and experienced many new things. I had to get myself up and get my own dinner, manage my money, and so on. These are all things I'd never done before." The requirements of her courses have "definitely taught me responsibility and dedication."

Ted said he was satisfied with his college experience, but his satisfaction "has nothing to do with school. I have experienced so many different things, become much more responsible for myself and have become more grounded in my views and beliefs." Juggling classes, homework, and a part-time job "has made me manage my time better and work harder." He also feels he has "become more reflective on my life as a result of having a certain amount of freedom and privacy in college." Linda feels that "most of my classes have been relatively enlightening and beneficial," but what she has learned in them has consisted mostly of "useless, easily forgotten knowledge." Far more important is that "college has forced me to think, to question, and sometimes just to accept. All of these qualities I either didn't possess prior to college or had very little control over." Her college experience has been "full of revelations and growth. Because of college, I am closer to possessing the knowledge I need to be who and what I want to be."

A large body of research supports these students' accounts that college has multiple benefits. Ernest Pascarella and Patrick Terenzini have conducted research on this topic for many years.[36] They find a variety of intellectual benefits from attending college, in areas such as general verbal and quantitative skills, oral and written communication skills, and critical thinking. These benefits hold up even after taking into account factors such as age, gender, precollege abilities, and family social class background. Pascarella and Terenzini also find that in the course of the college years students become less "vocational" in their college goals—that is, they place less emphasis on college as a way to a better job—and more "academic"— that is, they place more emphasis on learning for its own sake and for the sake of enhancing their intellectual and personal growth.

In addition to intellectual, academic benefits, Pascarella and Terenzini describe a long list of nonacademic benefits. In the course of the college years, students develop clearer aesthetic and intellectual values. They gain a more distinct identity and become more confident socially. They become less dogmatic, less authoritarian, and less ethnocentric in their political and social views. Their self-concept and psychological well-being improve. As with the academic benefits, these nonacademic benefits hold up even after taking into account characteristics such as age, gender, and family social class background.

The long-term benefits of going to college are also well established, according to research by Pascarella and Terenzini as well as many others.[37] Emerging adults who attend college tend to have considerably higher earnings, occupational status, and career attainment over the long run, compared to those who do not attend college.

It seems clear, then, that going to college yields a variety of rewards for emerging adults, both personally and professionally. Is college too expensive? Yes. Is attending college at a big university often frustrating and alienating? Yes. Could the college experience offered to emerging adults be improved? Certainly. But despite these limitations, going to college pays off in multiple ways for emerging adults.

Conclusion: College as a Safe Haven for Exploration

Attending college has become a universal aspiration for young Americans, and a majority of them do attend college and experience college life, at least for a while. They take a wide variety of courses, especially during their first two years, and gain a foundation of general education that most of them missed in their generally undemanding, uninspiring high schools. They try possible majors, looking for something that matches their abilities and interests, and most of them eventually make a choice they find satisfying.

But college is more than simply vocational training for most emerging adults. They want to leave college with skills that enable them to find a good job, certainly, but that is not all they want from their college experiences. They want to have their share of collegiate fun, too, and take part in the friendships, camaraderie, romances, partying, and communal *joie de vivre* that is naturally generated by having so many unattached young people together in one place. Most are also open to being inspired by new ideas, and most find at least some professors who provide that inspiration. Above all, college is a place for experiencing personal growth. The social experiences, the intellectual experiences, and the experience of being on your own and learning to take responsibility for your day-to-day life combine to transform the green emerging adults who entered as freshmen into graduating seniors who have taken great steps toward maturity, toward becoming an adult.

In many ways, the American college is the emerging adult environment par excellence. It is expressly designed for the independent explorations that are at the heart of emerging adulthood. You have two years to try different courses before you commit yourself to a major. Even after you choose a major, you can switch to another major if you find something you like better. As you try out different courses and different majors, you explore a variety of different ideas that help you to develop your world view. Meanwhile, as you are exploring possible directions for your work future and possible ways of looking at the world, there are hundreds, probably thousands, of other people around you every day, having experiences similar to your own, few of them married, all of them with a considerable amount of unstructured time—the perfect setting for explorations in love. College is a social island set off from the rest of society, a temporary safe haven where emerging adults can explore possibilities in love, work, and world views with many of the responsibilities of adult life minimized, postponed, kept at bay.

Of course, it is not always so simple or idyllic as all this. The majority of students are employed part or full time in addition to their course work, which makes for a busy and sometimes stressful life. Students are often dissatisfied with some aspects of their college experience—large, alienating classes; indifferent professors who view undergraduates as a burden to be avoided—even as they are satisfied overall. Less than one third of 25–29-year-old Americans have obtained a four-year college degree, which means that more than half of the young people who entered college after high school failed to obtain one. Even those who do obtain a degree are often left with a daunting burden of debt from their college tuition and expenses that will take years, if not decades, to pay off.

All of these are serious problems. Undergraduate education, especially at large universities, has substantial room for improvement. The fact that half of freshmen fail to graduate is deplorable, especially since minorities disproportionately drop out, often for financial reasons. The cutbacks in funding and support for higher education in the past two decades are a disgrace in a country as rich as the United States.

Nevertheless, college persists as a universal aspiration for emerging adults in the United States. For all of its problems, the promise it offers in terms of career advantages, personal growth, and opportunities for exploration remains alluring.

7

Work

More Than a Job

S OME OF THE FUNNIEST AND MOST biting parts of the novel *Genera-tion X* involve work. To describe the jobs that many emerging adults take to pay the bills while they look for something better, Coupland coined the term "McJob," defined as "a low-paying, low-prestige, low-dignity, low-benefit, no-future job in the service sector. Frequently considered a satisfy-ing career choice by people who have never held one." At one point Dag, one of the main characters, complains, "I mean, really: why *work*? Simply to buy more *stuff*? That's not enough." Another character, Claire, is "a gar-ment buyer–daywear" at the beginning of the book, but says, "I don't think it's making me a better person. . . . I'd like to go somewhere rocky, and just empty my brain, read books, and be with people who wanted to do the same thing."

Although Coupland's characters are extreme types—at the end of the novel, all 3 quit their McJobs and move to Mexico, where they plan to buy a cheap hotel—they personify some of the themes that show up in the work lives of many emerging adults. Emerging adults often hold a series of McJobs in their early twenties while they look for something that will be more sat-isfying. They have high expectations for work. They expect to find a job that will be an expression of their identity. Merely being able to "buy more stuff" is not enough. Most want to find a job that will make them "a better person" and hopefully do some good for others as well.

Work follows a course similar to love from adolescence through emerg-ing adulthood. In love, as we have seen, the first explorations begin in ado-lescence, but explorations become more serious and enduring in emerging adulthood. With work, too, emerging adulthood is a time when choices become more serious, the stakes riding on those choices become higher, the foundation for adult life is being laid. And with work as with love, emerging adulthood is a time not only of exploration but of instability.

Work experiences begin in adolescence for most people growing up in American society. Over 80% of high school seniors have held at least one part-time job by the time they leave high school.[1] However, for the great majority of adolescents, their part-time jobs have little to do with preparing them for a future occupation. Most of their jobs are in the low-wage service sector of the economy—restaurant server, cook, retail sales clerk, and so on.[2] They take these jobs not with the intention of gaining important skills that will form the basis for the work they will do as adults, but mainly for the purpose of bringing in an income that will finance their current consumption and leisure—clothes, CDs, movie and concert tickets, fast food, travel, car expenses.[3] They work to provide for the pleasures of the moment, not to lay a foundation for the future.

Work takes on a much larger significance in emerging adulthood. Now emerging adults start to think seriously about what kind of work they want to do throughout their adult lives. Work becomes not simply a way of gaining extra cash to finance weekend and vacation fun, but a central part of life, the other pillar on which an adult life is built, along with love.

The rise of emerging adulthood has changed the nature of work for young people in their late teens and early twenties. A half century ago, when the typical age of marriage and entry to parenthood was in the very early twenties, most young women worked for only a short time, until their first child was born, and few of them had career goals, focusing their energies instead on being wives and mothers.[4] Most young men, meanwhile, were under pressure at an early age to find a job that would enable them to support a wife and children. Rather than taking years to look around for a job that would be satisfying and enjoyable, they had to focus on finding a job that would provide enough income to support a family.[5]

Now that the typical ages of marriage and entry to parenthood are in the late twenties, today's emerging adults have their late teens and early to mid-twenties to try out various possibilities in school and work in the hopes of finding an occupational direction that will fit well with their interests and abilities. Young women now generally expect to continue to work even after they have children, and most of them plan to have a career in addition to being a wife and a mother.[6] During the emerging adult years, both young men and young women can go to college, combine college and work, or move from job to job without the obligations that come with the roles of spouse and parent.

The other major difference between work for young people 50 years ago and work for today's emerging adults is that there has been a dramatic shift in the nature of the economy and the kinds of jobs available.[7] In the 1950s and 1960s, the U.S. economy had a vigorous and expanding manufacturing sector that provided abundant, well-paying jobs in areas such as the automobile and steel industries. Young men with no more than a high school education (or even less) could get manufacturing jobs that provided relatively high wages, enough to support a wife and children.

Since that time, however, most high-paying manufacturing jobs have disappeared, as companies have used new technologies to reduce the number of workers needed and have moved their manufacturing sites out of the United States to countries where they can pay lower wages to their remaining workers. The American economy has shifted from a manufacturing base to information and services. Many of the jobs in the new economy pay less than the manufacturing jobs of previous years. In fact, from 1973 to 1997, the average earnings for a full-time male worker under age 25 declined by almost one third, adjusted for inflation.[8]

The best jobs in the new economy require higher education. From the early 1970s to the late 1990s, inflation-adjusted incomes rose slightly for persons with a four-year college degree or more, but fell in all groups with less education.[9] Incomes declined steeply for workers with a high school degree or less over this period, and their unemployment rates were especially high. Thus even after the decade-long economic boom of the 1990s, in the early years of the 21st century emerging adults face a workplace situation that is in some ways formidable.

In this chapter the focus will be on how emerging adults go about searching for satisfying work. We will see that emerging adults are highly diverse both in the ways they search for satisfying work and in their success in finding it. I start by emphasizing that the ideal for emerging adults is finding a job that clicks with their developing identity, and by describing emerging adults who look for this identity fit in a systematic way. Then I describe emerging adults whose search for work is less than systematic, who "fall into" various jobs either because they are unsure of their work identity or because they need to find a job in order to pay their bills. Next we look at variations in being ready to make a long-term decision about work, with a focus on differences between emerging adults in their early twenties, who often remain uncertain, and those in their late twenties, who typically have made a definite choice. This is followed by a section describing influences on job choice, especially the complex influences that parents can have, and a section describing the dreams that some emerging adults have for an alluring and sometimes elusive work ideal. The chapter ends with a section on work and identity that attempts to integrate the previous material into a theoretical framework.

Finding the Right Job

Work in emerging adulthood focuses on identity questions: "What do I really want to do? What am I best at? What do I enjoy the most? How do my abilities and desires fit in with the kinds of opportunities that are available to me?" In asking themselves what kind of work they want to do, emerging adults are also asking themselves what kind of persons they are. In the course of emerging adulthood, as they try out various jobs, they begin to answer their identity questions, that is, they develop a better sense of who they are and what work suits them best.

Many young people have an idea, in high school, of what kind of career they want to go into.[10] But usually that idea dissolves in the course of emerging adulthood, as they develop a clearer identity and discover that their high school aspiration does not align with it. In place of their high school notions, many find another career that does fit their identity, something they really enjoy and really want to do.

For most emerging adults the process of finding the right job takes several years, at least. Usually the road to a stable, long-term job is a long and winding one, with many brief, low-paying, dreary jobs along the way. The average American holds seven to eight different jobs between the ages of 18 and 30, and one in four young workers has more than 10 different jobs during this period.[11] There were many examples of this pattern in my interviews, when I asked them what jobs they had held since high school. Wilson is only 24, but already since high school, he said, "I've had about five different jobs. I worked as a DJ; I worked in a bakery; I worked at a grocery store; I worked for a cleaner; I worked at a plant that made air filtration products." Now he is working in the circulation department at a newspaper and studying to be a meteorologist. Terry's job history was similarly diverse.

> I was a waitress for two years until I got burned out on it. And then I worked at a big warehouse, and through working there I got the job at a bookstore. Then after I graduated [from college,] I quit and I went on a little vacation and came back and just took the first job I could find, which

was at a daycare, like running a day camp. That was just for two weeks until I found a better job, which was with a newspaper as a classified ad rep. I was only there for about 3 months, and then I got a job working for a man who was doing research on fish. I did that for about 6 months.

Now she works in a job she enjoys, as a lab technician.

As these examples illustrate, not all of emerging adults' job-hopping is motivated by identity explorations. Sometimes it is simply to pay the bills, to help them pay their way through college or just to get from one month to the next. Their eventual goal is to find a job they love and that fits their interests and abilities, but virtually all of them have many jobs in their late teens and early twenties that have little or nothing to do with this goal.

Looking for a Job That Clicks

Often, the career choice that young people make as emerging adults results from having a job experience that clicks with their identity and leads them to change directions from the career path they had been following. Kim was majoring in journalism at college when she took a part-time job at a preschool to help pay her college expenses. "They asked me to teach a three-year-old classroom and I did it and I loved it, and I thought, 'You know, this is what I need to do.'" She changed her major to education and is looking forward to graduating soon and becoming a teacher. It is evident that she has found the right job to fit her identity. "I love teaching," she says. "I can't imagine doing anything else."

Leslie says that when she entered college she did not have any career direction in mind. "I had no idea. I had no clue. I went in undecided." Then, in her second year of college, she started working in an x-ray research lab in a hospital. Her experiences with that job led her to choose a career in medicine. "As I worked with my job and slowly got more exposure to patients and medicine in general, I got more and more interested in it."

Cliff majored in political science in college and then entered law school, but law did not seem to fit his identity. "I decided that wasn't really what I wanted to be doing." He went to graduate school in business for a while and got a job in corporate banking. It was a decent job and it paid well, but he still felt he had not found the right fit. However, through his job at the bank he worked with builders, and in their lives he saw a vision for his own future. "They had a great life. They were doing what I wanted to be doing and making good money at it. I talked to them and went to work for a while for a builder just to get a good idea of what I was getting myself into." After that apprenticeship he went off on his own, and now he builds homes in the town where he grew up.

Although most emerging adults go through a process of exploration before finding a line of work that fits their developing identity, some know what they want to do from an early age and stick with it all the way. This seems to be especially common for people with technical abilities. Raul said, "Ever since I was little, I always liked messing with things. Radios at my house that were broken, I'd try to see if I could fix them." His love of "messing with things" has led him to become a computer technician. Craig has always been driven by "the fascination of how things work, what makes them tick. Basically, I took everything apart I could. Anything that's mechanical or works, I want to figure out what makes it work; there's got to be a reason." By the time he was in 10th grade, he had a job doing electrical wiring for new houses, and now he is a maintenance electrician, which involves repairing machines and working on "high-tech electrical problems." "I love it," he says. "That's what I've always wanted to be. I love problems. It's the challenge of if you can fix it or not."

Of course, some people think they know at an early age what they want to do as their adult work, but find the door closed to them when they reach emerging adulthood. This is especially common for people who have aspirations in athletics, the arts, or entertainment, fields that are attractive to many but also extremely competitive, in which only the people at the very top are able to make a decent living. Isaiah had hopes of playing professional basketball, as he was growing up. By now, "I thought I was going to be in the NBA, to be honest with you." But "things didn't work out," and he had to give up his basketball dream. Instead he is a district manager for a food company, but he is dissatisfied, perhaps in part because his job is such a long way down from his dream. "It's really not what I want. It's stressful, underpaid."

Beth grew up with a grandfather who "almost worked for Disney. He was always creative. I watched him when I was a child." Soon she discovered that she also "liked to make things." She majored in art in college, with an emphasis in sculpture. After college, however, she discovered that her skill as a sculptor "has nothing to do with money, unfortunately." Now she works as a library clerk, but she still does sculpture on the side, hoping someday to "get discovered, where somebody actually buys your things."

There are also people who discover in emerging adulthood that the job they dreamed of in childhood is not all they imagined it would be. Clive said, "I've liked trucks all my life, since I was a little kid. You know, trucks just fascinated me." However, when he began to look into truck driving seriously as a possible occupation, he discovered, "I really didn't want to have anything to do with it. It's like, you just live in this big metal machine with wheels. Just sitting and staring at the road like a zombie all the time. And I want more for my life than that, you know." Instead, he does yard work, but he hopes eventually to design and build houses. Chalantra recalled, "I always knew I wanted to be a doctor. I liked kids." She planned to become a pediatrician and was awarded a college scholarship as a pre-med major. However, she soon became disillusioned. "Pre-med took up too much time and I didn't have a life. And I figured that once I became a doctor I still wouldn't be able to spend time with my kids, and I want to have kids and be around them." Now she is working as a nurse's aide and thinking about studying to be a nurse.

Chalantra's remarks illustrate the kinds of work-family tensions that young women face today. Although they have much broader career opportunities than in the past, nearly all of them also plan to have children, and most of them want to be the primary caregiver when their children are very young.[12] While they are still emerging adults, still years away from having their first child, young women often anticipate the crunch they are likely to face as they try to balance their roles as worker, spouse, and mother. This realization affects their occupational choices, in that it makes them less likely to choose jobs that will be highly demanding and time-consuming, even if the job is high paying, high status, and in an area they enjoy and for which they have talent.[13] Women who do enter demanding, high-status professions are considerably less likely than their peers to have children.[14] Thus, for many women in emerging adulthood, choosing a career direction means not simply making a choice that clicks with their identity but making a choice that will allow them to balance their dual identities as workers and mothers.

"Falling Into" a Job

I have been using the word *exploration* to describe how emerging adults go about looking for a career path they wish to settle into for the long term, and for many of them that word applies—they think about what they want to do, they try a job or a college major in that area to see if the fit is right, and if it is not, they try another path until they find something they like better. But for many others, *exploration* is a bit too lofty a word to describe their work history during their late teens and early twenties. Often it is not nearly as systematic, organized, and focused as *exploration* implies.[15] *Meandering* might be a more accurate word, or maybe *drifting* or even *floundering*. For many emerging adults, working simply means finding a job, often a McJob, that will pay the bills until something better comes along.

This is especially true for emerging adults who don't have a clear idea of where their interests and abilities lie. Katy has been working as an assistant manager in a music store for the past year and a half. She says it is a decent job, it pays the bills, but "I don't want to do it for too much longer." She does it now only because of the lack of a promising alternative. "I've always been real clear about what I don't want to do, but not coming up with what I actually do want to do." She has a bachelor's degree in psychology, but she does not know where that might lead, if anywhere. "I want to go back to school at some point and get a Ph.D., but I don't know exactly in what area. So I'm taking a little time off to try to figure that out." Until her interests become clearer, she will simply mark time in her job at the music store.

Many emerging adults express a sense that they did not really choose their current job; they just one day found themselves in it, like a ball that rolls randomly on a pocked surface until it lands in one of the holes. "I just fell into it" is a frequently used phrase among emerging adults to describe how they found their current job. That's how Patrick described how he got his job as an audio engineer for radio advertisements. "I kind of fell into it. I got this job through a friend. Like, I had some computer experience and I do sound work, so I got the job." He has mixed feelings about the job, but "it's better than when I was working [as a server] in a café and not making any money." Bridget used similar language to describe how she got her current job as a supervisor at a temp agency. She was a temp herself while she looked around for something more enduring, and her supervisor for the temp jobs decided she had the right qualities and experience to be a supervisor, even though she was not looking for that job. "I kind of fell into this position. . . . this just kind of fell in my lap."

For the most part, emerging adults who got their jobs in this random fashion are looking for something else. Falling into a job rarely results in the kind of fit with one's identity that makes a job fully satisfying. Most emerging adults want to find that kind of fit, and any job that does not provide it is viewed as a way-station on the road to it. "I didn't really choose it. It chose me," Wendy says of the job as a bank teller she has had for the past five years. She got the job through a job placement service, not because she wanted to be a bank teller. Now she is taking night classes to become a nurse, which is what she has finally decided she really wants to do. Tamara is a graduate of an Ivy League university, but she took a job as a legal assistant in a law firm only because "I needed the money. I was so broke! And they pay well." Still, the money is not enough. "I hate my job!" she said. "There's no opportunity for growth there." She is planning to go to graduate school to train herself to do something she likes better, but she is not sure what, maybe "the health-care field or fashion industry."

It may be this instability and uncertainty in work that gives many emerging adults a sense of experiencing a "quarterlife crisis,"[16] as they bounce from one job to another without any sense of how to find their way. In part this is simply an identity crisis—it is hard to choose a direction in work until you know yourself well enough to decide what you really want to do, and it takes many emerging adults until their mid-twenties to develop a clear identity. However, this crisis may be especially common in the United States, where there is little assistance in making the school-to-work transition, and there are few programs or institutions that provide emerging adults with information and guidance. Some scholars have argued that the American system results in a "tyranny of freedom" that leaves emerging adults with too many choices and too little direction in how to sort through them.[17]

As I mentioned in the previous chapter, there are distinct differences between the United States and European countries in this area, with the American system allowing for greater choice but providing less help and the European system providing greater structure but allowing for less freedom to change direction.[18] Perhaps the decades to come will see both extremes move toward a hybrid system: structure and assistance for emerging adults who would like to move directly into the kind of work they know they want, freedom of exploration for emerging adults who want to take their time and try different options before committing themselves to one career.[19]

Deciding on a Long-Term Direction

Even for emerging adults who meander or drift through various jobs rather than exploring their options in a systematic way, the process of trying various jobs often serves the function of helping them sort out what kind of work they want to do. When you are in a dead-end job, at least you find out what you do *not* want to do, as Katy put it. You may also find out that a job has to be more than a paycheck, that you are not willing to do something boring and pointless in the long run even if it pays the bills, that you are willing to keep looking until you find something interesting and enjoyable. And there is also the possibility that as you drift through various jobs you may happen to drift into one you enjoy, one that unexpectedly clicks.

One way or another, most emerging adults eventually find a satisfying line of work. In my study, 73% of emerging adults reported being satisfied with their current job. But there is a definite difference by age in the extent to which emerging adults feel they have found a line of work they want to be in for the long run. People in their late twenties are more likely than those in their early twenties to have reached this point. In fact, this stability in work, marking an end to their work-related identity explorations, could be taken as an indication that they have left emerging adulthood and have entered young adulthood.

In my interviews, this age difference was evident in responses to the question "How do you see your life 10 years from now?" Most people gave a work-related response to this question, and those in their late twenties almost always had a definite answer. They had chosen their line of work, so they simply imagined how they would be likely to progress in it over the next 10 years. Russell, 28, who owns an electronics repair store, said that in 10 years he expects to be "hopefully doing what I'm doing now. I hope the business grows." Mason, 26, an attorney, said he expected to be "still practicing law." Tina, 26, a nurse, saw her life in 10 years as "continuing working in the nursing field at a higher level, whether with management or a higher clinical level of practice." Joyce, 28, who works in human resources for a large company, saw herself "probably going up even farther in my job, or moved up to a higher position maybe."

In contrast, emerging adults in their early twenties often answered, "I don't know," in response to the question of what they would be doing in 10 years. Still in the process of exploring job options, or still meandering through a series of short-term jobs, they found it difficult to extrapolate from their current work situation to their future work. Still in the process of resolving identity issues about their true abilities and interests, they found it difficult to answer a question that required a clear work identity.

So they said they did not know or gave a vague response when asked to imagine what life would be like in 10 years. Leslie, 20, who had just changed her college major to nursing, said of her life in 10 years, "I have no idea. It's changed so much since I've started school, I can't even imagine." Amos,

20, said, "I don't know. I haven't thought that far ahead." His only work goal was the vague one of "hopefully have a high-paying job." Leah, 23, said, "I don't know. It's really hard for me. I'm really not sure. I'm not sure what will happen, and at this point in time, there's not anything specific that I really want to happen." Jerry, 24, said, "That's hard. I don't know. I can't really see that far. I don't like to make plans for next week, really." Ariel, 24, said, "I have no idea. I think one of the things that I've noticed in the last couple of years is that there's no telling what can happen between now and then. I think I've had a lot of things that have occurred that were unexpected, and I try to plan things out and a lot of times it just doesn't work out that way."

Ian, 22, was still trying to reconcile his ambitions in writing and music, or maybe combine them. "I don't know what I'm going to be doing because I've got a lot of things I want to pursue, and I don't know which ones will pan out and which ones won't. Probably have a pretty good journalism job, be in a local band hopefully, and hopefully by then I will have written a novel." Renee, 24, said, "I don't even know where I'm gonna live next year. I just really have no idea what my future is." She was optimistic, however, that she would know in 10 years. "Hopefully by then I will be established, know what I want to do."

For the most part, emerging adults in their early twenties are unperturbed by not knowing what they will be doing in 10 years. They understand themselves to be at a period of life when they are still finding out what they want to do, and they are sanguine that they will find the answer before too much longer. As the examples above illustrate, they use the word "hopefully" a lot to describe how they see their lives in 10 years, and that word fits; they are hopeful that eventually they will find the kind of work that is right for them. Although they may not yet have found what they want, few doors seem closed for good to them and many options still seem possible.

Even in their late twenties, many people are still looking and still hopeful of finding a job that fits better than the one they have now. But the options often start to narrow once people reach their late twenties, as they leave emerging adulthood and take on the responsibilities of adult roles, especially marriage and parenthood. Being married means they have to coordinate their decisions about what job to pursue with a spouse. They can no longer simply leave their job and move somewhere else in hopes of finding something better. Maybe the spouse will support them in their desire to do something else, but maybe not.

Having children, even more than marriage, makes it difficult to change jobs or go back to school. Once you have a child, much of your life becomes structured around caring for and providing for that child, and that means your own options become limited. Harry is an auto mechanic who would like to retrain to be an electrician. But it would take three to four years, and that is time he does not have. "I've got a one-year-old son, so it's kind of hard right now. That makes it real tough." Patty would like to go back to school. "I wish I had a college degree, and I don't. Now that we have a mortgage and two kids, it's really hard to go back." In work as in other ways, having a child is the point of no return into adulthood, the event that marks the definitive end to the relatively free explorations of emerging adulthood. We will discuss this more in chapter 10.

Influences on Job Choice

Developing a work identity and making a long-term job choice is a solitary process for most emerging adults. Finding the right career path is a matter of clarifying for themselves what they most want to do and then seeking out a job that fits, and no one else can answer the question of what they most want to do. However, some emerging adults describe how they were influenced by others in their search for work.

Sometimes this influence comes in the form of what sociologists call "social capital,"[20] meaning social ties that entail mutual assistance, including help in finding a job. An emerging adult may know somebody who knows of a job opening, and get a job that way. Although this rather random way of finding a job is unlikely to yield the kind of job that provides a satisfying identity fit, it may be welcomed by emerging adults who do not yet know themselves well enough to be able to decide what to look for. Alex works as a file clerk in a law office, a job he obtained through his college roommate's father, who is an attorney in the firm, but he views it as temporary. "I just figured I would do it for a little while, while I'm figuring out what else to do." Lonnie obtained an associate's degree in drafting but soon lost interest in it; now he works at his mother's dry-cleaning store until he decides what to do next. "I'm kind of like taking it easy and not doing anything stressful and stuff like that."

Some emerging adults are willing to take a job that happens to come along through personal connections because they have set their sights low and are not very ambitious, but are happy with a job that pays decently and is reasonably pleasant. Kurt works as a clerk in a hospital, a job he learned about through his father, who is a security guard at the same hospital. He does not get any particular satisfaction or fulfillment from the job, but it beats his previous one unloading trucks for a discount department store, which was "just hard work and very low pay for what you did."

However, it is rare for emerging adults to be satisfied with a job that is not identity-based. When emerging adults take such a job through friends or family, it is usually as a temporary way of supporting themselves while they pursue a job they really want. Gabriella helps her father manage his apartment building while she attends college in fashion merchandising. Tory has a part-time job at United Parcel Service that he got when his mother, working at a job placement center, tipped him off to the opening, but he took it only to support himself while he pursues a degree in travel administration with the goal of becoming a travel agent.

In addition to finding a job through social connections, another form the influence of others may take is that emerging adults may be inspired to pursue a particular work path by the example of someone they admire. Teachers are mentioned quite often as providing such inspiration. Monte is studying music education in college and planning to be a music teacher. He decided on this area from "just looking at my high school band director. I saw how he really enjoyed his job, and he was really having fun. I enjoyed band, so I figured if I can get paid for doing that kind of stuff for the rest of my life, I'll be pretty happy."

For some emerging adults, it is a parent who provides the inspiration. Trevor is working as a clerk in a hospital while he works on a degree in radiology, a field he chose because "both my father and my stepmom are in the medical field, and I've always been kind of exposed to it that way." Vernon is a partner with his father in an insurance agency, and it is evident that his admiration and affection for his father led him into the business. "It's nice having him there in the office so I can learn from him and ask him questions. His dad was an agent before him, so I'm [the] third generation." Vernon also sees his connection to his father as a boost to his own status. "You kind of feel like you have power when you go to the home office and you go, 'That's my dad.' He gets automatic respect." Tina, a nurse, said her mom influenced her in a more general way, "just the fact that she did work all through my growing up probably influenced me to want to do that as well." This fits with research indicating that adolescent girls whose mothers work have higher career aspirations than girls whose mothers do not work.[21]

Some emerging adults find that the kind of work their parents do happens to fit well with their own identity. Louis is in the construction business, as his father was, but he says this was "my own idea," not something his father influenced. It's just that, like his father, he enjoys the kind of work that means "just being outside all the time, working with your hands." Similarly, Gus is studying graphic art, and he denies that his father influenced his choice of occupations—but he adds that "the things that my dad does, he's got mechanical skills like drawing and engineering. I guess I got some of that, because I'm good at stuff like that."

However, parents are figures of work inspiration less often than one might expect. In response to the question "Did your parents' occupations influence your own choice of occupation?" emerging adults were about twice as likely to answer "no" as "yes." Some of the "no" responses were adamant, from emerging adults who viewed their parents' jobs as the last thing they would want to do. This may have been because they saw how miserable and ungratifying their parents' work was. Leonard's mother "always either cooked or did custodial type things. That's why I'm like, 'Oooh, get it away from me,' because I don't want any of that. It's not that I'm above it. I'll do it if I have to, but this is what I'm trying to get away from. It stinks." Rocky said that from watching his father in his job as a salesman, "I realized I never wanted to be a salesman. That was one thing that I realized from my dad's job. I didn't want to have to go out and rub elbows and smile to people I absolutely didn't want to be around. He sucked up to so many people, I don't even want to talk about it. I just couldn't stomach that whatsoever."

Sometimes emerging adults start out following the work path blazed by their parents, but veer off when they come to realize it does not fit with their identity. Ken, whose father is a successful businessman, said, "I originally thought I might like to do something like what he does, but as I got into school, I found I didn't like business. I didn't have a mind for business." Barry, whose father is an accountant, said that because of his father's example, "When I was a kid, I thought I wanted to be an accountant or a stockbroker. I think when I was in 10th grade I took a business class and I was just so turned off by it, and I knew I didn't want to do that." Now he is a graduate student in English. Craig initially went into the family painting business, like his brothers, his father, and his grandfather, back "six or seven generations." But he eventually decided that his heart was in electrical work, not painting. The decision was not easy to break to his family, but he eventually "kind of came out in the open and said, 'I don't want to paint. I want to do this.' I felt I had to do it."

Even if parents have been highly successful in their work, emerging adults sometimes wish to avoid following in their footsteps if the costs of that success seem too high to them. Ian has a father who is a wealthy physician, but according to Ian, "He has so much stress it's amazing." Ian has chosen to go into journalism, even though he knows "if I'm a journalist making $20,000 a year, my dad makes vastly more than that." More important than the money is to have a job he loves. "If I enjoy thoroughly doing what I'm doing in life, then I would be better off than my dad."

We can see again that what is most important to emerging adults in work is finding the right identity fit, the right match between a job and their interests and abilities, so that they will "enjoy thoroughly" the work they do. They have high expectations for work, higher perhaps than previous generations. For most of them, it is not enough simply to have a job, even a well-paying job. They want to have a job that is enjoyable and gratifying, a direct expression of their identities. Sometimes their parents provide them with opportunities to find a job with the right identity fit; other times their parents provide them with a model of an anti-identity job to avoid.

Dreams, Pipe Dreams, and the Dreamless

Because emerging adulthood is a time of open possibilities, when little has been decided for certain, it is a time when dreams flourish. They may not yet have found a job they love, they may in fact be working at a lousy, stressful, low-paying job, but they can still hope and plan for bigger things, they can still imagine that the work they eventually settle into will be something wonderful. Just as they hope to find their soul mate, they hope to find their dream job.[22]

A common dream among emerging adults is owning a small business. Perhaps this is a distinctly American dream, more common in a society that encourages free enterprise and individual initiative than it would be elsewhere. The reality of owning a small business is often harsh, in that many small businesses fail and the ones that succeed often require long hours and relentless responsibilities on the part of the owners. Nevertheless, for some emerging adults it is an attractive dream, seeming to hold the promise of independence and self-sufficiency, of being your own boss and being in control of your fate. It also holds an identity allure, because they can choose as their business area something that is central to their identity.

Ned had tattoos of eagles, monsters, and women all over his arms and chest, and he planned to get more. He was working as a truck driver, but his real dream was "to open up my own business. That's what we're thinking about now, you know, a tattoo business." He said the person who did his tattoos was "making well over $200,000 a year," and Ned did not see any reason why he could not be successful as well. "I think if you put into it what you can do, and don't do friends for free like a lot of people I know do, but do it as a business, then I think you'll make money."

Perhaps the most common small-business dream for emerging adults is owning a restaurant. Derek, currently working as a server in a restaurant, said that this was his "long-term plan. Even in the last year, I've talked to some people, like the chef from the café I used to work at, who's planning on starting something, and he said he wanted me to be with him when he started it, which wouldn't be bad." They knew of some potential investors. "There's customers that used to come into the old café that are willing to put money into it. So we're starting the wheels in motion for that, like actually making a legitimate plan. And people are legitimately interested."

Other common work dreams in emerging adulthood involve music or sports.[23] Charles, who was profiled in chapter 2, was doing temp jobs to support himself while he focused on promoting his a cappella singing group, the Jump Cats. Brock was working as a bartender, but soon he was moving to Kentucky to play for a semi-pro soccer team. "It's been my dream to play professional soccer since I was five years old," he said. "I played all through youth leagues and all through high school and I played in college, and I was successful at every level I played." In fact, he was an All-American in college, which was also something he had dreamed of. Now he hopes to extend the fulfillment of his soccer dreams. "This is just the next step hopefully on the ladder that goes up a little further."

Of course, there are dreams, and then there are pipe dreams. That is, there are dreams that emerging adults like Charles and Brock are working toward, pouring their hearts into every day, and then there are dreams that are only the wistful wishes of emerging adults who enjoy imagining a glorious future but are doing little to make it happen. Albert works in an ice cream store, but he says, "What I really want to do is play professional baseball." However, he did not play baseball in high school, nor is he playing organized baseball now. How is he planning to make his way into playing professionally? "I don't know," he says. "I'll see what happens."

There are also emerging adults who are dreamless, who have already, at a relatively young age, nearly given up hope of finding fulfilling work that will be the basis of a satisfying life. For some, this unfortunate status is a consequence of being unable to develop a clear identity that could serve as a guide through the maze of occupational choices. Carrie is working as a library assistant. It started out as an assignment from a temp agency, and she continued with it because "they hired me full time and it's easy." But, she says, it is "not really what I'm interested in." What *is* she interested in? That's the problem. She doesn't know. "I'm totally floundering right now," she admits. "I don't know what I had hoped for, and I think that's part of the reason that I'm floundering because I still don't know what I'm hoping for." She had once hoped to do something in international relations or politics, but that dream is "long gone." Now she has "no idea what I'm gonna do." She has more or less given up on finding satisfying work. "In my plans for my life what I'm probably gonna end up doing is like working at a yucky job like this for a year or so and like saving money and then traveling."

In contrast to Carrie, Curtis, a 29-year-old African American, knew just what he wanted to do, but his problem was finding a good job doing it. He learned how to be a printer while in prison in his late teens, and by now "I've been operating presses for close to 10 years." It's work he enjoys. "I like doing things with my hands. I couldn't be an office person. I like working with machinery and that kind of stuff." However, he has been frustrated by the inconsistency of the work. "It's not really like solid, you know. You get in there, and then all of a sudden it gets slow and you probably have to lay off a couple of weeks." So he went to work for a Kinko's copy center. He liked that job, too. "It's more stable, and the benefits is excellent. And plus they got shares, you know, you can invest in this and get a little share of this. And they have a lot of good things going. So I wanted that. Plus, the opportunity to become something else, you know, like a manager."

But Kinko's let him go after 90 days because he made personal calls on company time and came in late "a couple of times." Now he has taken a job with a different copying company, for lower pay with fewer benefits, and he is starting to lose hope, as he feels himself sliding down in pay and status from his printing job to his Kinko's job to his current copying job. He can see his dreams fading.

> I would like for myself to be established in my little house, you know, and everything is together. But I know it's not gonna be that way. It's too hard, you know, the way things is changin'. It ain't gettin' no better, you know. There's a lot of things that gets in the way at times, breaks you down. So I don't know. Ten years from now, hopefully I'll still be alive. That's all I have to say.

Curtis's story is a microcosm of the plight that many young men in urban areas have faced in recent decades. As noted in the introduction to this chapter, beginning in the 1960s, high-paying manufacturing jobs became scarcer as technology was developed to require fewer workers and as factories moved overseas for cheaper labor or to suburban areas for cheaper land.[24] That left young men like Curtis, who "like to work with [their] hands," with limited job options. Increasingly, the better paying jobs have required higher education. But as the economies of urban areas declined, so did the quality of the public schools, leaving children attending those schools ill prepared for going on to college. Thus in emerging adulthood many of them find themselves like Curtis, in a low-paying, unpromising job, struggling to keep their hopes up but sliding toward the despairing conclusion that "it ain't gettin' no better."

Work and Identity

In the course of this chapter, we have seen that the work paths taken by emerging adults are extremely diverse. Some go through a period of exploration during which they try out various possibilities, through college courses or through work experiences, and then decide on the path that seems right for them. Others explore various possibilities, but as emerging adults they are still looking for a work path to settle into. Still others know from an early age what they want to do, and they stay on that course to its fulfillment in emerging adulthood. And some seem to be adrift in the work world, wandering from one unsatisfying job to another, unsure of what kind of work they want or how to find it.

One way to make sense of this diversity is to use the ideas about identity formation developed by Erik Erikson and James Marcia.[25] As I mentioned in chapter 1, in Erikson's theory of development through the life course, he postulated a central challenge or crisis for each developmental stage, and the challenge he described for adolescence was identity versus role confusion. According to Erikson, adolescence is the period of life when people are most focused on identity questions of who they are and what they want out of life. Central to these questions is exploring possibilities in love, work, and ideology, and eventually making enduring choices in these areas. Those who fail to make choices by the end of adolescence can be said to be suffering from role confusion. Erikson originally presented his theory in 1950; today, the identity explorations Erikson discussed take place mostly in emerging adulthood.

James Marcia and other scholars researched Erikson's ideas about identity and came up with a classification system for identity status containing four categories, each with a different combination of exploration and commitment, as shown in Table 7.1.

Identity moratorium is the status that involves exploration but not commitment. This is the status that most characterizes emerging adulthood, because it is a stage of active exploration, the active trying-out of different possibilities in love, work, and ideology. However, in this identity status, enduring decisions have not yet been made.

Identity foreclosure is the classification for those who have not experimented with a range of possibilities but have nevertheless committed themselves to certain choices—commitment, but no exploration. In love, this would be the classification for someone who ended up marrying the first person he or she dated seriously, and in work this would be the classification for the person who decided on a career path at an early age and stuck with it through its fulfillment in emerging adulthood.

Marcia and most other scholars on identity tend to see exploration as a necessary part of forming a healthy identity and therefore tend to portray foreclosure in negative terms. However, as we have seen in this chapter, some people have a distinct ability they recognize when still young, and they happily build on it until it becomes satisfying work in emerging adulthood. In a way they are fortunate, because they have definitely found a kind of work they enjoy and wish to do as adults, whereas emerging adults who go through a process of exploration may find such work but may not.

Identity diffusion is the status that combines no commitment with no exploration. This term applies to the emerging adults we have seen who seem to be drifting aimlessly, not yet committed to any particular choices but also not seriously attempting to sort through potential choices and make enduring commitments. They seem to be overwhelmed by the range of choices available to them, and they do not know themselves well enough to use self-knowledge as a guide to sorting through their options.

Table 7.1. Categories of Identity Status

		Commitment	
		Yes	No
Exploration	Yes	Achievement	Moratorium
	No	Foreclosure	Diffusion

Finally, *identity achievement* combines exploration and commitment. This is the culmination of the process of identity formation, as young people make enduring choices in love, work, and ideology. In this chapter and the previous chapter we have seen examples of this in emerging adults who have tried out various possibilities in school and/or work, then made a choice that clicks, that seems to them to be the right fit with their abilities and interests. By definition, identity achievement is preceded by a period of identity moratorium in which exploration takes place. If commitment takes place without exploration, it is considered identity foreclosure rather than identity achievement.

Although identity achievement is the culmination of the process of identity formation, this does not mean that once this status is reached identity issues have been resolved, never to return. As Erikson observed, "A sense of identity is never gained nor maintained once and for all. . . . It is constantly lost and regained."[26] With regard to work, even when emerging adults find a kind of work they like, they may grow tired of it after some years, or their interests may change, or they may wish to find something they like even better, and their explorations will continue. Nevertheless, Erikson viewed the development of a definite identity as the basis for the initial commitments of adult life and as the foundation for later stages of development. Emerging adults who come to know themselves well, and who develop a clear idea of what their abilities are and what they want to do, have a good foundation for the decisions they will make as adults.

Conclusion: High Hopes and Hard Realities

In this chapter, the emphasis has been on work as an identity quest. Emerging adults want more out of work than a decent wage and a steady paycheck. They want their work to be an expression of themselves, to fit well with their interests and abilities, to be something they find satisfying and enjoyable. If necessary, they are willing to endure frequent job changes and a long series of relatively low-paying, short-term McJobs as they move closer to clarifying what kind of work they really want to do, what kind of work suits their developing identity. Even amid the instability and uncertainty of their work in emerging adulthood, most of them remain hopeful that their identity quest will end in success and they will find a job that clicks with their perception of themselves.

Arguably, they have a better chance of finding such a job than people did in the past. When people married and had their first child in their early twenties, men quickly experienced pressure to find a job that would enable them to support a family, and women experienced pressure to leave the workforce to devote themselves to caring for the children and running the household. Now, with the postponement of marriage and parenthood into the late twenties, young people can use their emerging adult years to seek out satisfying work without the pressure of family obligations. For young women, the range of possible occupations is suddenly vast, greater than it has been for any generation of women in human history.

However, there is a dark side to the work prospects of emerging adults. With such high expectations for what work will provide to them, with the expectation that their jobs will serve not only as a source of income but as a source of self-fulfillment and self-expression, some of them are likely to find that the actual job they end up in for the long term falls considerably short of this ideal. Also, the information- and services-based economy of today requires a high level of education for the best jobs, and emerging adults who lack the abilities or opportunities to pursue higher education often find themselves excluded from competition for these jobs and left with only the lowest paying and least rewarding service jobs.

Nevertheless, most young people manage by their late twenties to find a job that they enjoy, that provides a decent income, and that provides a reasonably satisfying fit with their identities. The road to that job is long and winding for most emerging adults, with many obstacles and detours along the way, but more often than not it ends with a reasonable degree of success.

8

Sources of Meaning

Religious Beliefs and Values

THE THIRD PILLAR OF IDENTITY, ALONG with love and work, involves developing an ideology, a world view, a way of making sense of the world.[1] A world view invariably includes religious beliefs, for example, beliefs about the ultimate origin of life, about the existence of a soul, about the existence of supernatural beings, and about our destiny after death. People in all cultures address questions about what theologian Paul Tillich called issues of "ultimate concern,"[2] that is, existential questions about what really matters and what our lives mean in light of our mortality. Because such questions are inherently part of being human, developing answers to them is invariably part of developing an identity.

This does not mean that human beings are invariably religious, only that we invariably address religious questions as part of our lives. Even to conclude that there is no soul, that there are no supernatural beings, and that we have no destiny after death is to address religious questions and to include the answers in a world view. People in various cultures have created a marvelously diverse array of religious beliefs, but virtually every culture has religious beliefs of some kind.[3] Forming religious beliefs appears to be a universal part of identity development.

Another essential part of a world view is a set of values, that is, a set of moral principles that guides decisions about the issues that come up in the course of daily life. Beliefs and values are often connected; religious beliefs often include a set of explicit moral principles that are meant to guide daily life, such as the Ten Commandments that are part of the Jewish and Christian faiths. But values can also be nonreligious. For example, individualism and collectivism are systems of values that do not necessarily have a religious basis. *Individualism* means guiding moral decisions on the basis of what is believed to be best for promoting individual growth, freedom, and personal development.[4] *Collectivism* means guiding moral decisions on the basis of the needs and interests of the group rather than the individual.[5] Most cultures have an overall orientation that leans toward either individualism or collectivism, but each person also forms a moral orientation that includes some combination of individualism and collectivism to guide the moral decision making of everyday life.[6]

Emerging adulthood is a crucial time for the development of a world view, as it is for other aspects of identity development. The process takes place throughout childhood and intensifies in adolescence as we develop the capacity for the kind of abstract reasoning that can be applied to world view questions about concepts such as God, death, and right and wrong. However, for most people, the process of forming a world view is not completed by the time they leave adolescence. It is during emerging adulthood that people address worldview questions most directly, and it is during emerging adulthood that most people reach at least an initial resolution to their worldview questions. Like love and work, forming a world view becomes more intensive and serious in emerging adulthood. Few people enter emerging adulthood at age 18 with a well-established world view, but few people leave their twenties without one, just as few people leave their twenties without a definite direction in love and work.

In this chapter, we examine some of the religious beliefs and values that are part of the world views of emerging adults. The section on religious beliefs examines both the diversity of emerging adults' beliefs and their common determination to think for themselves with regard to religious issues. In the section on values, the focus will be on emerging adults' responses to two questions concerning their values for their own lives and the values they wish to pass on to the next generation. Together, these two questions provide an outline of the extent to which emerging adults' values reflect individualism and collectivism.

Religious Beliefs

In this section we will explore the striking diversity of emerging adults' religious beliefs, from atheism and agnosticism to devout traditional beliefs and everything in between. We will see how emerging adults' religious beliefs have surprisingly little connection to their religious training in childhood and adolescence, a reflection of emerging adults' resolve to think for themselves and decide on their own beliefs. We will also see how ethnicity is related to religious beliefs in distinctive ways.

A Congregation of One: Individualized Religious Beliefs

It is difficult if not impossible to characterize emerging adults' religious beliefs in general terms, because their beliefs are so diverse. Table 8.1 provides a sense of this diversity, by presenting the responses of the emerging adults in my research to questionnaire items about their religious beliefs.

As the table shows, religious beliefs are important to a slight majority of emerging adults, both in a general sense and as part of their daily lives, but nearly half of them regard their religious beliefs as only somewhat or not at all important. A strong majority of emerging adults believes that God or some higher power watches over them and guides their lives, but one fifth of them are either skeptical of this or definitely do not believe it. The table also shows that many emerging adults are still in the process of forming their beliefs: only a little more than one-third said they were "very certain" about their beliefs. Participating in a religious institution is unimportant to most of them, and most of them rarely or never attend religious services, but over one third of them attend religious services at least once a month.

The diversity of their beliefs was also evident in response to the interview question about their current beliefs.[7] They fell fairly evenly into four categories:

Agnostic/atheist: 22%

Deist: 28%

Liberal believer: 27%

Conservative believer: 23%

Let's look at how emerging adults in each of these categories described their beliefs.

AGNOSTICS/ATHEISTS   Emerging adults in this category explicitly reject any belief in God (atheists) or are unsure what to believe about religious questions (agnostics). For example, when asked about his current religious beliefs, Stuart exemplified the atheist view when he responded, "I don't believe in a

Table 8.1. Religiosity of Emerging Adults, Questionnaire Items

How important to you are your religious beliefs?	Percentage
Very important	32
Quite important	26
Somewhat important	25
Not at all important	17

How important is religious faith in your daily life?	
Very important	30
Quite important	23
Somewhat important	21
Not at all important	26

To what extent do you believe that God or some higher power watches over you and guides your life?	
Strongly believe this	56
Somewhat believe this	23
Somewhat skeptical of this	13
Definitely do not believe this	8

How certain are you about your religious beliefs?	
Very certain	36
Quite certain	35
Somewhat certain	19
Very certain	9

How often do you attend religious services?	
About 3–7 times a month	25
About 1–2 times a month	12
Once every few months	17
About 1–2 times a year or less	46

How important is it to you to attend religious services?	
Very important	22
Quite important	13
Somewhat important	23
Not at all important	42

soul. I don't believe in a god. I don't believe in an afterlife." Wilson exemplified the agnostic view in responding, "I really don't know. I can't say for sure if I believe there is a supreme being out there or not. I just don't know."

Some emerging adults in this category are actively hostile to religion. Palmer said, "I think religion's probably one of the biggest problems this world has. I really do. Look at all the wars between people because they're one religion and somebody else is another. In India, you know, you've got cows walking across the damn street, and people starving to death. That just doesn't register with me at all." Some contrast religion with science and rationality, and choose the scientific world view as superior. Denny said, "I kind of lean more towards science and stuff like that. I can see how evolution happened easier than I can believe in some spiritual super-being." Others are still exploring religious questions and hope to find answers eventually. Sandy said she was an agnostic, but added, "I really think someday I'll figure it out. I hope. Someday I'll go one way or another, but right now I just really am not sure. I'm just kind of waiting for a flash of lightning. You know, someday something will probably spark a belief in something."

DEISTS   These emerging adults declare a general belief in God or a "higher power" or "spirituality," but only in a general sense, not in the context of any religious tradition. They do not call themselves "deists," but they fit the definition of a deist as someone who holds a general belief in God. For example, Amelia said, "I definitely believe in a greater being, but I don't think I could specify, you know, I'm Buddhist or I'm Presbyterian." Often, emerging adults in this category specify that their beliefs do not include participation in organized religion. As Don said, "I have my own unique relationship with God. I don't ascribe to any institutionalized religion right now, at all."

Many deists use the word "spiritual" in describing their beliefs, and contrast this with "religious," meaning part of organized religion. Rachel described her beliefs by saying, "I'm a very spiritual person. I don't consider myself a religious person because I don't claim one religion. I mean, I've experienced all sorts of different religions, and I've learned about a lot of different religions. But I basically consider myself a more spiritual person than religious." Although some reject all organized religion, others believe that each religion holds part, but only part, of the truth about religious questions. José said, "I kind of believe that if there's a God, I don't think that God is a Catholic. God is God and you can [get to] God [through] whichever religion you want to go through."

LIBERAL BELIEVERS   Liberal believers share with deists a skepticism of organized religion and an acceptance of different faiths. What distinguishes liberal believers from deists is that liberal believers nevertheless describe themselves as members of a specific religious tradition (e.g., Catholic, Baptist, Jewish). For example, Christy sounded very much like a deist when she said, "Religion is a shoe that fits everyone differently, and there isn't one good or bad religion. In fact, if you look at it, everybody worships the same God, whether they call him 'Buddha' or whatever." However, she also described herself as a Catholic and said, "I'm drawn to the very basic beliefs that Catholics hold true."

Even though they consider themselves part of a specific religious tradition, most liberal believers do not see participation in religious services as essential to the expression of their faith. Juan said, "I believe in God, but I don't go to church every Sunday. You know, very little. The role of the church in my life has been just a Catholic baptism, first communion, confirmation, and that's it." Liberal believers often state that they do not accept all aspects of their religious tradition. Trey said, "I belong to the Lutheran church. As far as religiously, I guess most of their teachings I go along with. There are certain ones that I question. Some people that belong to the church would say to me, 'No, you can't question it. If you belong to the church, you've got to take it all or nothing,' but I don't think that's right."

CONSERVATIVE BELIEVERS   Emerging adults who are conservative believers express belief in traditional Christian or Jewish doctrines, such as, for Christians, the belief that Jesus is the son of God and the only way to salvation. For example, Kurt said, "I believe that through Christ is how you have your eternal salvation. I believe that he died on the cross for our sins, and that you have to repent of your sins and be baptized into Christ for the remission of your sins." Conservative believers are highly conscious of issues of salvation and life after death, but they also use their faith as a guide to daily life. Manuela said, "Everything I try to do in life, I always try to see it how God is seeing it. You know, what I wear, the way I look, what I say, the way I . . . you know, just everything." They tend to have an especially strong sense that their lives are guided by God. Clive said, "Since I gave my life to Christ, I've been like a whole new person. I have something to live for. I feel that this higher power is over me, guiding my life. It's like the more faith I put in Him, the better my life goes." Unlike deists and liberal believers, who hold that there are many different legitimate ways of believing in God, conservative believers regard their faith as the only true faith. As Shalanda put it, "I believe if you're saved, you're goin' to heaven. If you're not, you're goin' to bust hell wide open."

Make-Your-Own Religions

These categories portray great diversity in emerging adults' religious beliefs, but the diversity is actually even greater than this, because there is also diversity within the categories, especially among the deists and the liberal believers, who together comprise about half of emerging adults. Atheists/agnostics are quite similar to each other, in rejecting religious beliefs (atheists) or in declaring that they do not know what to think about religious questions (agnostics). Conservative believers also sound highly similar to each other, because they all subscribe to a particular doctrine, and being conservative means, by definition, not deviating from that doctrine. But deists and liberal believers feel free to form their own individualized belief systems, constructed from a variety of religious and nonreligious sources, including popular culture.

For example, Leah's father was a minister in a Disciples of Christ church and she went to church every Sunday growing up, but by now her beliefs have become a singular pastiche of New Age, Eastern, and Christian ideas. "A lot of my beliefs border on what would be labeled as witchcraft," she said. "I believe that objects can capture energy and hold it. . . . I do believe it's possible to communicate with people who have died. . . . I do believe in reincarnation. . . . I believe I've had past lives. . . . I am what I would label a 'guardian angel,' and there are certain people that I'm supposed to help out."

Carl described himself as a Christian, but he also said, "I feel that there is kind of more like the *Star Wars* thing, 'the Force.' There's just this kind of planetary aura, that everyone's thoughts and actions and feelings generate this energy. . . . That's what influences other things around the universe." Like Carl, Jared invoked ideas from *Star Wars*, which he combined with ideas from a variety of religions.

I've read some Joseph Campbell, and just the theory that all these religions, Mohammed and Buddha and Jesus, all the patterns there are very similar. . . . And I believe that there's a spirit, an energy. Not necessarily a guy or something like that, but maybe just a power force. Like in *Star Wars*—the Force. The thing that makes it possible to live.[8]

One reason the beliefs of many emerging adults are highly individualized is that they value thinking for themselves with regard to religious questions and believe it is important to form a unique set of religious beliefs rather than accepting a ready-made dogma. For example, Nate described himself as a Christian, but he also said he believed that "You don't have to be one religion. Take a look at all of them, see if there is something in them you like—almost like an à la carte belief system. I think all religions have things that are good about them." Melissa said, "I was raised Catholic . . . and I guess if I had to consider myself anything I would consider myself Catholic," but she also said:

> I don't have any really strong beliefs because I believe that whatever you feel, it's personal. . . . Everybody has their own idea of God and what God is, and because you go to a church doesn't define it any better because you still have your own personal beliefs of how you feel about it and what's acceptable for you and what's right for you personally.

Emerging adults such as Melissa see it as their personal responsibility to develop a set of religious beliefs that is uniquely their own.

Skepticism of Religious Institutions

As Melissa's comments suggest, the individualism valued by many emerging adults makes them skeptical of religious institutions and wary of being part of one. The questionnaire results shown earlier indicate that religious participation is much less important to emerging adults than their religious beliefs are. Only 17% indicated that their religious beliefs were "not at all important" to them, but 42% indicated that it was "not at all important" to them to attend religious services. To most emerging adults, participation in a religious institution, even a liberal one, requires them to abide by a certain set of beliefs and rules and therefore constitutes an intolerable compromise of their individuality.

Charles grew up attending an Episcopal church with his parents, but stopped attending in emerging adulthood.

> I realized that I was not being encouraged to think for myself. And that has been my fundamental problem with certain forms of organized religion. It is not a matter of "take this service for what it is and integrate it into your own life for whatever it means to you." It is, literally, "This is black. This is white. Do this. Don't do that." And I can't hang with that.

Similarly, Burt said he believed in God, but "I'm just not real big on the church thing. I think that's a man-made thing. I don't need anyone telling me what's right or wrong. I know what's right and wrong." Dana grew up in a Jewish home and attended synagogue, but stopped attending as she reached emerging adulthood because "there was this pressure from the people at the synagogue to be, like, kosher, and I just didn't like having anyone telling me what my lifestyle should be."

Emerging adults tend to personalize their relationship with God in a way that makes participating in organized religion unnecessary or even an impediment to the expression of their beliefs. Jean, who was raised Catholic but rarely attends mass now, said, "I'm the kind of person that feels that you don't have to go to church just to be religious. I mean, it's not necessary to be in a certain place to be religious." Joseph said he felt stronger spiritual feelings in the outdoors than in church. "Just being outside in the woods or fishing is more spiritual to me than going in and sitting in a church with a bunch of people and somebody preaching from the Bible. I kind of like to be independent and free to think on my own." Corey also preferred to keep his religious independence. "I don't think you have to go to church to worship God and his teachings. I think God is in here, in how you feel, and not what somebody at the pulpit's telling you God is."

Their wariness of religious institutions is sometimes based on negative experiences that have led them to view such institutions as bastions of corruption and hypocrisy. Terry was disillusioned about organized religion because of "hypocritical things in Christians that I knew." She gave as an example her grandmother, who "only reads the Bible and has it in her lap every day," yet freely casts racist aspersions on Black people. Hayley described herself as "brought up Baptist" and said she "still believes in God," but she also said she rarely attends church. Based on her experience she has concluded that "I don't feel that going to church every Sunday makes you a good Christian. You can go to church every Sunday and be a hypocritical asshole, as far as I'm concerned."

Beth had unpleasant memories of her church experiences in childhood. "I remember going to church and being bored, and seeing everybody around me being bored." By emerging adulthood, she had rejected the Catholicism of her youth because of

the guilt. I got so sick of feeling guilty all the time. And, oh God, "lust is so awful." I really feel like there are things that are natural to us, because I really believe that yes, we are human, but we also still have animal tendencies, and you can't guilt those out of people. And that's pretty much when I decided that yes, I did have an animal in me, and I wasn't going to guilt my animal any more because it made me unhappy. So I gave up being Catholic.

Disillusioning experiences such as Beth's are quite common among emerging adults and have turned many of them away from religious institutions.

The Missing Link: Childhood Religious Training and Current Beliefs

Perhaps the most interesting and surprising feature of emerging adults' religious beliefs is how little relationship there is between the religious training they received throughout childhood and the religious beliefs they hold by the time they reach emerging adulthood. In my research, about 60% of emerging adults were classified as having "high exposure" to religious training in childhood, meaning their parents took them to religious services on a regular and frequent basis.[9] About 20% were classified as having "moderate exposure" (parents took them to religious services now and then, but without much involvement or commitment), and 20% had "low exposure" (parents rarely or never took them to religious services). In statistical analyses, there was *no* relationship between exposure to religious training in childhood and *any* aspect of their religious beliefs as emerging adults—not to their current classification as agnostic/atheist, deist, liberal believer, or conservative believer; not to their current attendance at religious services; not to their views of the importance of attending religious services, or the importance of their religious beliefs, or the importance of religion in their daily lives; not to their belief that God or a higher power guides their lives or to the certainty of their religious beliefs in emerging adulthood.

This is a different pattern than is found in adolescence. During adolescence, there does tend to be a relationship between the religiosity of the parents and the religiosity of their children. For example, studies have found that adolescents are more likely to embrace the importance of religion when their parents talk about religious issues and participate in religious activities.[10] Evidently, however, something changes between adolescence and emerging adulthood that dissolves the link between the religious beliefs of parents and the beliefs of their children.

I am not the first one to report this finding. For example, Dean Hoge and his colleagues at the Catholic University of America studied Catholics in their thirties and forties and found little correlation between their religious training in childhood and adolescence and their current religious beliefs and practices.[11] Still, how could it be that childhood religious training makes no difference in the kinds of religious beliefs and practices people have by the time they reach emerging adulthood? It doesn't seem to make sense. Parents take their children to religious services repeatedly over many years, have them baptized or confirmed or Bar Mitzvahed, and it all comes to naught in emerging adulthood?

Yet that seems to be the truth of it, surprising as it may be. Certainly, there are cases where children grow up to hold the same beliefs as their parents, but such cases are too rare to show up in statistical analyses of groups, because it is much more common for children to hold different beliefs from their parents by the time they reach emerging adulthood. Their own accounts of the change are persuasive. Wilson said, "I was brought up as a Christian. I was baptized when I was seven years old, went to church every Wednesday, every Sunday and Sunday night. I had to go for years and years in a row. . . . I'm surprised I'm not a complete saint right now, as much church as I was subjected to." Now, however, he says, "I'm not religious at all. Zero. I question the credibility of religion now. I can't say for sure if I believe there is a supreme being out there or not. I just don't know." Brady said that he "went to church every Sunday until I was 16." By now, however, he has decided, "I'm an atheist. . . . I look at the Bible as just being a myth. It doesn't make any sense. I don't see how there can be a God, with the condition of the world. Especially not an all-knowing, all-powerful God."

Keith was especially vehement in rejecting his childhood religious training. He was "raised Catholic," and he went to mass every Sunday and also went to Catholic schools. However, his current beliefs are far from Catholicism.

I don't believe in anything. I really don't, and it goes far beyond atheism for me. Organized religion, I mean, everybody's got a void to fill and that's just one way of filling it. I mean, we have to realize that these books that they're reading were written by men, you know, men just like you or I. And for somebody to take that literally and to call it a religion, to me that's just utterly ridiculous, completely ridiculous to take it as the only truth and totally close your mind to all other things. You make yourself stupid.

A typical pattern was attendance at religious services throughout childhood and early adolescence, but increasing resistance during adolescence, leading to a rejection of religious participation in late adolescence or emerging adulthood. Sandy said, "I was pretty much dragged to church every Sunday until I was 18. Finally, at that point I said, 'I'm not going any more.' I just didn't want to. I was going out on Saturday night and getting drunk, and the last thing I wanted to do was get up at 7:00 in the morning and go to church." Craig said he was a "full-blown Catholic" as a child, but when he was 17 years old, "I just flat told Mom I wasn't going to go any more. It was a waste of time. I didn't like it. I went because I was under Mom and Dad's rules. I did what they said to do, went to Sunday school and stuff like that. But I can go to church all you want, and I'm still going to believe what I believe. You're not going to change me."

Usually the change in late adolescence and emerging adulthood was away from religious beliefs and religious participation, but in rare cases it was in the other direction, toward greater faith. Bridget said, "My parents were atheists. They didn't believe in God." Now, in emerging adulthood, she attends an evangelical church and says her own beliefs are "definitely that there's a God, and that he controls every part of your life, of everyone's life. I believe in the Bible." But this course was unusual. It was more common for emerging adults to have high exposure to religious training in childhood but fall away from religious beliefs and practices by emerging adulthood.

Let's return now to the original question. Why does religious training in childhood and adolescence seem to make so little difference for religious beliefs and practices in emerging adulthood? One reason is that in the course of growing up, people gradually become exposed to more and more influences and ideas outside the family. Going to college, especially, can challenge the religious ideas that emerging adults learned in their earlier religious training.[12] Joan said she had been brought up to be a "very strong Catholic." However, she said, "I stopped practicing the Catholic religion somewhere during college when I took a class in theology, and I'm going, 'Wait a minute. These Catholics have lied to me my whole life.'"

Yvonne gave a similar account. "I used to be a strong Catholic," she said. "During high school I was very dedicated in church, went every Sunday to mass with my family. But then after college I guess I became more open-minded about different beliefs, from learning about Buddhism and just different religions. And I guess I had doubts of what's really true and what's not." Now she is a deist and no longer attends mass. "I know there is a being out there, God, you know, who has created this earth, but to actually go to church every Sunday and actually pray to him, I don't feel there's a need to."

Exposure to new ideas is part of the explanation for why religious beliefs often change by emerging adulthood, but probably even more important is the responsibility emerging adults feel to decide for themselves what they believe about religious questions. As discussed in chapter 1, "making independent decisions" is near the top of the list of criteria that emerging adults consider most important for becoming an adult. This includes decisions about religious beliefs. For most emerging adults, simply to accept what their parents have taught them about religion and carry on the same religious tradition as their parents would represent a kind of failure, an abdication of their responsibility to think for themselves, become independent from their parents, and decide on their own beliefs. Quite consciously and deliberately, they seek to form a set of beliefs about religious questions that will be distinctly their own.

Is the change in their beliefs temporary? Will they eventually resume participation in the religious institution of their childhood? There is some research evidence to suggest this pattern.[13] The main years of emerging adulthood, from age 18 to 25, are the nadir of religious participation in American society, and religious participation rises somewhat in the late twenties after many young people marry and have their first child. In my research, too, some of those whose religious participation had waned after high school saw their nonparticipation as temporary, to be resumed after they had children. Perry was among those who viewed religion as something he had no interest in now but wanted his future children to be exposed to. "Growing up, we went to church every Sunday. I don't go to church every Sunday now, just because the weekends now, to me, are a time to relax and sleep late. But I will come around. I firmly believe that a religion should be a part of a kid's growing up."

The people in my research who had become parents were more likely than nonparents to attend religious services, perhaps motivated by wanting to provide religious training for their child.[14] For example, Leila and her husband had recently begun attending church with their four-year-old daughter, because "we both decided that we better start going because we have a child now, and we need to give her some type of feeling of church." So, some of the emerging adults who have rejected religious participation— but by no means all of them—may return to it later, spurred this time not by their parents but by their children.

Ethnic Differences

So far we have been talking about emerging adults' religious beliefs and practices in general terms, but it is also important to discuss the ethnic differences in this area. Emerging adults in each of the major American ethnic minorities—African Americans, Latinos, and Asian Americans—have accounts of their religious experiences that are distinctive to their group. We should be careful not to generalize too much, because each ethnic group is diverse and every ethnic group has many emerging adults who sound like the ones we have been listening to in this chapter—the quotes so far were taken from emerging adults in all of the ethnic groups—but our focus in this section will be on the characteristics that make the ethnic groups unique.

African Americans have been called "the most religious people in the world,"[15] and the strength of their religious beliefs is evident among emerging adults. On every measure of religiosity in my research, they were more religious than other emerging adults. For example, 55% indicated that religious faith is "very important" in their daily lives, compared to 22–24% of Whites, Latinos, and Asian Americans. Eighty-two percent stated they believe that God or some higher power watches over them and guides their lives, compared to 44% of Whites, 46% of Latinos, and 63% of Asian Americans. Forty-six percent of African Americans reported attending religious services at least three to four times per month, compared to 14% of Whites, 20% of Latinos, and 35% of Asian Americans. Fifty-four percent were "very certain" about their religious beliefs, compared to 26–34% in the other three groups. Not one of the African Americans we interviewed was an agnostic or atheist (compared to 29% of Whites).

When African American emerging adults talk about their religious beliefs, they often do so in a way that is frank and uninhibited, reflecting the acceptance of open religious expression in African American culture. "I want to be one of God's prayer warriors," said Monique, who credits her faith with helping her break an addiction to crack cocaine. "I walk out on the street and pray if I feel weak or something, or just talk to God." Ray said, "I still believe in God all the way. I travel with my Bible everywhere I go. I read it when things aren't going my way and when they are going my way." Conservative believers in other ethnic groups sometimes use similar language to describe their religious beliefs, but in other groups conservative believers are on the fringe, maybe 20–25% of the group, whereas for African Americans conservative religious beliefs are the mainstream.

Like African Americans, Latinos are rarely agnostics or atheists, and in Latino culture as in African American culture the expression of religious beliefs is a common part of everyday life.[16] But Latino emerging adults talk less about their personal relationship with God and more about religious faith—usually the Catholic faith—as something that provides an organizing structure for their families and communities. Gloria was one of several Latinas who spoke glowingly of memories of their *quinciñera*, a kind of religious coming-out ceremony for girls when they turn 15. "Everyone always has a quinciñera when they're 15, and it's something that you get a big party and you have a mass and it's all about you. It's really special. It's kind of like a presentation to the community and to God."

Carlos viewed community service as the most important expression of his faith.

> I'm in a [church] group that when people need things, maybe like they're elderly or they're handicapped or they just don't have the time or the money to clean their yard or paint their house, we go out there on Saturday and we paint their house for them, clean up their yard. It's like a community effort, a church effort. Give back to the community.

Many Latino emerging adults expressed skepticism about or even rejected some of the teachings of the Catholic church, but virtually all of them considered themselves part of a Catholic faith community.

For many Asian American emerging adults, their religious experience is a combination of two very different influences. On the one hand, many of them have been exposed to Buddhist beliefs through their parents, who brought those beliefs with them to the United States from their Asian homelands (the Asian Americans in my research all had parents who were born outside the United States). On the other hand, many of them have been exposed to Catholic beliefs from years of attending Catholic schools. Their parents have often sent them to private Catholic schools in an effort to provide them with the best possible education.[17]

By the time they reach emerging adulthood, Asian Americans have responded in a variety of ways to these two influences. Many of them have become Catholics, which they acknowledge is the result of their Catholic school religious training. "My sisters and I all went to 12 years of Catholic school, so we're Catholic," as Cindy put it simply. Few consider themselves Buddhists, perhaps because Buddhism is so far out of the mainstream of

American society. Nevertheless, many of them said they join their parents in Buddhist practices of praying to their ancestors and engaging in various rituals that show their ancestors honor and respect.

Most often, they end up in emerging adulthood neither Catholic nor Buddhist but as deists, with a blend of beliefs that emphasizes a common theme of honoring a higher power and trying to live a morally good life. "I don't know what I am basically," said Jane. "I went to Catholic schools, I believe in God, I believe in Buddhism. I read everything, and for me, I came to the conclusion it really doesn't make a damn bit of difference as long as you're a good person. You can call it God, Buddha, Providence, Allah, whatever you want to call it."

Values

As noted at the outset of the chapter, the world view formed by emerging adults includes not only a set of responses to religious questions but also a set of values, that is, a set of moral principles that provides a guide for making life decisions, small and large. Your values come into play when you have a decision to make and you have to ask yourself, "What is really most important to me?" For example, if you chose someone to marry and your parents were opposed to the marriage, the decision you made about whether or not to marry that person anyway would be a reflection of your values, of what was of ultimate importance to you.

One useful way of thinking about values is in terms of individualism and collectivism.[18] Individualistic values center on the rights and needs of each person. Examples of individualistic values would be freedom, independence, self-sufficiency, self-esteem, individual achievement, personal enjoyment, and self-expression. Collectivistic values prize most highly the person's obligations and duties to others. Examples of collectivistic values would be duty, loyalty, kindness, generosity, obedience, and self-sacrifice. Individualism and collectivism have been used most often to describe cultural differences in values. For example, the United States is often described as individualistic, whereas Japan, China, and other Asian cultures are often described as collectivistic.[19]

I asked the emerging adults in my research two questions whose answers reflected their values:

1. When you get toward the end of your life, what would you like to be able to say about your life, looking back on it?

2. What values or beliefs do you think are the most important to pass on to the next generation?

Let's look at their responses to each of these questions to see what the answers reveal about the values they hold.

"When You Get Toward the End of Your Life . . . ?"

Virtually all of the emerging adults in my research had a ready response to the question "When you get toward the end of your life, what would you like to be able to say about your life, looking back on it?" I think this reflects the fact that emerging adulthood is a time for forming life goals and a rough timetable for achieving them. I can't say for sure if adolescents would also have a ready response to the question because I only asked it of emerging adults, but I suspect that adolescents would find it more difficult to answer. Adolescents are usually very wrapped up in the here-and-now, the social whirl of peers and popularity, fleeting romances and would-be romances. Emerging adulthood is a time for more serious self-reflection, for thinking about what kind of life you want to live and what your Plan should be for your life. Most emerging adults answered the "When you get toward the end of your life . . . " question as if they had already given it considerable thought.

Their answers sometimes reflected individualistic values, sometimes collectivistic values, sometimes a combination of the two.[20] It is not surprising that their answers were often individualistic. They live in an individualistic society, and emerging adulthood is in many ways a self-focused time of life, a time when people focus on their self-development before they have committed themselves to a marriage partner and a child. So, even though the question asks them to think about the perspective they will have as they near the end of their lives, and even though nearly all of them expect to marry and have children eventually, in emerging adulthood their answer to this question is often in terms of their individualistic pursuit of happiness.

For many emerging adults, pursuing individual happiness means obtaining a wide range of life experiences. Christy said that by the end of her life she hoped to say:

> I lived it to the fullest. That I didn't just sit back and wait to die. There's too much out there to enjoy and experience. So I want to look back and

say I traveled, I ate bizarre food, I met the neatest people. I want to be able to show people the things I brought home from my travels. And I want to say I ran a marathon this year, I went kayaking this year, and I skydived . . . because I think all those experiences give some sort of a color and taste to your life.

Nicole's comments were similar. "I'd like to say that I lived a good life, and I didn't limit myself. If there's something that I wanted to do, I did it, and I didn't let anything hold me back. If somebody says, 'I've got a ticket for you to go to Brazil for two weeks. Do you want to go?' If I felt like going, I did it, you know. Just live a sky's-the-limit life."

Some emerging adults spoke of individual accomplishments rather than experiences as their life goals. Dalton hoped to be able to say that he "started from the bottom and worked my way to the top and accomplished basically what I really set out to do." Larry had very specific accomplishments in mind. "I would hope that I have achieved all that I thought I could. I want that big house, four-car garage, 50 acres of land and [to] be able to go on vacation for a month out of the year."

For other emerging adults, their life goals were described less in terms of specific experiences or accomplishments and more in terms of whatever would bring them the most enjoyment. For example, by the end of his life, Jerry hoped to be able to say "that I had a good time, because if I'm having a good time, I'm happy, and that's pretty much what I've gathered that everybody wants to do is just live a happy life, you know. It's not going to be free from grief at all times, but I'd say just that I had fun. I'm a fun seeker." Burt also wanted to be able to say "that I had a lot of fun. We're only here for so long, 70 years, which is nothing, and I just want to make sure that I have the most fun that I can." Likewise, Joan hoped to say "that I had fun. I want to be able to say, 'If I wanted to do it, I did it.' I want to have tons of fun, and no regrets." That phrase, "no regrets," was used often by emerging adults to describe how they hoped not to let any opportunity for enjoyable and interesting experiences pass them by in the course of their lives.

It seems likely that for many of these "fun seekers," their life goals will change in the future. Once they marry and have children, their goals are likely to be focused less on their individualistic pursuit of happiness and more on their responsibilities to others, especially their spouses and children. But while they are in emerging adulthood, as long as their future spouses and children remain hypothetical, when they think of their life goals they often think mainly in terms of what they want for themselves.

It is understandable that emerging adults often have individualistic life goals. What is perhaps more interesting and more surprising is that many of them have life goals that reflect more collectivistic values, emphasizing what they hope to do for others in the course of their lives. Robert Bellah has argued that Americans have a "first language" of individualism, meaning that when they speak about moral values, Americans most typically and most easily speak in terms of individualistic values.[21] But for many emerging adults, especially in ethnic minority groups, it is collectivism rather than individualism that seems to be their primary moral language.[22]

Their collectivistic values are often reflected in what they hope to do for their families, both their current families (parents, siblings, etc.) and their families of the future (spouse, children). Amber, a 25-year-old African American, hoped that by the end of her life she could say "that I was a good and loving family member, and that goes for my mother, my brothers, my husband, my children, grandchildren, on down the line." Raul, a 25-year-old Latino, said, "Things I want to say about my life when it comes to the end are that I've contributed to having a family, a better life for my children and taking care of my parents when they get older." Elaine, a 20-year-old Chinese American, said, "I hope I have lots of nephews and nieces, and I hope that I've learned a lot of things in life by that time, and I can share my knowledge and my experiences with the younger generations."

Many emerging adults also hope to help people outside their families. Benny's main life goal was "to say that I helped lots of people, physically, mentally, helped somebody stuck on the road and changed a tire, or somebody's all sad and you give them a shoulder to cry on." Gerard hoped to be able to say "that I had a lot of friends, that I had a lot of people that I cared about and that cared about me, and that I feel like maybe I helped some people." Willie hoped to say, "I made a difference in people's lives, that I was able to help those who were less fortunate." Often, emerging adults plan to express collectivistic values of generosity and care for others through the work they choose. Sophie, studying to be a teacher, hoped to be able to say "that I was able to help the students that I'll be teaching through life and helping them if they had any trouble or problems or anything." Sylvia hoped to be able to say, "I've been able to help a lot of people in terms of being a nurse and caring for them when they're sick. That I was a good nurse, that I was able to do my job and comfort them."

There were emerging adults whose life goals reflected individualistic values and others whose life goals reflected collectivistic values, but there were also emerging adults whose life goals reflected both kinds of values.

Individualism and collectivism are not necessarily in opposition to each other, but can both be part of the ideal that emerging adults have for their lives.[23] Doug hoped to be able to say "that I was able to do things that I wanted to do, that I was still having a good time even at the end of my life," but also "that I was always there for the people I cared for." Rosa hoped to say "that I experienced as much as I possibly could, lived a full life" but also "that I spent as much time with my friends and my family as possible, and that people know how I feel about them. I tell my mom I love her every time I talk to her." Arthur said, "I'd like to say that I was really good at something. I'd like to say that I was happy and fulfilled," but he added, "I'd like to say that I made an impact on other people. I mean, I want to know that I have made other people's lives better in some way." Emerging adults may be individualistic, but their individualism is often leavened by collectivistic values of care and concern for others.

"What Values and Beliefs . . . to Pass On to the Next Generation?"

Like the question about life goals, the question "What values or beliefs do you think are the most important to pass on to the next generation?" typically evoked a thoughtful and articulate response from the emerging adults we interviewed. Perhaps this is because emerging adults are reaching the age when most of them will soon think about having children of their own, which has led them to think about what kinds of values they would want those children to learn. Also like the question about life goals, the question about the next generation evoked some individualistic responses, some collectivistic responses, and some responses that combined the two types of values.

Some emerging adults were distinctly individualistic. Catharine said, "I think it's important to teach them to be proud of themselves. I think personal self-confidence is very important. . . . Do what you want to do and be strong in what you want to do." Similarly, Don wanted to pass on the value of "independent thinking, and to really kind of just follow your own dreams, whatever those are, just really go after whatever it is that you hold in your heart." Gilbert wanted the next generation to know "that you don't have to rely on people to do things. If you want to be strong, be strong for yourself." Jake said he wanted the next generation to learn the value of "having a sense of purpose in yourself. I think a lot of people view taking care of themselves as being selfish, or doing things for themselves as selfish. But I have a perspective that if you don't take care of yourself, you can't help anybody else and you can't take care of anybody else."

For emerging adults who wished to pass on collectivistic values to the next generation, those values were most often spoken of in terms of some version of the Golden Rule. Roy thought the next generation should learn "just to treat others like you want to be treated yourself, and if you always do that, then I think you'll be fine. I guess that's the Golden Rule." Laurie said, "As long as you treat people the way you want to be treated, that is the biggest thing to me." Ryan also wanted to pass on the value of "do unto others as you would want them to do unto you. Just basically treat your neighbor kindly."

Some of the emerging adults who favored collectivistic values were actively hostile toward individualism. They equated individualism with selfishness and viewed individualistic values as a source of problems. Andrea said, "I think I'd like to pass on a sense of community. Our society has gotten so into 'Me-ism,' and everybody says that you need to do what's best for you. I don't think that's always necessarily true because everybody has to make sacrifices for other people. I think our generation needs to know that it's not all about you." Arthur said he wanted the next generation to learn that "the value of wanting to help other people is very important. I would hate for my own children to be self-centered people that only looked out for themselves." Tammy was especially vehement about what she wants the next generation to learn.

> Everything you do or say or believe or feel, every action, every thought, every movement you make affects everyone else. It's such a self kind of society. "You're first. You're number one. You're the best. No one will take care of you if you don't take care of yourself." It's all so self, self, self. And look what's happened. We're so into doing for ourselves that nobody is helping anybody else.

However, as with the life-goals question, so with the next-generation question many emerging adults reconciled individualistic and collectivistic values in their responses. Bob said, "I would hope that they could learn to balance loyalty to themselves, being true to themselves, with being good to the people around you. The bottom line for me is do whatever you want to do to make yourself happy, as long as it's contributing to other people's happiness, too." Nicole had a similar view. "I just say respect yourself and then that would make you more mindful of other people. Have self-esteem, but don't be selfish. If you see somebody that's down on their luck and you can help them, help them." Harry was succinct. "Do what you want for yourself, but keep an eye out for the next guy, too." Dylan said, "You need to have your own principles and your own value base so that you're independent," but added that he wanted the next generation to learn "the Golden Rule, to treat other people like you would want them to treat you. The love-your-neighbor kind of thing."

Religious values also came up in response to the next-generation question. I noted at the outset of the chapter that values are sometimes based on religious beliefs. For the one-third of emerging adults for whom religious beliefs are especially important, there is a strong connection between their religious beliefs and the values they would like to pass on to the next generation. Del said he would most like to pass on "the belief that God is the savior of the world, and if you believe in him you'll have everlasting life." Shonitra said she would advise the next generation that "you've got to have God in your life. I feel like you have to have him in your life in order to succeed. I know that the devil is here to really destroy us, and if you don't have that protection, then most people aren't going to make it." Rita also said she would emphasize the importance of religious faith, because "I just can't imagine a person who didn't believe in God, how they get through hard times." Deanna explicitly made a connection between values and religious beliefs. "Nothing else really does as much as the word of God, I believe. And that determines your values and how you live your life and how you treat your family and how hard you work at school. It's all shaped by your beliefs." Shalanda said she wanted to pass on to the next generation "salvation, Christ, having God number one in your life. It's a better way of life. It works in every aspect. If that's going good and that's going right, everything else will line up."

Conclusion: The Diversity of Beliefs and Values Among Emerging Adults

The freedom that emerging adults have to choose how to live results in a striking diversity of beliefs and values. Emerging adults are atheists, religious conservatives, and everything in between. Many of them have developed their own idiosyncratic beliefs by combining different religious traditions in unique ways and adding a dollop of popular culture. With regard to their values, some are avidly individualistic, some are collectivistic, and some combine the two ethics.

If there is a unifying theme in all of this diversity, it is their insistence on making their own choices about what to believe and what to value. In their religious beliefs, there is little relation between what they were exposed to by their parents in childhood and adolescence and what they believe now, as emerging adults. Even the one-fourth of emerging adults who are religious conservatives have come to those beliefs through a personal process of questioning and searching. Emerging adults' values, too, are self-chosen. Even for those who embrace collectivistic values, their values are the product of their own ruminations on their life experiences and observations.

However, the emphasis on independent thinking that is so characteristic of emerging adults does not mean that they are selfish, or alienated from society, or that they wish to live an atomistic life unconnected to others. Over half of emerging adults attend religious services at least now and then, and more plan to attend once they grow a bit older and have children. For those who reject religious institutions, it is usually not because they are self-absorbed but because they doubt the morality of those institutions. In their values, most emerging adults are not extreme individualists but are either predominantly collectivistic or try to live by both ethics, wishing to live a personally fulfilling life while also doing some good for others. Although emerging adults are at a self-focused time of life, independent of their parents but not yet committed to new family ties, most of them nevertheless seek to find a balance between living the kind of life they want and treating others as they wish to be treated.

9

The Age of Possibilities

Four Case Studies

I s EMERGING ADULTHOOD ONLY FOR the privileged? Being an emerging adult means exploring different possibilities in love and work before settling on long-term choices, and it is true that coming from a family with substantial resources might make it easier in some ways to extend your period of exploration. With regard to work, certainly, if your parents can give you financial support through college and maybe even graduate school, you have more of an opportunity to explore possible careers than someone who feels compelled to go to work full time after high school just to pay the bills, instead of going to college.

But this is only part of the story. In another sense, reaching emerging adulthood is even more important and more promising for someone from a difficult background than for someone from a privileged background. Children and adolescents are at the mercy of their parents, for better or worse. If their parents are well-off financially, happily married, and loving toward their children, the children benefit from those advantages. But if their parents fight often, are physically abusive, go through a bitter divorce, are alcoholics, or are mentally ill—just a few of the problems exhibited by the parents of emerging adults we interviewed—then the children inevitably suffer from the kind of family environment that the parents' problems create. They cannot escape; there is nowhere else for them to go.

In emerging adulthood, however, this changes. Now they are capable of leaving home and living on their own. Their parents' problems need no longer be their problems, too. When they reach emerging adulthood, they have a chance to transform their lives and set out on a different path from their parents. This is one of the most important features of emerging adulthood, that it represents a possibility for people from difficult backgrounds to transform their lives. Emerging adulthood is arguably the period of the life course when the possibility for dramatic change is greatest. Children and adolescents are too limited in what they can do on their own to have much opportunity for changing the direction of their lives. After emerging adulthood, once people make enduring choices in love and work and take on long-term obligations, especially the obligation of caring for a child, it becomes more difficult to change course. Emerging adulthood is the freest, most independent period of life for most people. For people who are unhappy, who feel their lives are headed in the wrong direction, who desire to make a dramatic change for the better, emerging adulthood is the time to do it.

But isn't it too late by then? If a person grows up in an unhealthy family environment, isn't that environment unfortunately but indelibly stamped on their personalities, for the rest of their lives? This is the view that has long been dominant in Western thought. "The child is father to the man," the poet William Wordsworth famously declared some two centuries ago. At the dawn of psychology a century ago, Freud declared that the personality, and therefore one's fate in life, is more or less fixed by age six. Even today, there is more research on infancy and early childhood than on the rest of the life course combined, indicating that the belief still reigns that it is in the early years of life that our fate is determined once and for all.

Clearly many people believe this, scholars and nonscholars alike. But maybe this claim is exaggerated. Even if it is generally true, even if there is a correlation between childhood experiences and later development, there may be many people for whom this does not apply. And the proportion of people for whom it does not apply may grow sharply in emerging adulthood, the age of possibilities, as people gain greater freedom to run their own lives.

In this chapter, we look at four emerging adults whose lives raise doubts that our early years permanently decide the path we will follow in the future. All of them experienced terrible events or circumstances in childhood, all of them had lives that were in disarray by adolescence, and all of them transformed themselves in emerging adulthood and turned their lives in a dramatically different direction, toward health and happiness. Their lives suggest that whatever may have happened from infancy through adolescence, emerging adulthood represents an opportunity—maybe a last opportunity—to turn one's life around.

Jeremy: "I'm Equipped to Make Better Judgments"

Jeremy, 25, was an imposing physical presence, six feet tall with a muscular build and a thick, strong neck. He had light reddish-blond hair and a beard to match, about one week's growth, neatly trimmed. We met at his sparsely furnished apartment near my office at the University of Missouri on a weekend afternoon, and he was dressed for leisure: black jeans and a T-shirt with a map of Australia on it. His warm smile made the big man seem gentle despite his size.

Hearing about his childhood, it was surprising that he smiled at all by now. From infancy through adolescence, his life was tumultuous and painful. His parents had divorced, remarried each other, then divorced again by the time he was three. Shortly after they divorced the second time, his mother married again, a different man this time. While she was at work, his stepfather "threw me in the closet as soon as she'd leave for the day."

That marriage lasted only a year, and then he and his mother were on their own for a few years. He remembers that period as "probably the happiest time of my life," even though his mother "had to leave me alone a lot because she couldn't afford baby-sitters." What made it happy was that they "always got along. My mom was always more like my big sister than my mom."

However, by the time he was eight his mother had married again, and his second stepfather was even more abusive than the first. "He'd come in and beat on me while she was in the bathtub or when she left. He'd hide it from her." His mother and stepfather quarreled often, and the worst beatings took place when he tried to intervene to protect his mother. "They were fighting all the time, and I couldn't handle it. I couldn't ever help my mom, and I felt frustrated and helpless there. I'd go in and yell at him, and I'd get sent to my room. And then she'd leave, and he'd come beat the hell out of me for interrupting."

This was the beginning of "the whole cycle, where I went from one abuse to the next." At age 11, he moved to Arizona to live with his father and stepmother, but there he fought constantly with his stepmother. He "hung out with a bad crowd" of kids who "kind of accepted me when my parents didn't." The younger boys in the gang went "back and forth with backpacks full of drugs" for the older boys, who paid them in pizza and video games. He got in fights and "got beat up real bad once." He had altercations with the police, and spent time in a juvenile jail.

Jeremy's father and stepmother got fed up and sent him back to his mother and stepfather, but they did not want him either, and he went to live with his grandparents for a while. They were Jehovah's Witnesses, and they set about "trying to take control of me and make me a Jehovah's Witness, which I didn't want to do." Suspicious of outsiders, they would not let him have friends over, and he spent a lot of time alone. "It was hard enough to make friends, moving here from Arizona, but not being able to ever have anybody over made it harder."

He tried moving in with his mother and stepfather again, but the old pattern of conflict soon reemerged. Finally, all his other options exhausted, he moved out on his own. He was 15 years old.

How could Jeremy live on his own at age 15? His mother and stepfather were willing to pay the rent on his apartment to get rid of him, and he got a job to supply himself with food and other necessities. Not surprisingly, his school work "kind of took a back burner" to his job and the responsibilities of daily life on his own. With no parents around to keep an eye on him, throughout high school he got drunk often, smoked pot often, "just a lot of wild things." He lived for the moment and gave little thought to the future. "When I was in high school, I didn't really think I'd make it to this age. I didn't really think about where I wanted to go or what I was going to do."

To look at Jeremy's life as he entered emerging adulthood, you would have thought it was unpromising, to say the least. As he puts it, "Everybody says I should be some kind of a mass murderer or something after all the things I've gone through." The physical abuse, the bitter divorce of his parents, the hostility from his stepparents, the experience of being "bounced around" from one household to the next, the substance abuse, the school problems, the gang involvement—any one of these experiences might have predicted a troubled future, and in combination, you would think his fate was sealed.

Yet here he is at age 25, engaged to be married, attending college full time while working 20–30 hours a week, no longer a substance abuser, seemingly at peace with himself and the world, an all-around good guy. What was it about his experiences in emerging adulthood that enabled him to overcome the influences of his childhood?

Meeting his fiancée three years ago was a big turning point. Their relationship "pushed me in a totally different direction than where I was headed." He calls her "my best friend" and says, "She meets every requirement I could ever have in a friend. I feel like I can trust her. We just click and get along." Research on criminals has indicated that a solid love relationship is one of the strongest influences against future crime,[1] and Jeremy's story suggests that maybe it works in a similar way for noncriminals who also have a troubled past. Love gives people something to live for, a compelling reason to plan for the future and stay out of trouble, and structures daily life in a way that makes opportunities for deviance less likely.

But the change in Jeremy's life is perhaps due even more to simply reaching emerging adulthood, because it meant gaining a new maturity in his understanding of his life. To Jeremy, becoming an adult entailed learning how to handle whatever life throws at him.

> There's a lot of things that people say makes you an adult that I don't agree with, because I was doing those things when I was 16 or 17, and I was definitely not an adult then. Once you know how to handle most things that come your way and nothing really throws you for a loop and you don't get upset every time something goes wrong, I think that's one of the first steps toward being an adult.

This new maturity in his thinking has enabled him to see the potential benefits of his past trials. "Hopefully, with what I've got behind me and the experiences I've had, I'm equipped to make better judgments to push my life in a better direction." He believes that coming through such difficult times has made him stronger and more resilient. "There's a lot of bad things that have happened in my life, and I just kind of feel like, anymore, they kind of roll off."

It is not only that he has become better equipped to handle what others might do to him. He also takes a share of responsibility for the troubles he has had in the past, and he has tried to change how he treats others. "I take a lot more care to think about other people and think about how my actions are going to affect them, where before I was more interested in what I could get for myself. I've just become a lot less self-centered."

As a consequence of these changes in himself, the changes in Jeremy's life have been profound. For several years out of high school, he worked in semiskilled manual labor for a company that did flood and fire restoration. At the time, he was happy enough to make some money and did not think much in terms of a long-term plan, but by his early twenties he started thinking about what his life would be like 10, 20, 30 years down the road, and he realized he wanted to do something other than manual labor. So he entered college at age 23 to pursue a business degree, and he has stuck with it and maintained "a straight B average," something that he does not think he would have been capable of doing when he was younger. "Before, it was difficult for me to put any energy in anything that I didn't get a paycheck out of. If I didn't get something immediately back for it, I didn't want to put the effort into it. I couldn't look far enough ahead. I wanted instant gratification." Now, however, "I just kind of feel that I can see a goal. I'm much more prepared."

A profound change has also taken place in his relationships with his parents and stepparents. "I get along fairly well with my stepmother and my stepfather now. Let bygones be bygones, you know, and I've let them go. And I've really grown to like my mom and dad. Moving out helped. And time's helped. Time's helped a lot of things. Everybody's grown up."

Nicole: "I Needed to Experience Freedom"

Nicole, 25, met me for our interview at an outdoor café in Berkeley, California. She came straight from her job as a receptionist and medical assistant at a dermatology center, and she was dressed very professionally: a nice lavender dress and a silver necklace with matching earrings. An African American woman, her skin was very dark, and she had long, straight black hair. She was a small woman, but she had a large, expressive mouth.

To look at her, so polished and professional, and to listen to her, so thoughtful, articulate, and ambitious, you would never have guessed that she grew up in dreadful circumstances in what she called "the ghetto," the housing projects of Oakland, with no father and a poor, mentally ill, entirely incompetent mother. Nicole was just six years old when her mother had "her nervous breakdown." The functioning of the household was already shaky, but after her mother's collapse it totally disintegrated into disorganization and chaos. Nicole remembers "days, sometimes even weeks" when the only meal she got was the free lunch for poor kids at school.

It was Nicole, her mother's oldest of four children by three fathers, who took over and pulled the household together—*at age six*. "I became the mother. I had to be the strong one. It was never something that was put upon me. It was just, I saw it had to be done." She made sure her brothers and sister got washed, dressed, and fed each day. She cleaned the house and kept it in order. By the age of eight, she was working in order to make money that would enable her to buy food and other essentials for the household.

I swept stores, I baby-sat. I did whatever I could, because otherwise we went without. At like eight years old, I had neighbors who were like, "Oh, Nicole, can you watch my kid?" Everybody thought, "Well, she's older than her age. She can handle this." And I could. I made a couple bucks and helped my mother out, helped my family out.

Still, the help she gave to her family came at a personal cost to her. Because she was so consumed with family responsibilities, she rarely had time or energy left over for school work, and through high school her grades were low. She graduated from high school, but she was never regarded as a promising student, the kind who might go on to college or even get a graduate degree.

It was only when she reached emerging adulthood that she was able to turn her attention to her personal goals. She got a full-time job, found an apartment, and moved out on her own. Soon, she started taking college courses in the evening. Despite having a full-time job in addition to taking courses, she got excellent grades. Removing herself from the chaos of her family household was the key.

I needed to experience freedom. I needed to experience living out of my mother's home in order to study. I couldn't really get my studying skills down pat until I moved out, and when I moved, I'm like, gosh, I always knew I could excel in school. In order for me to go to school and function properly, I need to be on my own.

Because she works full time and can only take evening courses, her progress toward a degree has been slow, but she is undaunted. "I'm going to get my degree, however long it takes." She is within one course of an associate's degree, but that is just the beginning of her educational ambitions. She plans to get a bachelor's degree next, and eventually a Ph.D. in psychology. Talking about getting a Ph.D. sent her into rapture. "Ooooh, I love the word. I want to have it in 10 years, by 35. That's feasible."

Still, she tries not to look too far ahead.

I'm just trying to get through the day-to-day. If I focus so long-term, I'll like get crazy. I'm so hard on myself. I really set unrealistic goals at times. So now I'm just like, OK, take it one step at a time. Look ahead, but just for five seconds. You know, "your future's still there." It's like, "I'm just checking on you, Future." And then move on.

Her goal of getting a Ph.D. and becoming a clinical psychologist is inspired partly by her childhood experiences and partly by her interpretation of her mother's condition. Because of her own experiences, she plans to work with "so-called dysfunctional children and kids from broken homes." She hopes to help children avoid the problems that plague her mother.

> As a young child, I remember my mother working and just this beautiful woman. Then she had a nervous breakdown, and she went kind of crazy. She stopped working, she got on AFDC [Aid for Families With Dependent Children]. So that's something very important to me, to be constantly building a person's self-esteem and getting in touch with themselves and just accepting life, you know, no matter what happens to you. Just deal with it and move to the next level.

She talks about working with girls, in particular. "I'd like to have like a consultation agency, kind of like a wellness group—bring young girls in, talk to them about self-esteem and problems they were having at home."

Nicole is so focused on work and school that love has been moved to the back burner for now. "Right now, I'm not really focusing too much on guys," she said. "I don't have time. Most of the time, guys I meet, they're like time wasters or time thieves. So I'm just not into the whole dating scene right now." She realizes her reluctance to get involved with a man makes her different than most of the women she grew up with. "I see my friends, and they're like, 'Well, don't you want to get married? Don't you want children?' I mean, by this time, 25, I'm an old maid, I'm over the hill. I might as well be 50. You know, by this time I should have two kids by two daddies. But I'm not ready right now. I can wait."

She prefers to focus on her own goals and her own identity at this point in her life. Like many emerging adults, she feels that only after she has a fully formed identity and has learned to stand on her own will she be ready to commit herself to someone else.[2] She believes she needs to be self-focused during this time in order to succeed. "I'm just trying to focus on me and get my life together. Right now, I guess this is kind of like a selfish time for me. I'm just really trying to get into myself so that when I come out of that, I can deal with someone else. Right now, I just gotta keep the tunnel vision."

After so many years of being devoted to the needs of her mother and her siblings, she relishes the opportunity for her identity explorations and regards them as an exciting adventure.

Every day that I wake up, I learn something new about myself. Learning about yourself is a really emotional thing because it's like you wake up one day and you think you're living the way you want to live, and then the next day you get up and it's like, "Wait a minute, I'm doing everything wrong. I don't know who I am." And you have to be willing to take that step forward and say, OK, I'm going to get to know myself no matter if it's painful or if it's going to make me happy. I have to dig deep within myself and figure out who I am. And this is a learning process every day.

Nicole's optimism in the face of difficulties, her ability to see the potential benefits of even the most dire circumstances, is perhaps the most striking feature of her personality, and it is this ability that is at the heart of her resilience.[3] She calls her childhood of growing up with a deficit of resources and an overload of responsibility "a big learning experience. I don't think I regret it because had I not gone through it, I wouldn't be the person I am today." She believes the deprivations of her childhood have made her more appreciative of the things she has now. "It's like a blessing. If I see somebody on the street who's dirty and smelly, I think, gosh, at least I have some place to sleep. I mean, it always could be worse. Had I not experienced that, maybe I wouldn't think that way."

Similarly, she sees no reason to regret her delay in going to college and the slow progress she has made so far. "I don't think everyone is set to go to college as soon as they get out of high school. Some people have life experiences that they need to get, and that's something I needed to do." She sees her current job in the same optimistic light. Although she does not find much satisfaction in the work she does as a receptionist and medical assistant, seeing it as a step on the way to something better makes it less onerous now. "I just look at it all as temporary because I know what I want to do in the future."

Although Nicole is enjoying her emerging adulthood as a long-awaited chance to focus on her own goals and her own life, she still has a strong sense of duty and obligation to her family. I asked her if she had thought about working fewer hours in order to take more college courses. "The only thing is I would worry about my family because right now I think of them," she said. "That's one thing I still battle daily is like if I should just waitress or do something part time and go to school full time and just worry less about my family, supporting them. I just feel like I gotta take care of them."

Her ambitions are driven in part by the dream of taking her mother's worries away so that she might finally recover from her psychological problems.

> That's why it's so important for me to be really successful and make a lot of money, so I can buy my mother a house and put her in a situation where she doesn't have to worry about the bills. She doesn't have to worry about her clothes. She doesn't have to worry about having food. It will all be there. It's like, "now you've got everything—move on."

If only she could bestow on her mother some of her own steely determination. "I just wish I could give her that strength to say, 'I'm gonna take care of me. I'm gonna make a choice. I'm gonna do something with my life.' It's never too late." As for Nicole, in spite of a childhood full of adversity, in emerging adulthood her hopes are high, her optimism undiminished. "It's like, the more you come at me, the stronger I'm going to be."

Bridget: "Now I Answer to Myself"

Bridget, 23, arrived at my University of Missouri office one evening directly from her job as a supervisor at a temporary employment agency. She was sharply dressed in a green turtleneck, green plaid jacket, and blue skirt, and her shoulder-length blonde hair was nicely groomed.

"It wasn't a terribly happy childhood," she said of her first 18 years, and as she described her family life that sounded like an understatement. Physical abuse, emotional abuse, alcoholism, bitter conflict, estrangement— "My family is the role model for the dysfunctional family," she said. Her mother claims, "I caused her 18 years of unhappiness" just for being born, because the pregnancy forced her parents into a loveless marriage. Throughout her childhood her mother told her, "I would never have married him if it hadn't been for you." Needless to say, her parents' marriage was no garden of delights. "They fought like crazy," Bridget recalls. "It was very physically abusive. He hit her a lot. She has an alcohol problem. And he would come home from work sometimes and just beat the holy living crap out of her. He had the anger problem, and she had the alcohol problem."

When her parents were not abusing each other, they abused Bridget and her younger sister. "Mom was good at verbal abuse, and Dad was good at the physical. Of course, the verbal was worse." Bridget's mind still resonates with all the nasty things her mother told her as she was growing up. "You're ugly. You're fat. You'll never have any friends. You're stupid."

It is true she never had any friends as a child, mainly because her mother was so abusive to any kids who came around.

> I never really had neighborhood friends because my mom would always find fault with their families or find fault with them. She made it very difficult for me to have friends as a child. Very difficult. Because she didn't get along with the parents. She was jealous of everyone. Anyone who was thinner than her, prettier than her, had hair that was nicer than hers, had a car that was nicer than hers.

How did Bridget emerge from this nightmare to become the happy, healthy young woman she is today? One key was the development of her religious faith.[4] She had little exposure to religious training as a child. "My parents were atheists. They didn't believe in God." However, when she reached high school she became involved in a religious organization almost accidentally, and something about it resonated with her.

> I started going to church when I was a sophomore in high school, because I dated a boy that I had a really big crush on, and when he broke up with me I was devastated and I was like, "I'll just go to his church, and that way we'll have something in common." So I started going, and I thought, "My gosh, I like this. I like these people." And so by a year later, I was saved. Definitely, that was something that influenced my life.

Her church was a refuge for her during her otherwise painful high school years.

> I wonder now what my life would have been like had I not had this positive influence. All throughout high school, because of that church group I was always around happy people, people that had fun with their lives, people that really enjoyed living. And out of all this gloom that I had in my home life, I could always escape to my friends, and I'll always be grateful for that.

She continues to attend the same church, and she remains close to many of the people there, and grateful to them. "I am so close to some families at church that just really helped me out. They give this unconditional love.

That's something I still don't understand, how people that barely knew me could give me unconditional love because of Jesus, so much more than my own parents. That just didn't make sense, and it still doesn't and it never will."

Bridget's faith kept her afloat during high school, but the real turning point in her life came in emerging adulthood. Becoming an emerging adult made it possible for her to remove herself from her toxic family household. "It's always been bad, and now it's just not there, which I guess is good. I feel more peaceful. I don't have to deal with it on a daily basis. I don't have to worry about whether they would yell at me about something. Now I answer to myself." Once she had moved out, it was easier to avoid their destructive influence. "I tried not to be around them a lot, not spending a lot of time at home, going away to college, getting away for a complete year in Sweden, where I had to do it or die."

Her college year in Sweden was a watershed, "a huge turn of events," Bridget says. It was there that she realized that she no longer needed to rely on her family, that she could stand alone as a self-sufficient person—that, really, she had no other choice. "I got to Sweden and I called to try to talk to them, and they wouldn't accept my calls. So I think that when I was thousands of miles away from home in a strange country not knowing what I'm going to do when I get back, I knew that kind of thrust me into adulthood, whether I wanted to or not." It was then that she accepted responsibility for her life, it was then that she realized "that I had to be accountable for my actions, and that I am my own person and that what I do is going to directly affect my entire life."

In emerging adulthood, not only has Bridget separated herself from destructive family influences, but she has also reinterpreted her past family experiences, so that she sees her suffering as something that has built her up rather than torn her down. "There's been a lot of pain and a lot of hurt, but I've really grown from it," she says. She sees her experiences, even the bad ones, as an essential part of her identity. "It's made me the person who I am today," she says. "It all happens for a reason."

Coming back from Sweden, she knew she faced a challenge, being entirely on her own, but she accepted it with relish. "I could have, when I came back, worked at Wal-Mart for the rest of my life because, you know, I'd had the hard breaks or whatever." Instead, she finished her college degree, paid for with her own hard work, and laid the foundation for a promising future. "I'm very proud of what I've done and how I got there," she says. "I've worked my ass off to get where I am."

One of Bridget's definite dreams is to have a husband and children. Witnessing her parents' awful relationship has made her cautious about marriage, but not cynical. "I love the idea of falling in love and being with one person, and having someone to share your life with. I think I'd be ready for that if I found the right person. But I'm not going to rush it. I'm not going to settle for anything less than I deserve." She envisions providing her own children with a family environment much different than her own: "A real loving household. Open communication. No violence. I will never strike a child." Her resilience despite horrendous family conditions makes her optimistic about how her own children might fare in the world.

> Something that I've noticed around people my age is that they're very cynical about "well, I'm not going to have kids because I don't want to bring them up in a world like this." I don't really have that view because I look at myself growing up in a very bigoted household—prejudiced, backwards, any other negative term you could use—and I got out of it. So I have hope.

She also has career ambitions, although they are not clearly defined at this point. "I do want a career in something like human relations," she says, but shortly after she adds, "I would really like to teach high school. I think I would be a good teacher." She also remains open to new possibilities. "Tonight if someone called and said, 'You have an opportunity to go to Eastern Europe to teach English as a second language, would you do it?' I'd say, 'Yeah, when does my flight leave?'"

Although Bridget's life right now is uncertain, one thing she is certain about is that the future is bright. "I look at what's happened in the last 2 years of my life, and it's changed so much that I can't possibly see what's going to happen in 10 years. It'll be pretty exciting, I'm sure."

Derek: "I Feel I've Been Very Fortunate"

Derek was 28 years old, but he had the look of someone in no hurry to reach adulthood. He was African American, but he had dyed his hair blonde, which made for a striking contrast to his coffee-colored skin. He had silver studs in his chin and his tongue. His tan felt beret was on backward, and he wore a striped T-shirt and light pants. In short, he looked much more like he was in the role of his part-time job, as a DJ in a San Francisco nightclub, than of his full-time job, as a server in a restaurant.

His family history was so chaotic and tragic that if it were fiction it would be rejected as unbelievable. He was given up for adoption at birth, and after five months in a foster home he was adopted by a White, affluent New England family. But his adoptive father was an alcoholic, and when Derek was three years old his parents divorced, an event he calls "a catastrophe." Then, when he was five years old, his mother died in a car accident, along with a sister and an aunt. Derek was in the car, too, and he remembers that the accident seemed to happen in "slow motion, and it was basically loud and confusing."

Derek and his remaining two sisters and brother went to live with his father, but his father's alcoholism had worsened since the divorce, and he was in the midst of a downward spiral, in no condition to raise four children. "He started drinking more and spending his money and getting really extravagant," Derek recalled. He was soon forced to sell his share of the advertising agency that had made his fortune, and the downward spiral continued as "he gambled, sold his cars, hit rock bottom." Derek and his siblings were dispersed to other family members, and Derek was passed to an aunt and uncle, then to his grandparents, then to a boarding school for three years (from age 11 to 14), then to "a 60-acre organic commune" for a half year, then to another aunt and uncle through high school. His father did eventually stop drinking, when Derek was in fifth grade, but "the rest of his life was spent trying to recover, physically and financially," and Derek never lived with him again. He died the year after Derek graduated from high school, from years of too much alcohol and cigarettes.

As an African American growing up in "90% White" areas of New England, Derek had substantial experience with what he calls "the brutality of childhood." During recess at school, the other kids played a game they called "Chase the Nigger," starring Derek. After school he ran all the way home, trying to avoid kids who were hoping to beat him up and who sometimes succeeded.

By high school, Derek was filled with anxiety. "I was in a constant panic. I was depressed a lot. I didn't think about the future." His anxieties were projected outward in the form of fear of nuclear war.

> I had a very nihilistic attitude toward the world, and I thought it was going to end from a nuclear war. I was mortified and petrified by the whole prospect of nuclear war. If I looked up in the sky and I saw a trail from a jet, I was worried that it was a missile. Any incident that was reported in

the *New York Times* would panic me, like the Persian Gulf War and terrorism, the whole Soviet empire—anything would stimulate that fear.

In Derek's case, this seems like a projection of his personal anxieties rather than a politically informed concern, because he was not politically involved nor interested in world affairs except for this one issue. He was extremely anxious about sexual issues as well. "I was a virgin until I was 20, and I was scared of women because, like, the only thing worse than nuclear war would be losing my virginity."

How did he change from an adolescent wracked with anxieties to an emerging adult who is happy, confident, content with himself and his life, and hopeful about the future? For Derek, once he became an emerging adult, he was more in control of his life. He was no longer simply moved around from one place to another by other people. Perhaps for this reason, his anxieties about nuclear war eased soon after high school. "It just finally came to the point where I just had to let go of fearing war," he recalls. It also helped ease his anxieties when, early in emerging adulthood, he had an intimate relationship with a woman for the first time, and sex no longer seemed more terrible than a nuclear holocaust. "My first girlfriend, I went out with her for two years, and we lived together and it was fun. The timing was right."

For Derek, it has been important to have emerging adulthood as a self-focused time to recover from the upheavals of his childhood and get his psychological house in order.

> In the last year or two, I've focused more on myself for the first time, where before, as a child, I was afraid to be alone. I was afraid to be with people, but I was scared to be alone. Then I started to communicate with people, but I was still completely petrified of being alone. Now, I'm comfortable being alone and being with people, and I don't have to be with as many people as I used to.

Although he is 28 years old, an age when most others have left emerging adulthood for the long-term commitments of young adulthood, Derek remains unsettled at this point in both love and work. He does have many female friends. "I have a strong base of female intimate friends that I've known for 5 to 10 years," he says. And he now feels ready to find someone to commit himself to. "Lately, I've had ideas of marriage and engagement and long-term relationships. And I've just recently met a woman who has just broke off an engagement with somebody, so there's the potential for a relationship right there." As for work, he realizes that his jobs as a server and a DJ do not hold much potential as long-term careers. But his experience in his last restaurant job involved him in all aspects of the business, and he thinks of owning and running a restaurant or café as something he might want to do. Still, these dreams are amorphous right now, and he realizes that he is reaching a point in his life where it is time to focus his efforts. "I'm starting to feel like it's really time to explore my potentials."

Derek's success in prevailing over his difficult childhood and adolescence is reflected not so much in definite accomplishments in love and work as in the kind of person he is. Despite being subjected to frequent upheavals as he was growing up, in emerging adulthood he has developed a strong sense of himself. "As I get older, I have learned not to sell myself so short. That's one thing about growing older, [you] take more pride in who you are and don't feel that you're not valuable. That crosses over into relationships. That crosses into living situations." Despite being subjected to prejudice, he holds no grudges toward people of other ethnic groups. "My friends are so many different ethnicities and races and creeds that I forget what they are, as well as what I am. They're just my friends with a capital F. There are no hyphen-friends in my life." Despite suffering more chaos and tragedy by age 28 than most people suffer in a lifetime, he sees the good that has come out of his past experiences. "I've had a good life. I don't feel that a lot of people have wronged me. For every like 50% tragedy, there's been like 150% support. I feel I've been very fortunate."

Conclusion: Emerging Adulthood as a Second Chance

What is it that makes it possible for a person to transcend adverse family circumstances in childhood and adolescence and nevertheless become healthy and hopeful in emerging adulthood? Research on resilience has identified a number of factors that are echoed in the lives of the four emerging adults profiled in this chapter.[5] It helps to be intelligent, and a fierce intelligence is evident in Nicole and Bridget, who have succeeded academically in spite of numerous obstacles. It helps to have a loving relationship with at least one parent, as Jeremy did with his mother, or with an adult outside the family, as Bridget had. Religious faith can be a source of strength and hope, as it was for Bridget. Personality characteristics such as persistence, determination, and optimism can be invaluable, and for all four emerging adults described here, it is striking how they were able to interpret terrible experiences in positive ways. No matter what they suffered, they managed to see their experiences favorably and feel "very fortunate," as Derek put it. They have managed to construct a healthy identity, and they accept even their worst experiences as necessary to make them into what they have become.

But in addition to these characteristics, which have been known for some time to be related to resilience among children and adolescents, there is something about reaching emerging adulthood that opens up new possibilities for transformation for people who have had more than their share of adversity during their early years. Perhaps most important, reaching emerging adulthood makes it possible to leave a pathological family situation. This is not an option readily available to children and adolescents. They do not have the skills and resources to leave a destructive home and go off on their own. Those who try often move from the frying pan into the fire, as the case of Jeremy illustrates.

In contrast, for emerging adults, leaving home is normal and expected, and most of them are quite capable of living on their own. For emerging adults whose family lives have been damaging them and undermining them for years, simply leaving that environment represents a great liberation, a chance to wipe the slate clean and start anew. Now, instead of being subjected daily to the slings and arrows of an unhappy family life, their lives become their own.

In addition to the effect of moving out on their own, there is another change that is more subtle but may be equally important in making it possible for emerging adults to transform their lives. It is their growing self-knowledge and self-understanding, the gradual clarification of their identities. Gene Bockneck calls this their *sens de pouvoir*, meaning a sense of one's own capabilities, experienced as a feeling of inner power.[6] As they move away from the noise and confusion of adolescence, they become more capable of appreciating the power they have to change what they don't like about their lives. It is this that enables emerging adults to step back and assess their lives and to decide "this is why it is not working, and this is what I need to do to make it better."

Even when emerging adults' lives change for the better, this does not mean that none of the effects of the previous 18 years of their lives will remain with them, and it does not mean that the transformation of their lives once they move out will be easy and immediate. As we have seen, for all of the emerging adults described in this chapter, it has taken them years in emerging adulthood to gain solid footing after being buffeted around so much in their youth. But once they reach emerging adulthood, it is possible for people with difficult pasts to begin to take hold of their lives and make choices that will gradually enable them to build the kind of life they want.

Of course, it could be that some people's lives take a turn for the worse in emerging adulthood. Reaching emerging adulthood means making more of your own choices, and some people make choices that are unwise or unlucky. Others may suffer troubles in emerging adulthood that send a life once seemingly headed toward a bright future suddenly careening off the road—anything from an unintended pregnancy to a terrible automobile accident to an overdependence on alcohol or other substances. No one in my study seemed to have taken this path, but that could be because such people are too preoccupied with their current problems to be willing to take part in a study like this. I would predict that for emerging adults in general, the correlation between parents' characteristics and their own characteristics declines considerably from what it was in childhood and adolescence, as they make more of their own decisions and become responsible for constructing their own lives, sometimes for better, sometimes for worse.[7]

Nevertheless, there is evidence that in emerging adulthood life is more likely to take a turn for the better than for the worse. National surveys show that emerging adulthood is a time of rising optimism and well-being for most people,[8] whether they go to college or not, whether they have a stable job or not, whether they were doing well back in high school or not. Emerging adulthood is a time of looking forward and imagining what adult life will be like, and what emerging adults imagine is generally bright and promising: a loving, happy marriage and satisfying, well-paying work. Whatever the future may actually hold, during emerging adulthood, hope prevails.

10

From Emerging Adulthood
to Young Adulthood

What Does It Mean to Become an Adult?

THE END OF ADOLESCENCE AND THE beginning of emerging adulthood is fairly easy to define. Adolescence in American society ends at about age 18, because that is the age at which most Americans finish high school and move out of their parents' household. Nearly all adolescents have in common that they attend high school, they live with their parents, and they are experiencing the physical changes of puberty. None of these remain typical after age 18, so it does not make sense to call them adolescents any more. After age 18 comes the freedom, exploration, and instability that distinguish emerging adulthood.

But when does emerging adulthood end and young adulthood begin? This is a much trickier question. I have described emerging adulthood as lasting from about age 18 to age 25, but always with the caveat that the upper age boundary is flexible.[1] Twenty-five is an estimated age that does not apply to everybody. For some people, the end of emerging adulthood comes earlier, and for many people the end of emerging adulthood comes later. Part of the definition of emerging adulthood is that it is a period of being in between adolescence and young adulthood, a period of being in the process of reaching adulthood but not there yet. But how do you know when you have arrived? It all depends on how you define adulthood.

In this chapter, we look first at how adulthood has been defined in traditional cultures and in the past in American history, then at how emerging adults today define adulthood and assess their own progress toward adult status. Next they reflect on their mixed feelings about leaving adolescence— from the perspective of emerging adulthood, it seems like an easier time.

Then they describe their mixed feelings about becoming adults—from the perspective of emerging adulthood, reaching adulthood promises stability but evokes fears of stagnation. Finally, we examine their views of the future, and how they foresee a happy and successful life for themselves even as they believe the world in general is fraught with peril.

Making the Transition to Adulthood

Traditional and Historical Conceptions of Becoming an Adult

In other places and times, the crossing of the threshold to adulthood has been relatively clear, with the focus on a single event: marriage. According to anthropologists, cultures all over the world have shared a common belief that marriage marks not only the joining together of two persons in a lifelong partnership but also the attainment of full adult status.[2] After marriage, a young man is welcomed into the men's group, no longer kept with the boys. A young woman who marries is elevated to equal status with other women. Historians of American society have come to a similar conclusion.[3] Through most of American history, until late in the 20th century, getting married meant reaching full adulthood.

Marriage no longer has this meaning in American society. It is meaningful in other important ways, of course, but its status as a marker of adult status has passed. In the many studies I and others have conducted on what people of various ages believe defines the transition to adulthood, marriage consistently ranks near rock-bottom of the 40 or so criteria that I include on a questionnaire of possible markers of adulthood.[4] In interviews, when people are given a chance to state their views about what is important to them personally as markers of their progress toward adulthood, marriage is almost never mentioned—even by people who are married.[5]

What explains the demise of marriage as a marker of adulthood? Perhaps most important is that marriage is a much less dramatic transition than it used to be even 40 or 50 years ago. By the time they marry, the majority of today's emerging adults have already known each other for several years, had a regular sexual relationship, and lived in the same household. Being married may feel different to them psychologically than cohabiting did, as we discussed in chapter 5, but in fact not much changes in their daily lives. For example, Pam married four months ago but says it had nothing to do with making her feel more like an adult. "We had been together for four years, and I just felt like it was a continuation of our relationship. I mean, we lived together anyway, so I don't think it's changed much." Compare this to the situation historically—when getting married usually involved leaving your parents' household for the first time, having a sexual relationship for the first time, and living for the first time with someone outside your family—and it's easy to see why marriage would have had greater significance as a transition to adulthood in the past than it does now.

Adulthood Here and Now: Learning to Stand Alone

But if it is not marriage that marks adulthood, what is it? What do emerging adults today believe makes a person an adult? I have researched this question for 10 years, in many different parts of the United States, with people from a variety of ethnic groups and social classes, and I have found there is a remarkably strong American consensus across all these groups. Becoming an adult today means becoming *self-sufficient*, learning to stand alone as an independent person.[6]

There are three criteria at the heart of emerging adults' views of the self-sufficiency required for adulthood: *taking responsibility for yourself, making independent decisions*, and *becoming financially independent*.[7] Table 10.1 shows that these three criteria are favored by high percentages of emerging adults on a questionnaire that asks them to "indicate whether you think each of the following must be achieved before a person can be considered an adult."[8]

Responsibility is a word that comes up over and over again in interviews when emerging adults respond to the question of what it means to be an adult, and usually it means responsibility for yourself, not others. Tammy has begun to feel like an adult recently because "I finally realized that I'm responsible for everything I do and say and believe, and no one else is, just me. That's all, so I'm an adult." Ray said becoming an adult means "taking care of your own responsibilities and not having to lean on people for everything. If you can take care of your every need without relying on other people, then I really believe you should be pretty much an adult."

In part, taking responsibility for yourself means accepting responsibility for the consequences of your actions rather than looking for someone else to blame if things go wrong. "A boy doesn't necessarily take responsibility for his own actions," said Cliff. "It can be someone else's fault that he acts up. It's the parents' fault or it's society's fault. But a man is responsible for whatever he does, and his choices are his and he succeeds and fails on his own." Hoyt gave a specific example.

Table 10.1. Selected Criteria for Adulthood, Questionnaire Responses

Necessary for Adulthood?	% Indicating "Yes"
Accept responsibility for the consequences of your actions	93
Decide on personal beliefs and values independently of parents or other influences	81
Become less self-oriented, develop greater consideration for others	81
Financially independent from parents	74
Use contraception if sexually active and not trying to conceive a child	66
No longer living in parents' household	55
Avoid drunk driving	42
Make life-long commitments to others	40
Reached age 18	40
Reached age 21	34
Become employed full-time	26
Married	15
Finished with education	15
Have at least one child	14

Note: The questionnaire asked participants to "Indicate whether you think each of the following must be achieved before a person can be considered an adult."

> I bought a truck one time for $500. It was a junker. Put a new engine in it, put a new transmission in it, did all the work myself and spent some money on it, and it was still a junker when I got done with it. It's one of those things where you realize, "Well, I really screwed this one up. I'm going to have to take the responsibility for it. I can't put it off on anybody else this time. I'm an adult and I made the decision to buy the heap of junk. This is a learning experience."

Making independent decisions is the second most important marker of adulthood. Emerging adults believe that to be considered an adult a person has to use independent judgment in making the decisions, small and large, that come up in the course of daily life. To Arthur, becoming an adult means "having the freedom to make decisions about your own life, I think, as opposed to having someone else dictate them to you." Likewise for Vicky, reaching adulthood involves "actually making your own decisions. Not having someone always tell you what to do, but saying, 'This is what I want to do, and this is how I'm going to go do it.'" Wendy feels she has reached adulthood because "all the decisions I make are my own. I discuss them with other people for input, but they don't make the final decision for me."

The scope of independent decision making includes not only topics such as where to live and what career to pursue, but also the less tangible area of what your beliefs and values should be. The item on making independent decisions in Table 10.1 refers specifically to this: "Decide on personal beliefs and values . . ." For Mindy, this area was crucial to her sense of reaching adulthood.

> I was from a very religious background—Southern Baptist—and I had to learn to believe what I believe and not let my parents or anyone else tell me what to believe. And I think once you can establish your own beliefs and control your own life, then you're an adult.

For some emerging adults, there was one especially important decision that marked their transition to adulthood because they made it themselves. Chalantra, now 20, married young; she was just 18. Too young, as it turned out, because they divorced a year later. "When I decided to get divorced, I made that decision on my own," she says now. "And I feel like that makes you an adult, when you can sit down and weigh out things and realize that something is for you or isn't for you." For Laurie, choosing to have sex for the first time was the crucial decision. "I don't think that I really considered myself a woman until my first sexual experience. I grew up in a really strict home and always believed you should wait until you're married. And basically when I did it, that was a big turning point for me because it was my own decision. I didn't look to somebody else for answers." Notice that it was not the sexual experience itself but the independent decision that made her feel she had reached adulthood.

Financial independence is a third pillar of adult status for emerging adults. They believe they need to make enough money to "pay the bills" on their own before they can be considered fully adult. Sylvia feels she has not yet entirely reached adulthood because "I kind of feel that being adult should mean that you're financially independent, which I'm not. I'm very dependent on my parents in that way." In contrast, Melanie does feel adult because "I'm paying for everything. I'm paying for school, I'm paying for my car, and I'm paying for my credit card bills that were my fault a long time ago." In Tory's view, "I think financial independence has a lot to do with it. Paying your own bills, not going to Mom and Dad and saying, 'Can I have $300 to go to Florida with the guys for spring break?'"

As I noted in chapter 3, for all three of these top criteria for adulthood, becoming an adult is defined in terms of independence *from parents*. Establishing independence from parents is a gradual process that begins well before emerging adulthood, but a major thrust toward adulthood comes with moving out of the parents' household. Ariel said that for her, becoming an adult "started with just moving out of the house. I don't think that was the end of it, but I think that started me to build my own belief system and to question life in general, and figure out who I was and what I wanted and everything." Yvonne still lives at home, but she anticipates that she will enter adulthood "when I move out of the house. When I'm like finally in an apartment by myself, taking care of the bills, taking care of everything, depending on nobody but myself."

For many emerging adults, moving out is part of going off to college after high school. In Tom's view, his passage to adulthood "started when I went to college. I had to be on my own. It was the first time I'd ever really been away from my parents, and I had been real close to my parents. So having to be on my own then made me think that I was grown up." Hazel recalled that "moving off to college really made me feel adult just because of being able to be autonomous, being able to make all my decisions on my own and survive without the help of my parents except for the financial aspect."

As Hazel's comments suggest, it is not just moving out itself that is important as a marker of adulthood, but the way moving out requires emerging adults to take on new responsibilities, make independent decisions, and become more independent financially. Casey said he felt he was on his way to adulthood at 21

> when I first moved into the house I'm renting now. To pay my own rent, pay my utility bills, pay for my own car insurance. Being responsible for having to clean my own house, do my own laundry, do my own ironing, keep my own schedule, everything. When you're doing it all by yourself and you're generating all the money that makes it possible, and you're making all the decisions—I think that's when I started really feeling like an adult.

Because it is not so much moving out that matters but the taking on of responsibilities, the making of independent decisions, and the financial independence that moving out often requires, emerging adults can feel they have reached adulthood even if they have returned home or never left. Trey lived with his parents through college and for two years afterward, but he says, "I really considered myself an adult even living at home and being with my parents. I don't think that's a requirement to be considered an adult." I asked him what made him feel that he was an adult while he was still living at home. "Making independent decisions," he said. "I mean, I used my parents as support, but I was able to say, 'This is what I want to do,' or 'This is what direction I want to go.'" Palmer was able to consider himself an adult while living at home because he was capable of being financially independent if necessary. "I could afford rent, that wouldn't be a big deal. I couldn't buy some of the things I buy, but I don't really use my parents' home for anything except for a place to sleep. Other than that, I pay for everything."

Learning Consideration for Others

With their view of what it means to be an adult defined so much by learning to stand alone as a self-sufficient person, independent of parents or anyone else, emerging adults give the strong impression of measuring their progress toward adulthood strictly in terms of themselves and their personal development. I have noted that emerging adulthood is a self-focused age, and this self-focus is evident in their conceptions of adulthood. They live in an individualistic society and are at an individualistic time of life, and the combination makes their self-focus strikingly high. Eventually they do want to commit themselves to others through marriage and parenthood, but first they want to demonstrate to themselves and others that they can fend for themselves in the world.

Still, even during emerging adulthood they do not lose sight of the rights and concerns of others. On the contrary, the individualism of their view of what it means to be an adult is tempered by an emphasis on consideration for others. Being self-focused does not mean being selfish, and becoming self-sufficient does not entail becoming self-absorbed. Becoming an adult means learning to stand alone, but it also means becoming less self-oriented and more considerate of others.[9] As Table 10.1 shows, this is widely endorsed by emerging adults as a criterion for adulthood.

Some emerging adults place consideration for others at the heart of their conception of adulthood. Gerard said that in his view of what it means to be an adult, "I'd say not being selfish is a big part of it. Being able to look out for other people's interest[s] and not just think of your own." Similarly, Peggy holds the view that in order to be an adult, "I think you have to take into consideration how your actions will affect other people. You know, like drunk driving. I don't have problems with people drinking and I think that's fine, but when you drink and then you get in a car and drive and hurt some-one else, that's not taking into consideration other people that you might harm through your actions."

However, emerging adults who place concern for others at the center of their conception of adulthood are relatively rare. More often, they view self-sufficiency as the most important part of becoming an adult, but they temper this focus with concern for others. The word *responsibility* comes up often again here. Responsibility has an elastic meaning, the way emerging adults use the term. It can refer to taking responsibility for yourself, and that is how they use it most often, but it can also be used to refer to respon-sibility toward others.

According to Mindy, reaching adulthood means "being responsible and knowing what your priorities are. Not looking out just for yourself but when you have the well-being of others in mind, and knowing that you are not just responsible for yourself but for other people around you, and not harm-ing them." Corey said that becoming an adult involves "learning to take responsibility for yourself, and maybe also feeling somewhat responsible for the others around you instead of just being irresponsible and not worrying about anything but personal gratification." Paul said that to be an adult means to be "responsible for your actions. Beyond just yourself, but con-sider people around you, how your actions affect other people."

It is another paradox of emerging adulthood, that becoming more self-sufficient can also mean becoming less self-centered, that learning to stand alone can be combined with learning to be more considerate of others. We have seen, in chapter 3, how the same kind of change takes place in their relationships with their parents. As they move away from their parents, they also become closer to them. In the same way, as emerging adults take more responsibility for themselves, they often become more aware of the respon-sibilities they have toward others.

What Matters for Some: The Complex Meanings of Parenthood

Along with marriage, the other traditional marker of reaching adulthood is becoming a parent. Has parenthood suffered the same decline in signifi-cance as marriage? Yes and no. As you can see in Table 10.1, on the questionnaire of possible criteria for adulthood parenthood ranks near the bottom in the responses of emerging adults, right down there with marriage. In interviews, emerging adults sometimes preface their statements about what is important for adulthood by stating that simply having a child does *not* make you an adult. When I asked Cecilia what it means to be an adult, she said, "Certainly not having kids," then went on to talk about what did matter for her. Charles, too, began his response by saying, "You have to have a child? I don't think so. You don't have to have progeny to be an adult. I don't think that for a woman to be an adult she has to have a baby."

This might make it seem that becoming a parent is not an important part of reaching adulthood, but the meaning of parenthood in relation to adult status is more complex than that. Although few nonparents view having a child as a significant marker of adulthood, and even few parents would say that parenthood is a *requirement* for adulthood, for themselves personally those in their twenties who are parents usually regard it as the most important event in their passage to adulthood.[10] This is especially true if they have become parents relatively early, in their teens or early twenties. Those who become parents early do not have the luxury of moving gradually toward adulthood according to their personal assessment of their progress toward self-sufficiency. Instead, parenthood thrusts them into adulthood immediately and abruptly, as they are suddenly required to change their lives to care for their newborn child.

Sam, 23, had his first child when he was 19, and now recalls, "I grew up very fast, and what really shoved me into adulthood was becoming a father. You've got to basically get your act together. You grow up quick." Leanne, 23 and the mother of three children, had her first child at 18 and says, "That has a tendency to make you grow up real fast. Even when I was pregnant, it was like, 'I've got to plan for this baby's future. Things have got to be different now. I've got somebody else that has to depend on me.' And that tended to make me grow up a lot, just in my thinking." Celine, 22, had her first child at 20 and now has a four-month-old as well. Asked if she felt she had reached adulthood, she replied, "With kids, definitely! Adulthood overnight, you know! The focus is on them and not on you. You think of that other person before you think of yourself." Larry, 26, became a father at 23 and says, "If you want to grow up fast, that's a sink or swim. I went from happy-go-lucky to 'You've got a baby to take care of. You've got to put a roof over its head. You've got to do this and this and this.' It's not 'Well, you can if you want,' it's 'This is what has to be done, period.' It seemed like it just happened overnight."

We can see, then, that parenthood requires people to take on weighty new responsibilities whether they would have chosen to or not, whether they feel ready or not. It "has to be done," as Larry said. Unlike most emerging adults, who take on the responsibilities of adulthood gradually, at their own pace, as they feel ready for them, young parents must take on all at once the tremendous responsibility for the life of a tiny, extremely vulnerable child. They become adults because of what their new role as parents requires of them, *right now*, not because their long personal journey toward self-sufficiency is at last complete.

Does this mean that 40 or 50 years ago, when most people became parents by their early twenties, they had a sense of reaching adulthood at a much earlier age than most emerging adults do today? I think this is likely. We can only speculate, because we do not have studies on this topic going back that far, but it seems like a reasonable speculation. Back then, the *majority* of young people were in a situation like the young people just described, of being thrust into adulthood suddenly at the birth of their child rather than reaching adulthood gradually, at their own pace. Of course, it is also possible that they had their first child earlier because they already felt they had reached adulthood earlier and so they felt ready for parenthood. But either way, it is likely that they felt like adults at an earlier age than emerging adults do today.

Ambiguity and Ambivalence

Feeling In-Between

Although becoming a parent often has the effect of thrusting emerging adults into adulthood overnight, those who become parents in their late teens or early twenties today are the exception. Because parenthood does not come for most people until the late twenties or beyond, by the time they reach parenthood they already feel they have reached adulthood through other markers. Most emerging adults deliberately wait to marry and have children until they have first established their self-sufficiency and feel they have a definite sense of their identity as individuals.

Because for most people today the journey to adulthood is long and gradual, emerging adulthood tends to be experienced as a period of being in between adolescence and adulthood, on the way to adulthood but not there yet. As 20-year-old Leslie put it, "There's not a break and then you become an adult. It's just a long, gradual process. I'm more of an adult than

I was when I was 15 or 17, but in 5 years I'll probably be more of an adult than I am now." For most emerging adults, it takes at least until their mid-twenties until they feel they have made it all the way to adulthood, and sometimes later.

Often, the sense of being in-between occurs when emerging adults continue to rely on their parents in some ways, so that their movement toward self-sufficiency is incomplete. For example, Malinda says she feels she has "somewhat" reached adulthood. On the one hand, she takes responsibility for herself. "I think I behave responsibly. Now it's only me that I account to. No one's checking up on me, and anything I do has got to be up to me." But on the other hand, she does not yet make her decisions independently. "My parents are nearby, and I still depend on them for some things. I don't have them do things for me, but I ask for their advice." Holly feels like an adult in most ways, but her lack of financial independence holds her back from completely reaching adulthood. "When I have my mom pay half the rent, that makes me feel like a kid again, but otherwise I feel like an adult." Similarly, Dan said he had reached adulthood in "all but the financial part of it. I mean, I live my own life. I act like an adult, and I think of myself as an adult and act the way I feel I should. I consider myself an adult, but I guess I haven't crossed the line as far as money goes."

For other emerging adults, they have become entirely self-sufficient to all appearances, yet there is still some part of them that just doesn't feel adult. Terrell, a 23-year-old African American, gives a definite impression of adult maturity. He has a promising career with a computer software company, he is entirely independent from his parents, and he seems to have a clear idea of who he is and what he wants out of life. Yet when I asked him if he had reached adulthood, he replied, "Not absolutely, because I still sometimes get up in the morning and say, 'Good Lord! I'm actually a grown-up!' 'Cause I still feel like a kid. I've done things like just got up one morning and said, you know, 'I'm going to Mexico,' and just get up and go. And I should have been doing other things." Shelly, a college junior, feels she has come a long way toward adulthood since she left home for college three years ago, but also feels she has a long way to go.

> I feel like I'm much further than I was when I started college. I've made this huge jump, I think, in just being more comfortable with myself and just being more settled with myself. But then there are a lot of areas where I still haven't figured all this stuff out, and there's still so much more to

figure out. Like, when people call me "ma'am," I'm like, "Whoa!" So, not really totally yet.

The proportion of emerging adults who move from feeling in-between to feeling fully adult increases steadily in the course of the twenties, and by age 30, 90% feel they have reached adulthood and are no longer in-between.[11] However, during the twenties, age is only a very rough marker of whether or not a person feels like an adult. There are 21-year-olds who say they have definitely reached adulthood, and 28-year-olds who say they still feel in-between.

Adulthood: A Dubious Honor?

In most societies, reaching adulthood is a valued achievement. Being an adult means having a certain authority, commanding respect, and being allowed to participate in activities forbidden to children and adolescents. In American society, too, entering adulthood is something most emerging adults regard as an achievement. They take pride in being able to fulfill the responsibilities necessary for independent adult life: holding a job, paying their bills, running a household. They enjoy being able to run their own lives and make their own decisions about where their lives should go.

However, many emerging adults are ambivalent about reaching adulthood. Yes, it is nice to have the freedom to run your own life, and it is satisfying to be able to handle adult responsibilities competently. But mixed in with their pride in reaching adulthood is dread and reluctance.

In part, this ambivalence results from a realization that adult responsibilities can be burdensome and annoying. Laurie said she has reached adulthood "for the most part," but adds that her adult responsibilities seem "overwhelming sometimes. There are times when I really wish subconsciously that I was being taken care of by my mom and dad." Amber thought of a specific example. "I was just looking at this thing for my life insurance and naming beneficiaries. And I was thinking, you know, this is the kind of thing I want my parents to do for me. I don't want to be faced with these grim decisions myself."

The other source of their ambivalence about entering adulthood is that they associate becoming an adult with stagnation. Gerard said that, at 27, "I feel like I'm kind of teetering on the brink of adulthood, you know. I guess in some ways I feel like it and other ways I don't. I associate being an adult with being really boring, and I just don't feel quite that boring yet."

Dylan also had a bleak view of adulthood. "I think in some respects I feel like I'm an adult, and in some respects I kind of hope I never become an adult. Maybe I associate adultness with being overly constrained or something. Losing your fresh approach."

In this view, to reach adulthood means the end of fun, the end of spontaneity, the end of personal growth. Cindy said, "I don't think I'll ever feel that I've fully reached adulthood, because I think every day is going to be a quest for me. Every day you're going to learn new things in life. Once you accept that you're an adult and there's nothing else to learn, then your life becomes stagnant." Martin put it this way: "I don't know if I've reached adulthood yet because I don't know if I ever want to. How do you define an adult? Do you want an adult to never be childlike? Because I always like to play and I don't know if I ever want to quit playing, if that's what that means." Emerging adults like these idealize childhood, and adulthood looks pale in comparison. Trey said, "I always think it's best to have somewhat of a child in you, otherwise you get too set in things and you're not able to look at things in certain ways. So I don't think it's always good to say, 'I'm 100% adult.' I'm probably somewhere around 50% most of the time."

Emerging adults also realize that once they enter adulthood there will be no going back. Rob said, "I'd have to say that maybe I'm not 100% an adult. And maybe I don't want to be. What's the hurry? I have my whole life to be an adult, you know." Renée, 24, realizes she is not as mature as her parents were at her age, "obviously because they were married and having me." But she adds that at this point in her life, "It's not that I want to be that mature, you know. I guess I'm an adult as much as I want to be an adult."

Looking Back to High School: Those Were the Days?

The ambivalence that many emerging adults feel about reaching adulthood also comes out when they reflect on how their lives have changed since high school. We asked them, "Would you say your high school years were *less* stressful and difficult than your life now, or *more?*" I expected that most emerging adults would say their high school years were worse, because adolescence is well known to be stressful and difficult for many people.[12] By emerging adulthood, I expected most people would say they were happier and were glad to have left the upheavals of adolescence behind. This would fit with other research indicating that life satisfaction and overall well-being rise substantially from adolescence through emerging adulthood.[13]

However, their actual responses were more complicated. To my surprise, most of them (58%) said their high school years were *less* stressful and difficult; only 24% said high school was *more* stressful and difficult (with the rest responding, "about the same").

Some remember their high school years as simple, happy, and carefree. Like Sean, who said, "I didn't have the demands on my time then that I do now. I mean, in high school, you went to school for six or seven hours a day, and my parents didn't ask me to work, so basically I had all the time in the world on my hands to go to school and have fun, and that was basically it. Whereas now, that's not the case." Some, like Tom, appreciated the structure and security of daily life in high school.

> It was just "you get up, you go to school; you're going to go to school until May, and you're going to go to this class and this class." I mean, every day was just like a routine. And in the summer, I'd play baseball. It was a pattern, and I knew that I'd come home and the food was there, Mom would fix dinner. There weren't that many decisions and choices I had to make.

More often, however, emerging adults say that high school seemed highly stressful *at the time*. It's just that, from the perspective of their emerging adulthood, the stresses and difficulties of high school seem trivial. The high school years may have seemed stressful, said Lillian, "but they were that silly kind of stressful. Peer pressure stuff. You know, you worry about who's saying what about you, or are you going to have a date to this event or that event. That was all pretty stupid." Rocky finds it all mystifying now. "I look back and I'm like, why in the hell did I even care about that shit? Why did I care about if I was having a good hair day or a bad hair day? It was no big deal! I could care less now. But it was something back then where the slightest things would stress you out."[14]

Many emerging adults remember the pressure cooker of their peers' judgments as the most stressful thing about high school.[15] Tammy remembers high school as being all about thinking, "I'm just not OK, and everybody else is, and I look funny and I smell funny and I act funny and I dress funny. You think you're sticking out like a sore thumb, and that's pretty stressful. I hated it!" For Kim, high school involved "too much worrying about what other people thought. When you get older you don't have to worry about all that stuff. You can do what you want." On the questionnaire, three fourths of emerging adults responded that they worry less now about what their peers or friends think of them, compared to high school.

If only they had appreciated back then how good they had it! "When I was in high school, I thought what I was dealing with was stressful, but that was nothing," said Larry. "And now it's like, 'God, I wish I was a teenager, when everything seemed so carefree, and there was some order to things.'" Mandy had similar regrets. "Looking back at my teenage years, I think, 'Man, I've got a lot of responsibility. I should have enjoyed that freedom while I had it, you know, instead of trying to grow up.'" "No car payments or house payments," recalled Candace wistfully. "I had it made."

In contrast, the stresses of emerging adulthood are more serious and seem more legitimate. As Rita said, "The problems that I have now are a lot more real than they were in high school. I mean, [in] high school your problem is, you know, what you look like, what your hair turned out like, and whether or not to tuck your shirt in because it might make you look too fat, stuff like that. It's just a lot bigger problems now, problems that matter." Wendy made a similar contrast. "Back then, stress to me would have been 'What am I going to wear?' Now, it's like, 'How am I going to pay this bill?' and 'Where am I going in life?' It may be more stressful because the things that are stressful to you are major, more difficult to think about, harder decisions to make."

College students remark on how much tougher academically their college courses are, compared to high school. "High school was just a cakewalk," scoffed Martin. "It was easy. If you played the game in high school that the teachers wanted you to play, you could make A's. In high school it was rote memorization, and now it's more independent thinking." High school was easier, said Ian, "because there were no all-nighters or three finals in a week. Teachers pampered you. I think college is just a blast, but the workload is immense."

More than anything, emerging adults say their financial responsibilities are what make their lives stressful now compared to high school. Benny said high school was "less stressful because I didn't have the worries of paying the bills. You know, I did work but that money was mine. Now when I'm making my money it goes to the electric bill, the water bill, and all that." Denny also thought high school was easier because of fewer money worries. "You were at home and didn't have too many worries, just go to school and that was it. You didn't have all these bills. Now you've got to work and pay your bills."

Although moving toward adulthood means greater stress in some ways, it also means having greater abilities to deal with stress.[16] "The demands get harder, but you're a little more prepared to deal with them," said Malinda. Emerging adults take satisfaction in being able to handle the stresses of their new responsibilities. Heather described the change like this:

> In high school, I had no concerns. I just hung out with my friends all the time, school wasn't real tough, financially my parents took care of me. It was just fun. And now, I'm 24, I work all the time, I'm financially on my own, I take care of myself. It's scary, but it's nice, too. You feel a lot of satisfaction out of it.

Emerging adults also realize that new stresses are a cost of their new freedoms. Leslie says her life now is more stressful "because of just the extra pressures of things like money and stuff like that," but she knows that these are stresses she has freely chosen. "I kind of brought it on myself, too. I like the financial independence. And living away from home has relieved so much stress that it kind of balances out." Mike summed up well the emerging adult paradox of greater stress and greater freedom.

> I would say high school was less stressful and difficult, but I'm having a hell of a lot more fun now than I was then. It was less stressful then obviously because you don't have bills to pay. Really, if you get up in the morning and somehow find your way to school and can flop a warm body in a chair, you've covered all your responsibilities for the day. Now, you're expected to perform, and the bank wants their money on the first of every month and all that good stuff. So from that standpoint I'd say, yeah, it's a little more stressful. But driving nice cars is fun, and going to Cancun is fun without having to say, "Mom and Dad are going to Cancun. I think I'm going to tag along with them this year," you know. You can jump on a plane and go to Vegas, if you want to. That's why it's more fun. You're not living under someone else's rules.

High Hopes in a Grim World

Despite the stresses of emerging adulthood, it is for most people a time of high hopes and big dreams. When emerging adults look toward the future, they see the fulfillment of their hopes in love and work: a lifelong, harmonious marriage; happy, thriving children; and satisfying and lucrative work.[17] This is, in part, because their dreams have not yet been tested by real life. In their twenties, it is still possible for emerging adults to believe that everything will work out as they had planned, because even if things are going badly now, no doors are firmly closed, few decisions are irrevocable, their dreams may yet prevail. What Aristotle observed about the youth of his time more than 2 millennia ago is still true: "Their lives are lived principally in hope. . . . They have high aspirations; for they have never yet been humiliated by the experience of life, but are unacquainted with the limiting force of circumstances."[18]

Their high hopes are evident in their responses to the national survey I mentioned in chapter 1. In that survey of 18–24-year-olds, nearly all—96%—agreed with the statement "I am very sure that someday I will get to where I want to be in life."[19] In my study, in response to the questionnaire item "Do you think your life overall is likely to be better or worse than your parents' lives have been?" majorities in every ethnic group responded "better," and very few people responded "worse," as Table 10.2 shows.[20] The results were similar for separate questions about financial well-being, career achievements, and personal relationships.

I asked the same question in the interviews, and their responses indicated that an important reason for their optimism about the future was that they expected to receive more education than their parents did, and they expected their extended education to lead to a better life occupationally and financially. I have noted several times the expansion in recent decades in emerging adults' participation in higher education, and in chapter 7 I discussed the strong relation that exists between education and future income and occupational success. Emerging adults may not know the statistics, but they have a strong sense of the relation between education and future success. Gary, a 23-year-old African American who is working on a degree in business advertising, said:

Hopes tend to run high in emerging adulthood. (CATHY © 1996 Cathy Guisewite. Reprinted with permission of Universal Press Syndicate. All rights reserved.)

Table 10.2. "Do you think your life overall is likely to be better or worse than your parents' lives have been?"

	Percentage		
	Better	Same	Worse
African Americans	79	14	7
Latinos/Latinas	66	26	9
Asian Americans	65	30	4
Whites	52	36	12

My father, the only thing he had was a high school education. He never went to college. And he worked his way up from the bottom. I mean, completely got his hands dirty and worked his way all the way up— took him 30 years to do it. Me, I don't see myself being where he's at in 30 years. I'm going to do a lot better than my parents, 'cause I'm only going upwards.

Lance, who was about to complete a degree in history and government, said he expected his life would be "definitely better" than his parents' lives had been, because "my dad only graduated from eighth grade." Due to Lance's college degree, he anticipated that his life would be "much better educationally and financially both."

The rise in participation in higher education has been especially striking for young women,[21] and many of them are aware that their opportunities are much greater compared to women of the past. Becky, who is working on a graduate degree in biology, said her life would be better than her parents' lives because "attitudes have changed. Women are given much more respect and are given more opportunities as far as having a career." Amelia, a 24-year-old marine scientist, reflected, "I think for me, being a woman, I've definitely grown up with a lot more opportunities than my mom ever did."

Educational attainment is higher among Asian Americans than in any other ethnic group in American society,[22] a reflection of the high value placed on education in Asian American cultures.[23] In my study, many Asian American emerging adults spoke of how their parents had been motivated to immigrate to the United States primarily because of the educational opportunities that would be available to their children. Consequently, Asian

American emerging adults were especially aware of the importance of education as the foundation for happiness and success in adulthood.[24] Sylvia, a Chinese American who had just finished her degree in nursing, said her life would be better than her parents' "because we were able to have a really good education here. In Hong Kong there's only one college, and you have to be really smart and really rich to enter." Vanessa, working on a master's degree in teaching English as a second language, said that for her parents, "it was very, very difficult for them to get education" in Taiwan, their home country. For her, however, "I've got a chance to receive more education than my mom and my dad did, which is very important. Now I'll have more chances to reach a higher level later on in my life—my job, my career, my family, everything." Korena spoke of her Chinese father, who "started working when he was 10. He never had a chance to go to school, even though he likes to go to school and he likes to learn a lot." In contrast to his experience, "I have my chance, and I've got my bachelor's degree, and I have every possible criteria to pursue my Ph.D. So of course my life will be better than theirs."

In addition to anticipating more education and higher incomes than their parents, emerging adults also expect their personal relationships to be better. None of those whose parents divorced expect to repeat that debacle themselves. For example, Mason, in talking about how he expects his life to be better than his parents' lives, said, "I don't think about it so much financially, I think about it more from a personal standpoint. The fact that they got divorced, I consider that as not being successful, and therefore I obviously hope that does not happen to me. So in that respect, I expect it to be better." Even those whose parents have stayed married often expect to exceed their parents' personal happiness because they expect the quality of their marriage relationship to be higher. Mindy said her life would be better because "I think definitely that my relationship with my husband is a lot closer than my mom and dad's, and I think we have something stronger in that we're friends. My mom and dad, they're starting to be friends, but I don't think they were before. We have higher expectations of what we want out of marriage."

Even many emerging adults with parents who have had considerable financial and career success believe their lives will be better because they will have better personal relationships. Bruce was a singer in a struggling rock band and his father was a prominent biology professor at a major university, but Bruce thought his life would be better because "the things that I'm looking for in life aren't going to come with a bunch of money and a big house. I don't think I'll make as much money as him, but I don't need as much either."

Many of them believed their lives would be better because they would strike a better balance between work and family. Cliff said, "I'm going to make time in the future to spend with family and coach Little League and that type of thing that my parents didn't do, and if that means I'm financially less set for life, then I'll drive a truck rather than a BMW. Fine. So what? I'll make that trade." Barry said, "I'm not sure I'll make that much more money than they will, but I'm not going to have to work the grueling job day in and day out like they had to." These comments suggest that surveys indicating that emerging adults place a high value on making money may be misleading.[25] Yes, they would like to make a lot of money, but most of them are unwilling to sacrifice happiness in their personal lives in order to do so. A recent study found that more than 80% of emerging adults in their twenties said that having a work schedule that allows them to spend time with their family is more important than earning a high salary or holding a prestigious job.[26]

Some emerging adults mention their parents' early entry into marriage and parenthood as a disadvantage they will not have. Rita said she expected to be "better off financially because they had like four kids in their twenties and neither one of them had great jobs. They were always struggling." Jonna said:

> I think mine will be better just because they got married right out of college, [and then] they had kids. I guess what I'm trying to say is they did the job thing and the kid thing right when they got through college, and I guess maybe I don't want to do that. I guess the way I think it will be better is just because I will hope to have done the things that I want to do, and they didn't have the opportunity because they got married and had kids.

Sam thought his life would be better because "Dad and Mom got a real early start. My mom was 16 when she had my sister, and they went through hell for a real long period."

Even many emerging adults whose current lives seem unpromising believe that things will work out well for them in the long run. Bob has no current love partner and says, "I hate my job!" yet compared to his parents, he expects that his life will be better economically, better personally. I just think by the time my parents reached my age, they'd already run into some barricades that prevented them from getting what they wanted, personally and family-wise. And so far, I've avoided those things, and I don't really see those things in my life. I don't like my job. I'm frustrated about the lack of relationships with females. But in general, I think I'm headed in the right direction.

Although emerging adults believe their personal futures hold great promise, they are much less sanguine about the prospects for the world more generally. On the contrary, they believe the world is full of perils, and the future of their country and their generation is grim.[27] Their concerns are various, but the most common issues they mention pertain to crime, the environment, and the economy. Ariel said, "It seems like the world just isn't as safe a place any more. There's more violence on TV, and everywhere you go, it's there. People are more on guard much of the time." In Millie's view, "There's so many things going on in the world that are so horrible now that haven't always been going on, from the ozone layer, to overcrowding, to AIDS and hunger and poverty, all those things."

For the most part, however, emerging adults believe in the promise of their personal future even as they express doubt about the future of the rest of the world. Jared, considering the state of the world, concludes, "It's a big mess." But for himself personally, "I just try to deal with my little circle right in town here, and I'm having the time of my life, to tell you the truth, as far as the people, the friends I have and stuff, and I just love it." Even amid the world's problems, emerging adults persist in believing they will be able to carve out some measure of happiness for themselves and those they love.

Conclusion: Adulthood at Last, Ready or Not

We have seen in this chapter that the feeling of being in-between is a central part of being an emerging adult. Entering adulthood is no longer as definite and clear-cut as getting married. On the contrary, the road to young adulthood is long and winding, and the end of it usually does not come until the late twenties. They reach adulthood not because of a single event but as a consequence of the gradual process of becoming self-sufficient and learning to stand alone. As they learn to take responsibility for themselves, make independent decisions, and pay their own way through life, the feeling gradually grows in them that they have become adults.

However, they view this achievement with mixed emotions. The independence of emerging adulthood is welcome, and they take pride in being able to take care of themselves without relying on their parents' assistance. Nevertheless, the responsibilities of adulthood can be onerous and stressful, and emerging adults sometimes look back with nostalgia on a childhood and adolescence that seem easier in some ways than their lives now. Claims that most emerging adults experience a "quarterlife crisis"[28] in their twenties are exaggerated—life satisfaction and well-being go up from adolescence to emerging adulthood, for most people. But even if it is not really a "crisis," emerging adulthood is experienced as a time of new and not always welcome responsibilities, a time of not just exhilarating independence and exploration but stress and anxiety as well.

Despite the difficulties that come along with managing their own lives, most emerging adults look forward to a future they believe is filled with promise. Whether their lives now are moving along nicely or appear to be going nowhere, they almost unanimously believe that eventually they will be able to create for themselves the kind of life they want. They will find that soul mate, or at least a loving and compatible marriage partner; they will find that dream job, or at least a job that will be enjoyable and meaningful.

Eventually this happy vision of the future will be tested against reality, and for many of them the result will be an unpleasant collision that will force them to readjust their expectations. But during emerging adulthood everything still seems possible, and nearly everyone still believes their dreams will prevail, whatever perils the world may hold for others. This may be optimistic, but the belief that they will ultimately succeed in their pursuit of happiness gives them the confidence and energy to make it through the stresses and uncertainties of the emerging adult years.

NOTES

1. Arnett (2000a); Arnett & Taber (1994).

2. Arnett & Taber (1994). This applies to couples who marry. However, since the early 1970s, the rate of single parenthood has grown dramatically, to a current rate of about 25% of all American births. Consequently, the median age of entering parenthood used to be a year or so after marriage, whereas today the median ages of marriage and parenthood are very similar. Nevertheless, the point here remains valid, that the median ages of both marriage and parenthood have risen steeply over the past half century.

3. Michael, Gagnon, Laumann, & Kolata (1995).

4. National Center for Education Statistics (2002).

5. Mogelonsky (1996). This is perhaps not as large a proportion as it sounds from this statistic. Because only about one fourth of young Americans obtain a four-year degree (the rest drop out or attend only two-year schools), one third of this one quarter is only about 8%. Nevertheless, this percentage has risen steadily over recent decades. Also, there is an additional percentage who attend graduate or professional school not immediately after graduating with a four-degree but after spending some time out of higher education.

6. Modell (1989). There are no statistical data to confirm this, but this is the conclusion Modell draws on the basis of his insightful historical analysis.

7. Modell (1989).

8. Sommers (2001). The rise in participation in higher education has been especially dramatic for young women. Traditionally men were much more likely than women to obtain higher education—women were, in fact, barred from most colleges and universities—but young women surpassed young men in the 1980s, and in the past decade the gender gap favoring women has been persistent. See National Center for Education Statistics (2002), Table 20-2.

9. National Center for Education Statistics (2002).

10. Bianchi & Spain (1996); Dey & Hurtado (1999).

11. Arnett (1998); Arnett & Taber (1994).

12. Alan Reifman has developed a scale for assessing these five features, and initial results show empirical support for them. See Reifman, Arnett, and Colwell (2003).

13. Erikson (1950).

14. Erikson (1968, p. 150).

15. As Gene Bockneck (1986) notes, numerous developmental theorists in the 20th century have described something like what I am calling emerging adulthood. As far back as 1935, Charlotte Buhler described a "preparatory stage" following adolescence that involved entry into self-chosen and independent activity. More recently, Daniel Levinson and his colleagues (1978) delineated an "early adult transition," lasting from age 17 to 22, which is characterized by separating physically and psychologically from one's family, followed by a period of "entering the adult world" from age 22 to 28, in which people explore possible roles and relationships and make tentative commitments. But none of these theoretical ideas took root as a distinct area of scholarship on this age period, perhaps because up until recently only a minority of young people (mainly men) were able to use the late teens through the twenties for independent identity explorations.

16. Waterman (1999).

17. Feiring (1996); Furman, Brown, & Feiring (1999); Padgham & Blyth (1991).

18. Barling & Kelloway (1999); Csikszentmihalyi & Schneider (2000).

19. Bachman & Schulenberg (1993); Steinberg & Cauffman (1995).

20. See www.cns.gov/americorps and www.peacecorps.gov.

21. The idea about a Plan with a capital P is based on an essay by Elizabeth Greenspan (2000).

22. U.S. Bureau of the Census (2003).

23. Goldscheider & Goldscheider (1999).

24. Goldscheider & Goldscheider (1999).

25. Arnett (2000a).

26. The graph is from Arnett (2000a).

27. Arnett (1994, 1997, 1998, 2001, 2003); Nelson (2003).

28. Hornblower (1997).

29. A variety of scholars have commented on the increasing "individualization" of the self in "posttraditional" societies, meaning that social timetables for the life course have become less standardized and people now have a greater range of individual choice in when they make transitions such as finishing education, marriage, and retirement (e.g., Heinz, 2002). I agree, but I would add that the range of individual choice is greatest during emerging adulthood.

30. E.g., Hogan & Astone (1986); Shanahan (2000).

31. Keniston (1971).

32. Keniston (1971, pp. 8–9).

33. The data in Table 1.1 are from Population Reference Bureau (2000).

34. Heaton (1992).

35. Nelson (2003).

36. For a perspective on the darker side of emerging adulthood, including the limitations imposed by social class, see Côté (2000).

37. Saraswathi & Larson (2002).

38. Arnett (2002).

39. The data in Table 1.2 are from Population Reference Bureau (2000).

40. In the total sample there were 157 Whites, 56 African Americans, 48 Asian Americans, and 43 Latinos. All of them have been given pseudonyms to protect the confidentiality of their responses.

Chapter 2

1. Coupland (1991), p. 47.

Chapter 3

1. Laursen, Coy, & Collins (1998); Larson & Richards (1994). There is currently a widespread view in adolescent psychology that adolescents get along just fine with their parents, but I don't think this fits the evidence. It's true that adolescents often say they like and admire their parents, but it's also typical that conflict with parents rises sharply in adolescence and closeness sharply declines. For an analysis of this issue, see Arnett (1999).

2. Goldscheider & Goldscheider (1999).

3. Dubas & Petersen (1996).

4. For an excellent account of both current and historical patterns of leaving home, see Goldscheider & Goldscheider (1999). Most of the information in this section is from this source.

5. Goldscheider & Goldscheider (1999).

6. Goldscheider & Goldscheider (1999).

7. Goldscheider & Goldscheider (1999).

8. There is little research on this topic, but for related papers see the 1996 issue of *New Directions in Child and Adolescent Development*, "Leaving Home: Understanding the Transition to Adulthood," edited by Julia A. Graber and Judith Semon Dubas.

9. Fingerman (2000).

10. The ages are 23 for men and 21 for women; Silbereisen, Meschke, & Schwarz (1996).

11. Chisholm & Hurrelmann (1995).

12. Goldscheider & Goldscheider (1999).

13. Côté (2000).

14. Goldscheider & Goldscheider (1999).

15. Goldscheider & Goldscheider (1999).

16. Goldscheider & Goldscheider (1999).

17. Larson & Richards (1994); Richards, Crowe, Larson, & Swarr (2002).

18. Larson, Richards, Moneta, Holmbeck, & Duckett (1996). For a good account of how adolescents come to rely more on friends than on parents for some issues, see Youniss & Smollar (1986).

19. Fingerman (2000). Joseph Allen and his colleagues (1994, 1998) describe something similar in adolescence, a new balance of "autonomy" and "relatedness" between parents and adolescents, meaning that, for adolescents, becoming more independent does not necessarily mean becoming less attached to their parents. Also, as adolescent psychologists such as Collins (1990) and Smetana (1988) describe, changes in how parents understand their children also take place when the children first reach adolescence. However, in my view, the process is more mutual in emerging adulthood; both parents and emerging adults come to view each other with greater understanding and respect.

20. Buchanan (2000).

21. For an example of how vehement scholars can be on opposite sides of this issue, see the exchange between David Demo (1993) and Paul Amato (1993). For a more balanced appraisal of the issue, see Buchanan (2000), Emery (1999), or Cherlin (1999). Also see Hetherington, Bridges, & Insabella (1998) and Hetherington & Kelly (2002). One recent approach is an original and insightful attempt to reconcile the opposing sides of the debate. Laumann-Billings and Emery (2000) noted that research on divorce typically focuses on disorders of behavior—how divorce affects functioning in school or work, for example—whereas clinical case studies typically focus on the distress that results from divorce—how divorce feels to those affected by it. In two studies of emerging adults, one with college students and one with a low-income community sample, they found that emerging adults often reported painful feelings, beliefs, and memories concerning the divorce, even if in their behavior they seemed to have recovered from it. So, it may be that both sides are right—children usually recover from divorce in most respects by the time they become emerging adults, but the pain associated with divorce endures through emerging adulthood.

22. Lasch (1979).

23. Larson & Richards (1994, p. 164).

24. Buchanan (1997); Buchanan, Maccoby, & Dornbusch (1996); Cooney (1994).

25. Buchanan (2000).

26. See Wallerstein, Lewis, & Blakeslee (2000) for qualitative descriptions of the anger and anguish that often result from divorce.

27. The effects are stronger for fathers, but relationships with mothers are affected as well. For example, O'Connor and colleagues (1996) found that emerging adults whose parents have divorced have less positive relationships with both mothers and fathers, with regard to closeness and frequency of contact.

28. Ganong & Coleman (1999). Men are somewhat more likely than women to remarry.

29. Hetherington & Stanley-Hagan (2000).

30. Hetherington & Stanley-Hagan (2000). For example, Hetherington and Kelly (2002) report that only 20% of emerging adults feel close to their stepmothers.

31. Ganong & Coleman (1999).

Chapter 4

1. Bailey (1989).

2. Brumberg (1997).

3. Bailey (1989).

4. Arnett & Taber (1994).

5. Dreyer (1982).

6. Hatfield & Rapson (1996).

7. U.S. Bureau of the Census (2002).

8. Popenoe & Whitehead (2001) reported that in their focus-group interviews of 20–29-year-olds, "all the women and almost all the men expected to marry and stay in their first marriages" (p. 9). A poll of adolescents by the Gallup organization reported similar results (Popenoe & Whitehead, 2002). Among 13–17-year-olds, 88% said they expected to marry someday, compared to only 9% who expected to remain single.

9. See Popenoe & Whitehead (2002) for similar results.

10. Popenoe & Whitehead (2002).

11. Stone (2001). Internet dating services are growing rapidly; from 2001 to 2002 they tripled their annual revenue to $302 million and are now the most profitable services on the Web (Mulrine, 2003). The target audiences of Internet dating services tend to be older emerging adults (in their late twenties) and singles in their thirties and forties, just as in personal ads, but many younger emerging adults participate as well. For example, half of Match.com's members are under 30 (Mulrine, 2003).

12. In the focus-group interviews with young men conducted by Popenoe & Whitehead (2002), among those who had tried Internet dating services, "several commented that deception and misrepresentation were commonplace" (p. 9).

13. In focus-group interviews with young men age 25–33, Popenoe & Whitehead (2002) reported that most believe it is best to become friends with

a potential romantic partner and get to know each other by hanging out together before dating.

14. Berscheid (1994).

15. Laursen & Jensen-Campbell (1999).

16. Lykken & Tellegen (1993); Michael, Gagnon, Laumann, & Kolata (1995). It is notable that, according to national survey data, most young people age 20–29 do *not* see similarities as the key to lasting love; most believe similarities in areas such as religious beliefs are unimportant (Popenoe & Whitehead, 2001; Whitehead & Popenoe, 2002). Instead, they believe that lasting love is based on an intangible personality match with a "soul mate." Nevertheless, they tend to choose partners who are similar to themselves.

17. The information in this paragraph is from Bianchi & Casper (2000).

18. The quote by John Updike is from Michael, Gagnon, Laumann, & Kolata (1995, p. 57).

19. See Whitehead & Popenoe (2002).

20. The information on college dormitory policies is mostly from Michael, Gagnon, Laumann, & Kolata (1995).

21. Popenoe & Whitehead (2001). In another study, of college women, 64% of them agreed that sexual intercourse without commitment is wrong (Fletcher, 2001). Unfortunately, the study did not include college men.

22. Michael, Gagnon, Laumann, & Kolata (1995).

23. Centers for Disease Control (2002).

24. Michael, Gagnon, Laumann, & Kolata (1995).

25. Hatfield & Rapson (1996).

26. Gallup & Lindsay (1999).

27. "Teen Birth Rate" (2000).

28. Prince & Bernard (1998).

29. www.childstats.gov.

30. Civic (2000).

31. Civic (1999, 2000).

32. Miracle, Miracle, & Baumeister (2003).

33. Carroll & Wolpe (1996). The full term for genital herpes is herpes simplex virus 2.

Chapter 5

1. Popenoe & Whitehead (2002). This is the overall figure, but ethnic differences are quite substantial. Among females age 30–34 in 1998, 17% of Whites had never married, but for African Americans the figure was 47% (Smock & Gupta, 2000).

2. Putnam, Feldstein, & Cohen (2001).

3. In a recent national survey (Popenoe & Whitehead, 2001), only 42% of 20–29-year-olds responded that it is important to them to find a spouse who shares their religion. But this is a little misleading. Among that 42% are no doubt the ones for whom their religious faith is most important. So, another way to put it would be to say that virtually everyone for whom religious faith is of high importance looks for a spouse who shares his or her beliefs.

4. Popenoe & Whitehead (2001).

5. Popenoe & Whitehead (2001).

6. Bernice Neugarten and her colleagues examined views about the "best age" for a variety of life transitions, including marriage, in the early 1960s (Neugarten, Moore, & Lowe, 1965) and again in the early 1970s (Neugarten & Datan, 1973). In the early 1960s, a strong majority viewed the early twenties as the "best age" to marry, but by the early 1970s there was no consensus—less than half viewed any particular age period as the "best age." In my research, I asked "best age" questions on the questionnaire for Missouri participants (see Arnett [1998] for sample characteristics) and found a similar lack of consensus.

7. Popenoe & Whitehead (2001); Whitehead & Popenoe (2002).

8. Erikson (1950, 1968).

9. Phinney, Ong, & Madden (2000); Triandis (1995). In one reflection of the greater pressure to marry in Asian societies, Japanese media have recently referred to young people in their twenties who are in no hurry to marry as "parasite singles." See http://www.japantimes.co.jp/cgi-bin/getarticle.p15?fl20000525 a1.htm and http://lists.nbr.org/links/bbc5-03.01.asp.

10. As part of the research of the National Marriage Project, focus-group interviews were conducted in four cities with 60 single American men age 25–33. On the basis of the interviews, Popenoe & Whitehead (2002) described "ten reasons why men won't commit":

1. They can get sex without marriage more easily than in times past.
2. They can enjoy the benefits of having a wife.
3. They want to avoid divorce and its financial risks.
4. They want to wait until they are older to have children.
5. They fear that marriage will require too many changes and compromises.
6. They are waiting for the perfect soul mate and she hasn't yet appeared.
7. They face few social pressures to marry.
8. They are reluctant to marry a woman who already has children.
9. They want to own a house before they get a wife.
10. They want to enjoy single life as long as they can.

11. Figure 5.1 is based on Michael, Gagnon, Laumann, & Kolata (1995). It should be noted that there are ethnic differences in rates of cohabitation.

Latinos and African Americans are more likely than Whites to cohabit as their first union and more likely to have a child within the cohabiting relationship. African Americans are more likely to dissolve the cohabiting relationship than to end it in marriage; this is true even after accounting for socioeconomic status. Latinos are more likely than Whites to approve of cohabitation. Fifty-seven percent of African American children are projected to spend at least some of their childhood with cohabiting partners, compared to 42% of Latinos and 35% of Whites. For details and further information, see Smock & Gupta (2002).

12. Determining just how common are these two types are is complicated and depends on how long a cohabiting relationship should last without marriage before it is defined as "uncommitted." For example, in the United States in the 1990s, 33% of cohabiting relationships resulted in marriage within three years (Smock & Gupta, 2002), down from 60% in the 1970s, but of course others result in marriage after four or more years. Unfortunately, no surveys I have seen so far have actually asked cohabiters whether or not they intend to marry. However, based on the statistics available, I would estimate that in the United States slightly less than half of cohabiting relationships are "premarital" and slightly less than half are "uncommitted," with the remaining small percentage being "committed cohabiters," as discussed below. For further information, see Bumpass & Lu (2000) and Smock & Gupta (2002).

13. In the National Marriage Project's national survey of 20–29-year-olds (Popenoe & Whitehead, 2001), 43% agreed that "You would only marry someone if he or she agreed to live together with you first, so that you could find out whether you really get along."

14. Popenoe & Whitehead (2001).

15. Smock & Gupta (2002). However, there is evidence that for premarital cohabiters—those who plan to marry in the near future—the divorce rate is no higher than for noncohabiters (Cohan & Kleinbaum, 2002; DeMaris & Rao, 1992).

16. As noted in chapter 4, about 90% of Americans in their teens and twenties intend to marry eventually (Popenoe & Whitehead, 2001, 2002).

17. Kiernan (2002).

18. Kiernan (2002).

19. Nock (1995, 1998); Waite & Gallagher (2000).

20. Whitehead & Popenoe (2002), in their focus-group interviews with single 20–29-year-olds, also found parental disapproval of cohabitation.

21. As noted earlier in the chapter, in the National Marriage Project's national survey of 20–29-year-olds (Popenoe & Whitehead, 2002), 62% agreed that "Living together with someone before marriage is a good way to avoid an eventual divorce." In another national survey, the Monitoring the Future project's annual survey of American high school seniors, over 60% agreed in the 2000 survey that "It is usually a good idea for a couple to live together before

getting married in order to find out whether they really get along," a figure that has risen steadily over the past 25 years (see Popenoe & Whitehead, 2002; www.monitoringthefuture.org).

22. There is some ground for their belief that waiting until their late twenties to marry improves their odds of staying married. Popenoe & Whitehead (2002) observe that "age at marriage is one of the strongest and most consistent predictors of marital stability ever found by social science research" (p. 21). However, this finding is due mainly to the high rate of divorce for those who marry while still in their teens. The divorce rate for those who marry in their early twenties is no different from the divorce rate of those who wait until their late twenties or beyond. Although waiting until the late twenties or beyond makes it likely that partners will enter marriage more mature and more financially stable, as Whitehead and Popenoe (2002) observe, waiting that long makes marriage more problematic for some emerging adults, because by then they may be used to living life their own way and may find themselves reluctant to make the kinds of compromises and sacrifices that a successful marriage requires.

23. Amato (2001); Kiernan (2002); Smock & Gupta (2002); Wolfinger (2000). In one analysis, Amato & DeBoer (2001) assessed national, longitudinal data from two generations. They found that parental divorce made it twice as likely that children would eventually see their own marriage end in divorce. In contrast, children with maritally distressed parents who remained married did not have an elevated risk of divorce. Furthermore, divorce was most likely to be transmitted from parents to children if the parents reported a low rather than high level of discord prior to their divorce. The authors concluded that children of divorced parents have a higher risk of becoming divorced because they have a relatively weak commitment to the ideal of a lifelong marriage.

Chapter 6

1. See Pascarella & Terenzini (1991) for a comprehensive review and analysis.
2. Schneider & Stevenson (1999).
3. Arnett (2000a). Of American emerging adults who enter college in the fall following high school graduation, about one third enter two-year colleges and two thirds enter four-year colleges (National Center for Education Statistics, 2002, Table 20-2). Most of the material in this chapter applies more accurately to students in four-year colleges, whom I know better and on whom there is more research.
4. Larson & Richards (1994).
5. Astin, Oseguera, Sax, & Korn (2002); National Center for Education Statistics (2002); Steinberg (1996).
6. National Center for Education Statistics (2002); U.S. Bureau of the Census (2000).

7. Arnett (2003). According to the National Center for Education Statistics (1999), in 1996 the percentage of 25–34-year-olds who had completed higher education varied as follows: France 12%; Germany 13%; United Kingdom 15%; Canada 20%; Japan 23%; and United States 27%. This has been true traditionally but, especially in Europe, the proportion of emerging adults obtaining higher education is growing rapidly and is drawing close to Canada and the United States. Finland, for example, has rates of college entrance at least as high as the United States.

8. Hamilton (1994).

9. Arnett & Taber (1994).

10. The data in Figure 6.1 are from Arnett & Taber (1994) and National Center for Education Statistics (2002). Since 1970, the rise has been especially striking among women. As noted in chapter 1, in the past men were far more likely than women to attend college, but now there are more female than male undergraduates.

11. According to Csikszentmihalyi & Schneider (2000), most students entering college have a narrow range of professions in mind—doctor, lawyer, engineer, maybe athlete or musician. But these vague dreams bear little relation to the jobs most of them will end up having.

12. National Center for Education Statistics (2002).

13. National Center for Education Statistics (2002); Pollard & O'Hare (1999).

14. Dey & Hurtado (1999).

15. Sperber (2000).

16. Schulenberg & Maggs (2001).

17. Levine & Cureton (1998).

18. National Center for Education Statistics (2002).

19. Pollard & O'Hare (1999).

20. National Center for Education Statistics (1998).

21. Levine & Cureton (1998); National Center for Education Statistics (2002).

22. Mogelonsky (1996).

23. Levine & Cureton (1998); see Astin, Oseguera, Sax, & Korn (2002) for similar results. Of course, just as with aspirations for a bachelor's degree, not all of those who hope to get advanced degrees actually get one.

24. National Center for Education Statistics (2002).

25. Arnett (1997, 1998, 2001). In a recent survey by the National Opinion Research Center (Associated Press, 2003), "finish education" actually appeared to be the most highly valued criterion for adulthood. However, in my view this was because the survey provided participants with only a narrow range of possible criteria to choose from, all of which were demographic criteria (marriage, parenthood, etc.), none of which have rated highly in the many surveys I

and others have conducted on this topic. This issue will be explored in more detail in chapter 10.

26. Hamilton (1994).

27. As Côté & Allahar (1994) argue, for many college graduates the work they end up doing after college bears little relation to their college education. The important thing is to get the credential, the degree itself, because that is what is valued in the workplace rather than any specific knowledge.

28. Europe has a long tradition of apprenticeships, but it is interesting to note that in the 19th century, at the height of Romanticism, there was an ideal, especially in Germany, of young men having a *wanderschaft* (also sometimes called a *wanderjahre* or *wandervogel*), that is, a period in their late teens or early twenties that would be devoted to travel and self-exploration before settling into adult commitments. Similarly, in Britain many upper-class young men had a "continental tour" or "grand tour" of Europe before entering long-term adult roles. These ideas are similar in some ways to what exists today as emerging adulthood, but they were only for the elite and rarely for young women.

29. Schneider & Stevenson (1999, pp. 109, 84).

30. Clark & Trow (1966).

31. Sperber (2000).

32. Sperber (2000).

33. Magolda (1997); Sperber (2000).

34. Levine & Cureton (1998).

35. Sperber (2000).

36. Pascarella & Terenzini (1991). An opposing view has been presented by Côté & Allahar (1994), who argue that college is not worth it for the time and money spent on it. In my judgment the evidence is on the side of Pascarella and Terenzini, but Côté and Allahar's critique is worth reading.

37. E.g., Schneider & Stevenson (1999).

Chapter 7

1. Csikszentmihalyi & Schneider (2000).

2. Loughlin & Barling (1999).

3. Bachman & Schulenberg (1993); Bachman (1983).

4. Modell (1989).

5. Modell (1989).

6. Schneider & Stevenson (1999).

7. Wilson (1996).

8. Halperin (1998).

9. Halperin (1998); National Center for Education Statistics (2002, Table 16-4).

10. Schneider & Stevenson (1999).

11. U.S. Bureau of the Census (2000).

12. Dey & Hurtado (1999). Once married, young women also spend about twice as much time on household work as their husbands do—37 hours/week, compared to 18 hours/week for men (Smock & Gupta, 2002), even if both work full time. This is what sociologist Arlie Hochschild (1990) calls "the second shift" faced by working women.

13. Hochschild (1990).

14. Hewlett (2002). Of course, men are affected by this conflict as well, if not as widely. In Hewlett's study of highly successful businesspeople, 42% of the women were childless, but so were 25% of the men.

15. James Côté (2000) has argued that the life course in most industrialized societies today is characterized by "individualization," meaning that there has been a "general *destructuring* of forms of traditional culture with their civil and collective supports" (p. 29; emphasis in original), with the result that individuals are left to rely on themselves, because there are "pressures for each person to be a self-determining agent" (p. 29). He emphasizes that individualization is especially pronounced with respect to the transition to adulthood. Compared to traditional societies, in "late modern" societies such as the United States, Canada, and most of Europe, young people are not provided with enough support from adult society as they make the transitions to adult roles, especially with respect to work. Consequently, many of them stumble along in a state of what he calls "default individualization," which "involves a life course dictated by circumstance and folly, with little agentic assertion on the part of the person" (p. 33). The more favorable alternative is "developmental individualization," which involves "extensive deliberation on the alternatives and life courses available in late modern society," resulting in "a life course of continual and deliberate growth" (p. 33). However, this favorable path requires the cultivation of what Côté calls "identity capital," which includes "a stable sense of self, which is bolstered by social and technical skills in a variety of areas, effective behavioral repertoires, psychosocial development to more advanced levels, and associations in key social and occupational networks" (p. 209). As a consequence of building identity capital, "the personality takes on a complexity and a flexibility so that it can adapt to the multidimensional contexts of late modern society" (p. 210). But because of the pervasive influence of poor school systems and popular culture, and the diminished influence of religion and the family, Côté views this challenge as beyond the powers of many if not most emerging adults, and in his view they suffer from a lack of identity capital and end up floundering indefinitely in a state of default individualization. I view Côté's portrayal of the emerging adult years as much too bleak, but he's always provocative and worth reading. And he certainly has a valid point that most American and Canadian emerging adults get little assistance from their societies in trying to sort through a dizzying array of work options to find one that suits them well.

16. Robbins & Wilner (2001). In *Generation X*, Coupland (1991) anticipated this term, in his usual sardonic fashion, with what he called the "Mid-
Twenties Breakdown" (p. 27), which he defined as a "period of mental collapse
occurring in one's twenties, often caused by an inability to function outside of
school or structured environments coupled with a realization of one's essential
aloneness in the world. Often marks induction into the ritual of pharmaceuti-
cal usage." Elsewhere, he calls it a "mid-twenties crisis" (p. 73).

17. B. Schwartz (2000).

18. Alfeld (2003); Hamilton (1994).

19. It seems more likely that the Europeans will move toward the American system than vice versa. Already most European countries have added more
flexibility to their systems and made it easier to change tracks. Meanwhile, in
the United States, it is unlikely that there would be public or political support
for a nationwide school-to-work system, given how much it would likely cost
to implement one.

20. Côté (2000). Côté (2000) also talks about "identity capital," meaning
the self-direction and flexibility needed to succeed in a society that changes
rapidly and provides little institutional guidance for finding a job.

21. Hoffman (1984).

22. Daniel Levinson and his colleagues (1978), in their theory of adult
development, proposed that the main developmental task of the twenties is to
develop The Dream, meaning an ideal for one's occupational future.

23. According to Csikszentmihalyi & Schneider (2000), dreams of musical or athletic stardom are also common in high school. Although I am not aware
of any data comparing adolescents to emerging adults on this issue, I would
predict that fewer emerging adults have such dreams, as they are more likely to
have begun to find out just how difficult success in these fields can be.

24. Wilson (1996).

25. Erikson (1950, 1968); Marcia (1980, 1994). Also see Berzonsky &
Adams (1999).

26. Erikson (1959, p. 118). It should also be noted that research using
Marcia's categories has found that by their early twenties, most people are cat-
egorized as having not yet reached identity achievement (Waterman, 1999).
At this point, research does not show a clear developmental progression through
stages of identity formation, culminating in identity achievement. However,
little research has extended beyond the very early twenties.

Chapter 8

1. Erikson (1968) used the term *ideology*, but he conceded that this term
has pejorative connotations he did not intend. *World view* has come into use
more recently (e.g., Jensen, 1997), and I think it is preferable.

2. Tillich (2001).

3. Smith (1991).

4. Triandis (1995).

5. *Collectivism* is sometimes called "sociocentrism"; e.g., Shimizu (2000).

6. See Killen & Wainryb (2000) for a discussion of individual differences in individualism and collectivism.

7. The responses were coded by me and two colleagues. Rate of agreement was over 80%. Discrepancies were resolved through discussion. See Arnett & Jensen (2002).

8. It would be interesting to study the pervasiveness of people's belief in a *Star Wars*–type "Force." In Great Britain, there has been a debate recently about whether to include this belief as an official religion, because so many people mentioned it in the official polling the government does on religious beliefs.

9. Responses to this question were coded by me and two colleagues. Rate of agreement was over 80%. Discrepancies were resolved through discussion.

10. King, Furrow, & Roth (2002). Also see the Website for the National Study of Youth & Religion, www.youthandreligion.org.

11. Hoge, Johnson, & Luidens (1993).

12. Perry (1970/1999).

13. Gallup & Castelli (1989); Hoge, Johnson, & Luidens (1993); Stolzenberg, Blair-Loy, & Waite (1995). However, in my study, age was not related to any of the religious variables in statistical analyses (see Arnett & Jensen, 2002).

14. See Arnett & Jensen (2002) for the statistical analyses on this and other questions in this chapter.

15. Gallup & Castelli (1989, p. 122).

16. Suarez-Orozco & Suarez-Orozco (1996).

17. Attending Catholic schools was common among the Asian Americans in my San Francisco sample, but I am not aware of any statistics indicating how common it is for Asian Americans nationally. I mention it here as in intriguing possibility for further study.

18. Triandis (1995).

19. Triandis (1995). Scholars increasingly recognize that every culture is diverse, and most cultures are not pure types of either individualism or collectivism but have a combination of the two types of values in various proportions. Also, even a culture that is individualistic overall is likely to have some people who are more collectivistic than individualistic, due to differences in personality, age, and other factors. For a discussion of these issues, see Killen & Wainryb (2000).

20. For a detailed analysis, see Arnett, Ramos, & Jensen (2001).

21. Bellah, Madsen, Sullivan, Swidler, & Tipton (1985); also see Jensen (1995).

22. The results of some surveys have suggested that American emerging adults have become more individualistic and less collectivistic since the 1960s. For example, in the Monitoring the Future studies, which survey high school students annually, it has been found that in the late 1960s, 24% of high school seniors indicated that "being a success" was important, while 85% indicated that it was important to them to "make a contribution to society." By the late 1990s, these numbers had reversed: 89% stated that "being a success" was important, compared to 22% for "making a contribution to society." UCLA's annual survey of college freshmen has reported similar results (Astin, Oseguera, Sax, & Korn, 2002). However, in a recent study, Joos (2003) interviewed high school seniors and found that their definition of "success" included not only an overall sense of happiness and achieving personal goals, but also "helping others and making a difference." Thus, it may not be that values have changed since the 1960s so much as that definitions of "success" have changed and are now viewed among young people as including both collectivistic and individualistic elements.

23. S. H. Schwartz (1990).

Chapter 9

1. Sampson & Laub (1990).

2. This pattern is in accordance with Erikson's (1950) theory: first identity, then intimacy.

3. See Seligman (2002) for more on optimism as a characteristic of resilience.

4. There is by now a substantial literature on the relation between religious faith and a variety of positive outcomes. For information related to young people on this issue, see the Website for the National Study of Youth & Religion, http://www.youthandreligion.org.

5. Masten (2001).

6. Bockneck (1986). Bockneck's book, a comprehensive look at the age period I call emerging adulthood, is a neglected gem, full of insights and information, and I highly recommend it.

7. This lack of correlation seems to be true for religious beliefs at least, as we saw in chapter 8.

8. E.g., Schulenberg, O'Malley, Bachman, & Johnston (2004).

Chapter 10

1. Arnett (1998, 2000a).

2. Schlegel & Barry (1991).

3. Kett (1977); Rotundo (1993).

4. Arnett (1994, 1997, 1998, 2001, 2003); Mayseless & Scharf (2003); Nelson (2003). Other traditional markers, such as obtaining a full-time job or finishing education, also rank consistently near the bottom in my studies of the most important criteria for adulthood. In 2003 a study conducted by the National Opinion Research Center (NORC) claimed that "finish education" was in fact the top criterion for aulthood (Associated Press, 2003). However, the study did not allow people to state their own view of what was most important for adulthood, but gave them a narrow range of choices that included only demographic criteria (e.g., in addition to "finish education," there was marriage, parenthood, and obtaining a full-time job). I and others have conducted numerous studies on this topic, in many parts of the United States, using a variety of different methods (interviews as well as questionnaires), and "finish education" has never been anywhere near the top criteria, so I do not believe the NORC findings are valid.

5. Arnett (1998).

6. For an analysis of the historical and cultural roots of the importance of self-sufficiency in the transition to adulthood, see Arnett (1998). For results comparing American ethnic groups, see Arnett (2003). The differences among ethnic groups on criteria for adulthood are few. However, African Americans, and to a lesser extent Latinos, often feel they have reached adulthood earlier than emerging adults in other ethnic groups, evidently because they often take on family responsibilities at an early age, due to family poverty or to having a child at an early age.

7. Arnett (1994, 1997, 1998, 2001, 2003); Nelson (2003).

8. The full questionnaire contained 39 criteria; only a portion of those are shown here.

9. Once I put an item for "becoming less self-centered" on the questionnaire, after my first several studies, it immediately rose to the top two or three most widely endorsed items, below "responsibility" but above "financially independent" and right up there with "independent decisions" (e.g., Arnett, 2003). However, it has not come up in interviews as often as "responsibility," "independent decisions" and "financially independent" have (Arnett, 1998). I think this area—how emerging adults change in their social understanding (compared to adolescents)—is one of the most fascinating and promising for future research. See Bockneck (1986) for a rich theoretical discussion of this area.

10. In the Missouri sample (Arnett, 1998), one-fourth of participants had had at least one child, and among them parenthood was mentioned by 61% as a marker of their own transition to adulthood, more than any other criterion.

11. Arnett (2001). The other 10% remain in a state of what James Côté (2000) calls "youthhood," extending their emerging adulthood indefinitely past age 30, often with no particular desire to become adults and take on adult roles.

12. For a discussion of the "storm and stress" of adolescence, see Arnett (1999). Some scholars on adolescence deny that it is stormy or stressful, but I have argued that there is evidence that adolescence is more difficult than childhood or emerging adulthood, especially in terms of emotional upheaval and conflict with parents. Also see Larson & Richards (1994), who show that in the transition from childhood to adolescence, there is an emotional "fall from grace" as happiness declines and anxiety and unhappiness increase.

13. E.g., Helson & Kwan (2000); Roberts, Caspi, & Moffitt (2001); Schulenberg, O'Malley, Bachman, & Johnston (2004).

14. Larson and Richards (1994), using the Experience Sampling Method, in which people are beeped at random times during the day and then fill out a questionnaire about their moods and experiences at that moment, have found that adolescents have more emotional upheavals than either preadolescents or adults, partly because they experience more frequent stressful events but partly because of how they respond to stress.

15. This observation is confirmed by research on adolescents, e.g., Larson & Ham (1993); Larson & Richards (1994).

16. Bockneck (1986).

17. Arnett (2000b). Also see Reifman, Arnett, & Colwell (2003).

18. Quoted in Hall (1904, Vol. 1, pp. 522–523).

19. Hornblower (1997).

20. In binomial tests, the differences for each ethnic group were significant at $p < .001$. If anything, the findings here understate the optimism of emerging adults; "the same" was often a highly optimistic response, because it tended to come from emerging adults who admired their parents and wanted to emulate their parents' lives. See Arnett (2000b).

21. National Center for Education Statistics (2002).

22. Pollard & O'Hare (1999).

23. Asakawa & Csikszentmihalyi (1999); Lee & Larson (2000); Fuligni & Tseng (1999).

24. For similar findings, see Fuligni & Tseng (1999).

25. See Astin, Oseguera, Sax, & Korn (2002); Joos (2003).

26. Grimsley (2000).

27. See Arnett (2000b).

28. Robbins & Wilner (2001).

REFERENCES

Alfeld, C. (2003, November). A dream deferred: Effects of delayed career pathways during emerging adulthood in the USA and Germany. Poster presented at the Conference on Emerging Adulthood, Cambridge, MA.

Allen, J. P., Hauser, A., Bell, K., & O'Connor, T. (1994). Longitudinal assessment of autonomy and relatedness in adolescent-family interaction as predictors of adolescent ego development and self-esteem. *Child Development, 65,* 179–194.

Allen, J. P., Moore, C., Kuperminc, G., & Bell, K. (1998). Attachment and adolescent psychosocial functioning. *Child Development, 69,* 1406–1419.

Amato, P. R. (1993). Family structure, family process, and family ideology. *Journal of Marriage & the Family, 55,* 50–54.

Amato, P. R. (2001). What children learn from divorce. *Population Today.* Washington, DC: Population Reference Bureau.

Amato, P. R., & DeBoer, D. D. (2001). The transmission of marital instability across generations: Relationship skills or commitment to marriage? *Journal of Marriage & the Family, 63,* 1038–1051.

Arnett, J. J. (1994). Are college students adults? Their conceptions of the transition to adulthood. *Journal of Adult Development, 1,* 154–168.

Arnett, J. J. (1997). Young people's conceptions of the transition to adulthood. *Youth & Society, 29,* 1–23.

Arnett, J. J. (1998). Learning to stand alone: The contemporary American transition to adulthood in cultural and historical context. *Human Development, 41,* 295–315.

Arnett, J. J. (1999). Adolescent storm and stress, reconsidered. *American Psychologist, 54,* 317–326. Reprinted in M. Gauvain & M. Cole (Eds.). (2001). *Readings on the development of children* (3rd ed.). New York: Worth.

Arnett, J. J. (2000a). Emerging adulthood: A theory of development from the late teens through the twenties. *American Psychologist, 55,* 469–480.

Arnett, J. J. (2000b). High hopes in a grim world: Emerging adults' views of their futures and of "Generation X." *Youth & Society, 31,* 267–286. Reprinted in T. C. Lomand (Ed.). (2002). *Social science research: A cross section of journal articles for discussion and evaluation.* Los Angeles, CA: Pyrczak.

Arnett, J. J. (2001). Conceptions of the transition to adulthood: Perspectives from adolescence to midlife. *Journal of Adult Development, 8,* 133–143.

Arnett, J. J. (2002). The psychology of globalization. *American Psychologist, 57,* 774–783.

Arnett, J. J. (2003). Conceptions of the transition to adulthood among emerging adults in American ethnic groups. *New Directions in Child and Adolescent Development, 100,* 63–75.

Arnett, J. J., & Jensen, L. A. (2002). A congregation of one: Individualized religious beliefs among emerging adults. *Journal of Adolescent Research, 17,* 451–467. Reprinted in T. C. Lomand (Ed.) (2003), *Social science research: A cross section of journal articles for discussion and evaluation.* Los Angeles, CA: Pyrczak.

Arnett, J. J., Ramos, K. D., & Jensen, L. A. (2001). Ideologies in emerging adulthood: Balancing the ethics of autonomy and community. *Journal of Adult Development, 8,* 69–79.

Arnett, J., & Taber, S. (1994). Adolescence terminable and interminable: When does adolescence end? *Journal of Youth & Adolescence, 23,* 517–537.

Asakawa, K., & Csikszentmihalyi, M. (1999). The quality of experience of Asian American adolescents in activities related to future goals. *Journal of Youth & Adolescence, 27,* 141–163.

Associated Press (2003, May 9). University of Chicago survey says adulthood begins at age 26. *Available:* http://www.msnbc.com/news/911377.asp?0cv=CB20.

Astin, A. W., Oseguera, L., Sax, L. J., & Korn, W. S. (2002). *The American freshman: Thirty-five year trends.* Los Angeles, CA: Higher Education Research Institute, University of California, Los Angeles.

Bachman, J. G. (1983). Premature affluence: Do high school students earn too much? *Economic Outlook USA,* 64–67.

Bachman, J. G., & Schulenberg, J. (1993). How part-time work intensity relates to drug use, problem behavior, time use, and satisfaction among high school seniors: Are these consequences or just correlates? *Developmental Psychology, 29,* 220–235.

Bailey, B. L. (1989). *From front porch to back seat: Courtship in twentieth-century America.* Baltimore: Johns Hopkins University Press.

Barling, J., & Kelloway, E. K. (1999). *Young workers: Varieties of experience.* Washington, DC: American Psychological Association.

Barry, D. (1995). *Dave Barry's complete guide to guys.* New York: Fawcett Columbine.

Bellah, R. N., Madsen, R., Sullivan, W. M., Swidler, A., & Tipton, S. M. (1985). *Habits of the heart: Individualism and commitment in American life.* New York: Harper & Row.

Berscheid, E. (1994). Interpersonal relationships. *Annual Review of Psychology, 45,* 79–129.

Berzonsky, M. D., & Adams, G. R. (1999). Reevaluating the identity status paradigm: Still useful after 35 years. *Developmental Review, 19,* 557–590.

Bianchi, S. M., & Casper, L. M. (2000). American families. *Population Bulletin, 45*(4), 1–44.

Bianchi, S. M., & Spain, D. (1996). Women, work, and family in America. *Population Bulletin, 51*(3), 1–48.

Bockneck, G. (1986). *The young adult: Development after adolescence.* New York: Gardner.

Booth, A., & Crouter, A. C. (2002). *Just living together: Implications of cohabitation on families, children, and social policy.* Mahwah, NJ: Erlbaum.

Brumberg, J. J. (1997). *The body project: An intimate history of American girls.* New York: Random House.

Buchanan, C. M. (1997). Issues of visitation and custody. In G. Bear, K. Minke, & A. Thomas (Eds.), *Children's needs II: Development, problems, and alternatives* (pp. 605–613). Bethesda, MD: National Association of School Psychologists.

Buchanan, C. M. (2000). The impact of divorce on adjustment during adolescence. In R. D. Taylor & M. Weng (Eds.), *Resilience across contexts: Family, work, culture, and community* (pp. 179–216). Mahwah, NJ: Erlbaum.

Buchanan, C. M., Maccoby, E., & Dornbusch, S. (1996). *Adolescents after divorce.* Cambridge, MA: Harvard University Press.

Buhler, C. (1935). The curve of life as studied in biographies. *Journal of Applied Psychology, 19,* 405–409.

Bumpass, L. L., & Lu, H. H. (2000). Trends in cohabitation and implications for children's family contexts in the United States. *Population Studies, 54,* 29–41.

Carroll, J. L., & Wolpe, P. R. (1996). *Sexuality and gender in society.* New York: HarperCollins.

Centers for Disease Control. (2002). Trends in sexual risk behaviors among high school students: United States, 1991–2001. *Mortality and Morbidity Weekly Report, 51*(38), 856–859.

Cherlin, A. J. (1999). Going to extremes: Family structure, children's well-being, and social science. *Demography, 36,* 421–428.

Chisholm, L., & Hurrelmann, K. (1995). Adolescence in modern Europe: Pluralized transition patterns and their implications for personal and social risks. *Journal of Adolescence, 18,* 129–158.

Civic, D. (1999). The association between characteristics of dating relationships and condom use among heterosexual young adults. *AIDS Education and Prevention, 11,* 343–352.

Civic, D. (2000). College students' reasons for nonuse of condoms within dating relationships. *Journal of Sex & Marital Therapy, 26,* 95–105.

Clark, B., & Trow, M. (1966). The organizational context. In T. M. Newcomb & E. K. Wilson (Eds.), *College peer groups: Problems and prospects for research* (pp. 17–70). Chicago: University of Chicago Press.

Cohan, C. L., & Kleinbaum, S. (2002). Toward a greater understanding of the cohabitation effect: Premarital cohabitation and marital communication. *Journal of Marriage & the Family, 64,* 180–192.

Collins, W. A. (1990). Parent-child relationships in the transition to adolescence: Continuity and change in interaction, affect, and cognition. In R. Montemayor, G. Adams, & T. Gullotta (Eds.), *Advances in adolescent development: Vol. 2. The transition from childhood to adolescence* (pp. 85–106). Beverly Hills, CA: Sage.

Cooney, T. M. (1994). Young adults' relations with parents: The influence of recent parental divorce. *Journal of Marriage & the Family, 56,* 45–56.

Côté, J. (2000). *Arrested adulthood: The changing nature of maturity and identity in the late modern world.* New York: New York University Press.

Côté, J. (2003, June). *Understanding the prolonged transition to adulthood: An empirical approach.* Paper presented at the Nordic Youth Research Information Symposia 8 conference, Roskilde, Denmark.

Côté, J., & Allahar, A. (1994). *Generation on hold: Coming of age in the late 20th century.* New York: New York University Press.

Coupland, D. (1991). *Generation X: Tales for an accelerated culture.* New York: St. Martin's.

Csikszentmihalyi, M., & Schneider, B. (2000). *Becoming adult: How teenagers prepare for the world of work.* New York: Basic.

DeMaris, A., & Rao, K. V. (1992). Premarital cohabitation and marital instability in the United States: A reassessment. *Journal of Marriage & the Family, 54,* 178–190.

Demo, D. H. (1993). The relentless search for effects of divorce: Forging new trails or stumbling down the beaten path? *Journal of Marriage & the Family, 55,* 42–45.

Dey, E. L., & Hurtado, S. (1999). Students, colleges, and society: Considering the interconnections. In P. G. Altbach, R. O. Berndahl, & P. J. Gumport (Eds.)., *American higher education in the twenty-first century: Social, political, and economic challenges* (pp. 298–322). Baltimore: Johns Hopkins University Press.

Dreyer, P. (1982). Sexuality during adolescence. In B. Wolman (Ed.), *Handbook of developmental psychology.* Englewood Cliffs, NJ: Prentice Hall.

Dubas, J. S., & Petersen, A. C. (1996). Geographical distance from parents and adjustment during adolescence and young adulthood. *New Directions for Child Development, 71,* 3–19.

Emery, R. E. (1999). *Marriage, divorce, and children's adjustment.* Newbury Park, CA: Sage.

Erikson, E. H. (1950). *Childhood and society.* New York: Norton.

Erikson, E. H. (1959). Identity and the life cycle. *Psychological Issues, 1,* 1–171.

Erikson, E. H. (1968). *Identity: Youth and crisis.* New York: Norton.

Feiring, C. (1996). Concepts of romance in 15-year-olds. *Journal of Research on Adolescence, 6,* 181–200.

Feldman, S. S., Mont-Reynaud, R., & Rosenthal, D. (1992). When east meets west: The acculturation of values of Chinese adolescents in the U.S. and Australia. *Journal of Research on Adolescence, 2,* 147–173.

Fingerman, K. L. (2000). "We had a nice little chat": Age and generational differences in mothers' and daughters' descriptions of enjoyable visits. *Journal of Gerontology, 55B,* 95–106.

Fletcher, M. A. (2001, July 26). Campus romance, unrequited: Dating scene fails women, study says. *Washington Post,* p. A3.

Fuligni, A. J., & Tseng, V. (1999). Family obligations and the academic motivation of adolescents from immigrant and American-born families. *Advances in Motivation and Achievement, 11,* 159–183.

Furman, W., Brown, B. B., & Feiring, C. (1999). *The development of romantic relationships in adolescence.* New York: Cambridge University Press.

Gallup, G., Jr., & Castelli, J. (1989). *The people's religion: American faith in the '90s.* New York: Macmillan.

Gallup, G., Jr., & Lindsay, D. M. (1999). *Surveying the religious landscape: Trends in U.S. beliefs.* Harrisburg, PA: Morehouse.

Ganong, L. H., & Coleman, M. (1999). *Changing families, changing responsibilities: Family obligations following divorce and remarriage.* Mahwah, NJ: Erlbaum.

Goldscheider, F., & Goldscheider, C. (1999). *The changing transition to adulthood: Leaving and returning home.* Thousand Oaks, CA: Sage.

Graber, J. A., & Dubas, J. S. (Eds.) (1996). *Leaving home: Understanding the transition to adulthood.* San Francisco: Jossey Bass.

Greenspan, E. (2000, September 3). I had a plan: It just fell apart. *Washington Post,* p. B4.

Grimsley, K. D. (2000, May 28). For today's college grads, it isn't just about the money. *Washington Post,* pp. H1, H3.

Hall, G. S. (1904). *Adolescence: Its psychology and its relation to physiology, anthropology, sociology, sex, crime, religion, and education* (Vols. 1–2). Englewood Cliffs, NJ: Prentice Hall.

Halperin, S. (1998). *The forgotten half revisited: American youth and young families, 1988–2008.* Washington, DC: American Youth Policy Forum.

Hamilton, S. F. (1990). *Apprenticeship for adulthood: Preparing youth for the future.* New York: Free Press.

Hamilton, S. F. (1994). Employment prospects as motivation for school achievement: Links and gaps between school and work in seven countries. In R. K. Silbereisen & E. Todt (Eds.), *Adolescence in context: The interplay of family, school, peers, and work in adjustment* (pp. 267–283). New York: Springer-Verlag.

Hamilton, S. F., & Hamilton, M. A. (2000). Research, intervention, and social change: Improving adolescents' career opportunities. In L. J. Crockett & R. K. Silbereisen (Eds.), *Negotiating adolescence in times of social change* (pp. 267–283). New York: Cambridge University Press.

Hatfield, E., & Rapson, R. L. (1996). *Love and sex: Cross-cultural perspectives*. Boston: Allyn & Bacon.

Heaton, T. B. (1992). Demographics of the contemporary Mormon family. *Dialogue, 25*, 19–34.

Heinz, W. R. (2002). Self-socialization and post-traditional society. *Advances in Life Course Research, 7*, 41–64.

Helson, R., & Kwan, V. S. Y. (2000). Personality development in adulthood: The broad picture and processes in one longitudinal sample. In S. Hampton (Ed.), *Advances in personality psychology* (Vol. 1, pp. 77–106). London: Routledge.

Hetherington, E. M., Bridges, M., & Insabella, G. M. (1998). What matters? What does not? Five perspectives on the association between marital transitions and children's adjustment. *American Psychologist, 53*, 167–184.

Hetherington, E. M., & Kelly, J. (2002). *For better or worse: Divorce reconsidered*. New York: Norton.

Hetherington, E. M., & Stanley-Hagan, M. (2000). Diversity among stepfamilies. In D. H. Demo & K. R. Allen (Eds.), *Handbook of family diversity* (pp. 173–196). New York: Oxford University Press.

Hewlett, S. A. (2002). *Creating life: Professional women and the quest for children*. New York: Miramax.

Hochschild, A. R. (1990). *The second shift*. New York: Morrow.

Hoffman, L. W. (1984). Work, family, and the socialization of the child. In R. D. Parke (Ed.), *Review of child development research* (Vol. 7, pp. 223–281). Chicago: University of Chicago Press.

Hogan, D. P., & Astone, N. M. (1986). The transition to adulthood. *Annual Review of Sociology, 12*, 109–130.

Hoge, D., Johnson, B., & Luidens, D. A. (1993). Determinants of church involvement of young adults who grew up in Presbyterian churches. *Journal of the Scientific Study of Religion, 32*, 242–255.

Hornblower, M. (1997, June 9). Great Xpectations. *Time*, pp. 58–68.

Jensen, L. A. (1995). Habits of the heart, revisited: Autonomy, community, and divinity in adults' moral language. *Qualitative Sociology, 18*, 71–86.

Jensen, L. A. (1997). Different worldviews, different morals: America's culture war divide. *Human Development, 40*, 325–344.

Joos, K. (2003, November). What does it mean to be a success? The future goals and values of emerging adults. Paper presented at the Conference on Emerging Adulthood, Harvard University, Cambridge, MA.

Keniston, K. (1971). *Youth and dissent: The rise of a new opposition*. New York: Harcourt Brace Jovanovich.

̄77). *Rites of passage: Adolescence in America, 1790 to the present*. New

. Cohabitation in western Europe: Trends, issues, and implica-
ḍooth & A. C. Crouter (Eds.), *Just living together: Implications of*

cohabitation on families, children, and social policy (pp. 3–31). Mahwah, NJ: Erlbaum.

Killen, M., & Wainryb, C. (2000). Independence and interdependence in diverse cultural contexts. *New Directions for Child & Adolescent Development, 87,* 5–21.

King, P. E., Furrow, J. L., & Roth, N. (2002). The influence of families and peers on religiousness. *Journal of Psychology and Christianity, 21,* 109–120.

Larson, R., & Ham, M. (1993). Stress and "storm and stress" in early adolescence: The relationship of negative life events with dysphoric affect. *Developmental Psychology, 29,* 130–140.

Larson, R., & Richards, M. H. (1994). *Divergent realities: The emotional lives of mothers, fathers, and adolescents.* New York: Basic.

Larson, R. W., Richards, M. H., Moneta, G., Holmbeck, G., & Duckett, E. (1996). Changes in adolescents' daily interactions with their families from ages 10 to 18: Disengagement and transformation. *Developmental Psychology, 32,* 744–754.

Lasch, C. (1979). *Haven in a heartless world.* New York: Basic.

Laumann-Billings, L., & Emery, R. E. (2000). Distress among young adults from divorced families. *Journal of Family Psychology, 14,* 671–687.

Laursen, B., Coy, K. C., & Collins, W. A. (1998). Reconsidering changes in parent-child conflict across adolescence: A meta-analysis. *Child Development, 69,* 817–832.

Laursen, B., & Jensen-Campbell, L. A. (1999). The nature and functions of social exchange in adolescent romantic relationships. In W. Furman, B. B. Brown, & C. Feiring (Eds.), *The development of romantic relationships in adolescence* (pp. 50–74). New York: Cambridge University Press.

Lee, M., & Larson, R. (2000). The Korean "examination hell": Long hours of studying, distress, and depression. *Journal of Youth & Adolescence, 29,* 249–271.

Levine, A., & Cureton, J. S. (1998). *When hope and fear collide: A portrait of today's college student.* San Francisco: Jossey-Bass.

Levinson, D., Darrow, C., Klein, E., Levinson, M., & McKee, B. (1978). *The seasons of a man's life.* New York: Knopf.

Loughlin, C., & Barling, J. (1999). The nature of youth employment. In J. Barling & E. K. Kelloway (Eds.), *Youth workers: Varieties of experience* (pp. 17–36). Washington, DC: American Psychological Association.

Lykken, D. T., & Tellegen, A. (1993). Is human mating advantageous or the result of lawful choice? A twin study of mate selection. *Journal of Personality and Social Psychology, 65,* 56–68.

Magolda, M. B. B. (1997). Students' epistemologies and academic experiences: Implications for pedagogy. In K. Arnold & I. C. King (Eds.), *Contemporary higher education: International issues for the 21st century* (pp. 117–140). New York: Garland.

Marcia, J. (1980). Identity in adolescence. In J. Adelson (Ed.), *Handbook of adolescent psychology.* New York: Wiley.

Marcia, J. (1994). The empirical study of ego identity. In H. A. Bosma, T. L. G. Graafsma, H. D. Grotevant, & D. J. De Levita (Eds.), *Identity and development*. Newbury Park, CA: Sage.

Masten, A. S. (2001). Ordinary magic: Resilience processes in development. *American Psychologist, 56*, 227–238.

Mayseless, O., & Scharf, M. (2003). What does it mean to be an adult? The Israeli experience. *New Directions in Child and Adolescent Development, 100*, 5–20.

Michael, R. T., Gagnon, J. H., Laumann, E. O., & Kolata, G. (1995). *Sex in America: A definitive survey*. New York: Warner.

Miracle, T. S., Miracle, A. W., & Baumeister, R. F. (2003). *Human sexuality: Meeting your basic needs*. Upper Saddle River, NJ: Prentice Hall.

Modell, J. (1989). *Into one's own: From youth to adulthood in the United States, 1920–1975*. Berkeley: University of California Press.

Mogelonsky, M. (1996, May). The rocky road to adulthood. *American Demographics*, 26–36, 56.

Mulrine, A. (2003, September 29). Love.com: For better or worse, the Internet is radically changing the dating scene in America. *U.S. News & World Report*, pp. 52–58.

Naito, T., & Gielen, U. P. (2003). The changing Japanese family: A psychological portrait. In J. L. Roopnarine & U. P. Gielen (Eds.), *Families in global perspective*. Boston: Allyn & Bacon.

National Center for Education Statistics. (1998). *The condition of education, 1998*. Washington, DC: U.S. Department of Education.

National Center for Education Statistics. (1999). *The condition of education, 1999*. Washington, DC: U.S. Department of Education.

National Center for Education Statistics. (2002). *The condition of education, 2002*. Washington, DC: U.S. Department of Education. *Available:* www.nces.gov.

Nelson, L. J. (2003). Rites of passage in emerging adulthood: Perspectives of young Mormons. *New Directions in Child and Adolescent Development, 100*, 33–49.

Neugarten, B., & Datan, N. (1973). Sociological perspectives on the life cycle. In P. B. Baltes & W. Schaie (Eds.), *Lifespan developmental psychology: Personality and socialization*. New York: Academic Press.

Neugarten, B. L., Moore, J. W., & Lowe, J. C. (1965). Age norms, age constraints, and adult socialization. *American Journal of Sociology, 70*, 710–717.

Nock, S. L. (1995). A comparison of marriage and cohabiting relationships. *Journal of Family Issues, 16*, 53–76.

Nock, S. L. (1998). *Marriage in men's lives*. New York: Oxford University Press.

O'Connor, T. G., Allen, J. P., Bell, K., & Hauser, S. T. (1996). Adolescent-parent relationships and leaving home in young adulthood. *New Directions in Child Development, 71*, 39–52.

Padgham, J. J., & Blyth, D. A. (1991). Dating during adolescence. In R. M. Lerner, A. C. Petersen, & J. Brooks-Gunn (Eds.), *Encyclopedia of adolescence* (pp. 196–198). New York: Garland.

Pascarella, E. T., & Terenzini, P. T. (1991). *How college affects students*. San Francisco: Jossey-Bass.

Perry, W. G. (1970/1999). *Forms of ethical and intellectual development in the college years: A scheme*. San Francisco: Jossey-Bass.

Phinney, J. S., Ong, A., & Madden, T. (2000). Cultural values and intergenerational value discrepancies in immigrant and nonimmigrant families. *Child Development, 71,* 528–539.

Pollard, K. M., & O'Hare, W. P. (1999). America's racial and ethnic minorities. *Population Bulletin, 54,* 1–48.

Popenoe, D., & Whitehead, B. D. (2001). *The state of our unions, 2001: The social health of marriage in America*. Report of the National Marriage Project, Rutgers, NJ. *Available:* http://marriage.rutgers.edu.

Popenoe, D., & Whitehead, B. D. (2002). *The state of our unions, 2002*. Report of the National Marriage Project, Rutgers University, Rutgers, NJ. *Available:* http://marriage.rutgers.edu.

Population Reference Bureau (2000). *The world's youth 2000*. Washington, DC: Author.

Prince, A., & Bernard, A. L. (1998). Sexual behaviors and safer sex practices of college students on a commuter campus. *Journal of American College Health, 47,* 11–21.

Putnam, R. D., Feldstein, L. M., & Cohen, D. (2001). *Bowling alone: The collapse and revival of American community*. New York: Touchstone.

Reifman, A., Arnett, J. J., & Colwell, M. J. (2003, August). *The IDEA: Inventory of the Dimensions of Emerging Adulthood*. Paper presented at the annual meeting of the American Psychological Association, Toronto, Canada.

Richards, M. H., Crowe, P. A., Larson, R., & Swarr, A. (2002). Developmental patterns in the experience of peer companionship in adolescence. *Child Development, 69,* 154–163.

Robbins, A., & Wilner, A. (2001). *Quarterlife crisis: The unique challenges of life in your twenties*. New York: Tarcher/Putnam.

Roberts, B. W., Caspi, A., & Moffitt, T. E. (2001). The kids are alright: Growth and stability in personality development from adolescence to adulthood. *Journal of Personality and Social Psychology, 81,* 670–683.

Rotundo, E. A. (1993). *American manhood: Transformations in masculinity from the revolution to the modern era*. New York: Basic.

Sampson, R. J., & Laub, J. H. (1990). Crime and deviance over the life course: The salience of adult social bonds. *American Sociological Review, 55,* 609–627.

Saraswathi, T. S., & Larson, R. (2002). Adolescence in global perspective: An agenda for social policy. In B. B. Brown, R. Larson, & T. S. Saraswathi (Eds.), *The world's youth: Adolescence in eight regions of the globe* (pp. 344–362). New York: Cambridge University Press.

Schlegel, A., and Barry, H. (1991). *Adolescence: An anthropological inquiry*. New York: Free Press.

Schneider, B., & Stevenson, D. (1999). *The ambitious generation: America's teenagers, motivated but directionless*. New Haven, CT: Yale University Press.

Schulenberg, J., & Maggs, J. L. (2001). *A developmental perspective on alcohol use and heavy drinking during adolescence and the transition to adulthood*. Washington, DC: National Institute on Alcohol Abuse and Alcoholism.

Schulenberg, J. E., O'Malley, P. M., Bachman, J. G., & Johnston, L. D. (2004). Launching into early adulthood: Multiple pathways and their relation to trajectories of well-being and substance use. In F. Furstenberg, R. Rumbaut, & R. Settersten (Eds.), *Transitions to adulthood*. Chicago: University of Chicago Press.

Schwartz, B. (2000). Self-determination: The tyranny of freedom. *American Psychologist, 55*(1), 79–88.

Schwartz, S. H. (1990). Individualism-collectivism: Critique and proposed refinements. *Journal of Cross-Cultural Psychology, 21,* 139–157.

Seligman, M. (2002). *Authentic happiness*. New York: Free Press.

Shanahan, M. J. (2000). Pathways to adulthood in changing societies: Variability and mechanisms in life course perspective. *Annual Review of Sociology, 26,* 667–692.

Shimizu, H. (2000). Beyond individualism and sociocentrism: An ontological analysis of the opposing elements in personal experiences of Japanese adolescents. *Human Development, 43,* 195–211.

Silbereisen, R. K., Meschke, L. L., & Schwarz, B. (1996). Leaving the parental home: Predictors for young adults raised in the former East and West Germany. *New Directions in Child Development, 71,* 71–86.

Smetana, J. G. (1988). Concepts of self and social convention: Adolescents' and parents' reasoning about hypothetical and actual family conflicts. In M. Gunnar & W. A. Collins (Eds.), *Minnesota symposium on child psychology* (Vol. 21, pp. 79–122). Mahwah, NJ: Erlbaum.

Smith, H. (1991). *The world's religions*. New York: HarperCollins.

Smock, J. (2000). Cohabitation in the United States: An appraisal of research themes, findings, and implications. *Annual Review of Sociology, 26,* 1–20.

Smock, P. J., & Gupta, S. (2002). Cohabitation in contemporary North America. In A. Booth & A. C. Crouter (Eds.), *Just living together: Implications of cohabitation on families, children, and social policy* (pp. 53–75). Mahwah, NJ: Erlbaum.

Sommers, C. H. (2001). *The war against boys: How misguided feminism is harming our young men*. New York: Touchstone.

Sperber, M. (2000). *Beer and circus: How big-time college sports is crippling undergraduate education*. New York: Holt.

Steinberg, L. (1996). *Beyond the classroom: Why school reform has failed and what parents need to do*. New York: Simon & Schuster.

Steinberg, L., & Cauffman, E. (1995). The impact of employment on adolescent development. In R. Vasta (Ed.), *Annals of child development* (Vol. 11). London: Kingsley.

Stolzenberg, R. M., Blair-Loy, M., & Waite, L. J. (1995). Religious participation in early adulthood: Age and family life cycle effects on church membership. *American Sociological Review, 60,* 84–103.

Stone, B. (2001, February 19). Love online. *Newsweek,* pp. 46–51.

Suarez-Orozco, C., & Suarez-Orozco, M. (1996). *Transformations: Migration, family life and achievement motivation among Latino adolescents*. Palo Alto, CA: Stanford University Press.

"Teen Birth Rate Continues to Drop" (2000, January). *Population Today,* p. 3.

Tillich, P. (2001). *Dynamics of faith*. New York: HarperCollins.

Triandis, H. C. (1995). *Individualism and collectivism*. Boulder, CO: Westview.

U.S. Bureau of the Census (2000). *Statistical abstracts of the United States: 2000*. Washington, DC: Author.

U.S. Bureau of the Census (2002). *Statistical abstracts of the United States: 2002*. Washington, DC: Author.

U.S. Bureau of the Census (2003). Geographic mobility: March 1997 to March 1998. *Current Population Reports* (Series P-20, No. 520). Washington, DC: U.S. Government Printing Office.

Waite, L. J., & Gallagher, M. (2000). *The case for marriage: Why married people are happier, healthier, and better off financially*. New York: Doubleday.

Wallerstein, J. S., Lewis, J. M., & Blakeslee, S. (2000). *The unexpected legacy of divorce*. New York: Hyperion.

Waterman, A. S. (1999). Issues of identity formation revisited: United States and the Netherlands. *Developmental Review, 19,* 462–479.

Whitehead, B. D., & Popenoe, D. (2002). *Why wed? Young adults talk about sex, love, and first unions*. Report of the National Marriage Project, Rutgers University, Rutgers, NJ. *Available:* http://marriage.rutgers.edu/pubwhywe.htm.

Wilson, W. J. (1996). *When work disappears: The world of the new urban poor*. New York: Knopf.

Wolfinger, N. H. (2000). Beyond the intergenerational transmission of divorce. *Journal of Family Issues, 21,* 1061–1086.

Youniss, J., & Smoller, J. (1986). *Adolescent relations with mothers, fathers, and friends*. Chicago: University of Chicago Press.

INDEX OF NAMES

SUBJECT INDEX

Italicized page numbers refer to figures, tables, and cartoons.